THE COMMUNITY INDUSTRIES OF THE SHAKERS

By
EDWARD D. ANDREWS

Introduction by
CYNTHIA ELYCE RUBIN

Reprint of
New York State Museum Handbook 15
by Emporium Publications

INTRODUCTION

In the year 1774, Ann Lee arrived in New York from Liverpool. With her were eight loyal followers who believed she was Christ incarnate.

Ann Lee was a Quaker whose visions and prophecies had been the source of persecution and imprisonment in England. One vision had enjoined her to leave for America and a free climate where she could gather her loyal band together to live as they pleased.

Once arrived, they separated to find employment, but were finally reunited on a donated piece of land, north of Albany, called Niskayuna.

Here they made their home. Some five years later, their obscure wooded house became a center during a fanatical religious revival which took place in the Lebanon Valley, not far from Niskayuna. Visitors who came from New Lebanon were deeply moved by what they saw in the Shakers. Soon Mother Ann's powers were avowed as miraculous; her motions were mysterious signals to those who believed in her. These new Shaker converts, plus her own proselytizing helped spread the word of Mother Ann.

Later, in 1784, the Society of Believers at New Lebanon completed their first Shaker meeting house. It was also in that year that Mother Ann died, leaving behind the roots of Shakerism.

Communities were formed in New Hampshire, Maine, and Massachusetts. In 1805, three Shaker brethren left for the Midwest to establish communities there. In the following ten to fifteen years, communities were established in South Union and Pleasant Hill, Kentucky, as well as in Union Village, North Union, and Whitewater, Ohio. Only the Busro, Indiana Community was deemed ill-fated and closed in 1827.

COMMUNAL FAMILIES FORMED

The organization of these communities is interesting in a modern context because living was communal. Although people were divided into "Families," the word itself had a very broad meaning. All were brothers and sisters in a consecrated communion of the spirit. This spiritual link related every Shaker to Mother Ann as well as to every other Shaker.

The original Elders were appointed by Mother Ann. They were responsible, in the beginning, for setting up the Order of the Ministry, a self-perpetuating organ. Trustees, appointed by the Ministry and Elders, were named to handle business dealings with the "outside world." These Trustees were assisted by Deacons and Deaconesses who were responsible for different trade shops. The Shakers never let religious zeal make them blind to the fact that they must get along with the people around them and that they must trade to survive. Although they were self-sufficient to a great extent, they could never produce everything necessary for survival.

The divisions of the community into families had distinct advantages for communal living. Each family had its own store as clearinghouse for incoming and outgoing articles. Families were small enough to contain a "collective individuality," and if there were a misfortune such as a fire or epidemic, other families in the community would come to their aid. Because of the variety of agricultural work and craft industries engaged in, Shakers often had more than one occupation. This led to great flexibility of production and labor.

INDUSTRIES FLOURISH

Once the organization of the Societies was well established, various business endeavors were commenced with the "outside world." Fine craftsmanship, high quality, and honesty led to success and an unsullied reputation. In 1790 the Shaker seed industry began; it lasted for well over a century. Broom corn was introduced and Shaker brooms became a well-known product. They were also soon involved in collecting, growing, and packaging herbs and herb medicines. Many communities had their own herb-drying houses. Quality livestock and sheep were raised, giving rise to the famous Shaker flannels and cloaks.

Many communities had their own specialities. Mt. Lebanon produced chairs. South Union canned fruit. Shirley and Harvard, Massachusetts were the leading producers of apple products such as cider and applesauce. In 1874 Canturbury, New Hampshire, produced between three to four thousand pounds of maple sugar. Oval boxes were manufactured in Mt. Lebanon and Sabbathday Lake, Maine. Poplar wood sewing boxes were also made in many communities.

The Shakers' sole purpose in life was to establish God's Kingdom on earth. Their minds, hearts and hands were devoted to this ideal. It is not surprising, therefore, that their kitchens became as holy as were their many workshops. Here, industry and efficiency turned to meal preparation.

Like their architecture and dress, Shaker cookery expressed simplicity and a high standard of perfection. The Shakers practiced organic gardening; their plain and wholesome meals tended more and more toward vegetarianism. In the early days of development, separate tables were laid for meateaters and nonmeateaters. Meat was generally considered less beneficial than other types of foods. Pork was forbidden. Nordhoff, in (The Communistic Societies of the United States) says, "Many use no food produced by animals, denying themselves even milk, butter and eggs. They consume much fruit, eating it at every meal; and the Shakers have always fine and extensive vegetable gardens and orchards."

LIFE ATTRACTS MANY

Restraint and temperance were key concepts in all affairs. Waste was frowned upon. Hospitality was bountiful. There was always a place for the poor who might knock at the door — and many did knock, knowing what good fortune awaited them. It is said that the communities in Ohio received many converts from among travelers who stopped for dinner and stayed till death. Many liked the security which the community provided. There was want for nothing. "Put your hands to work and your hearts to God" is a well-known Shaker motto. But they made no religion of work — spiritualism was its base. Eldress Marguerite Frost of Canturbury said, "Its (Shakerism's) very essence is that of conscious action and reaction between the realm of the spirit and its human counterpart."

The original Shakers were instructed by visions and mystic experiences. In a way, there was always a dichotomy between the practical and the spiritual in their lives. Visions were not uncommon. Often during worship they would fall into ecstasies and frenzies, completely oblivious to their surroundings. Worship was universally characterized by a formidable religious fervor. Their songs and intricate dancing patterns and marches exemplified this.

There was no art for art's sake. Instead, their pictures were called "Spirit drawings." These pictorial manifestations of inner spirituality are presently admired from an artistic point of view as attractive primitive pieces, but this reaction is only a by-product of contemporary fashion, not a result of Shaker intent.

Nor was beauty admired for its own sake. Only "the world" could find enlightenment in the appearance of an object. Esthetics had no intrinsic value, but craftsmanship did. Much Shaker furniture can be compared to contemporary Danish designs that have lately become widely popular. Lines were straight and simple. No ornamentation obscured basic design. Functionalism and simplicity were inherent in Shaker perspective, not for lack of imagination, but because they were integral to the search for the Perfection of God's Kingdom on earth.

FUNCTIONALISM REIGNS

Technical problems challenged creativity. The Shakers were always looking for the most practical and most efficient timesaving devices and techniques. Their furniture and architecture reflected this search. Rooms had pegboards on walls so that chairs could be hung up to permit easy cleaning. There were no moldings or ornaments to catch dust, and houses contained many built-in wall units and cupboards.

Shaker furniture was designed for utility. Combination pieces were common. Benches enlarged to become tables; wood boxes had attaching towel racks. Inventive genius lent large wooden rollers to beds so they could be moved easily for cleaning. Ball-and-socket devices on the back legs of early sidechairs allowed a person to "tilt" his chair after a good meal. Simplicity and utility were values inherent in form and from which one could perfect the unity of the whole — justification enough for Shaker workmanship.

To succeed, Shakerism required separation from the world. As revealed by Mother Ann, the Shakers' spiritual life was superior to man's as typified by Adam after the fall. Celibacy was essential as abstinence from the sins of the flesh. In a sense man's intercourse with woman signified a need for private property. Lacking this desire for property and aided by divine communication, the Shakers believed they could strive more successfully for a higher spiritual echelon.

By means of "consecrated labor" the foundation of Heaven was laid. Work was beneficial for the soul, for it taught humility and a sense of order. Order in external affairs aided the quest for order in the internal and spiritual existence. From youngest to oldest, Shakers worked at some occupation. Only the infirm were exempt from labor.

THE SHAKER ADVENTURE

Margaret Melcher writes in The Shaker Adventures, "Everything the Shakers made was looked upon as a practical instrument for a spiritual end. Celibacy, separation from the world, community of goods; these modes of attaining the spiritual perfection that was their goal dictated the whole pattern of life."

How then did the Shakers fail?

Today, there are only some dozen Shakers living, whereas there were approximately six thousand a century ago.

MOVEMENT LACKS CONVERTS AND OFFSPRINTS

The most important factor in their eventual extinction is celibacy, the major tenet of their religious beliefs. During the Civil War, there were no formal orphanages, and many orphans came to live in Shaker communities. Although these orphans could always leave by choice at age sixteen, many remained. But as their industrial age took hold and manufacturing led to the accumulation of material goods and to jobs in the cities, many chose to depart. Converts became fewer and fewer in number.

Eventually, the original religious fervor was spent; revivals and fanatical sermons became fewer and less meaningful. Older Shakers could no longer maintain religious enthusiasm; the younger ones were less interested.

In a sense, Shakerism was a result of its times, and later inevitably gave way to times of industrial surge, railroads and big-city glitter. The Shaker peddler with his homely horse and buggy, a common sight around 1840, would be an anachronism in today's advanced technological age, when man can be totally eradicated from the earth by the madness of nuclear war.

CONTENTS

ILLUSTRATIONS

The community at New Lebanon was generally known, between 1861 and 1931, as Mount Lebanon. The early name for the Watervliet community was Niskeyuna. In the illustrations, the older names have been retained.

The photographs for these figures were taken as follows: By *William F. Winter,* figures 1, 5, 6, 8–13, 17, 19–46, 51, 52, 59–65; by *Edwin J. Stein,* figures 3, 4, 7, 14–16, 18, 47–50, 54–58, also the drawing for figure 2.

Figure 53 is from a photograph made previous to 1893.

FIGURE 1 General view of the New Lebanon community of Shakers, looking southeast toward the Taconic range of the Berkshires. The three groups of buildings in the middle distance part way up the mountain are the North, Church and Center families. Despite the apparently wooded nature of the terrain, broad open tracts are visible, especially to the west of the Shaker road. At the foot of the other side of the range lies the Hancock (Mass.) community.

THE COMMUNITY INDUSTRIES
OF THE SHAKERS
BY EDWARD D. ANDREWS PH.D.

The rôle played by the communistic order of Shakers
in the early industrial and social development of New
York State, New England and the Kentucky-Ohio country is of such interest and importance that it seems
strange that the subject has not hitherto been treated by
the many observers who have written about this unusual
sect. Although this religious society believed in separation from the world, so enlightened and forceful was its
economic policy and so efficiently prosecuted were its complex industrial and agricultural activities that it influenced opinion and practice in many places and over a span
of time reaching from the first formation of the American
republic until well after the middle of the last century. In
working out a satisfactory industrial system which would
insure the welfare of their institution and the survival of
their faith, the Shakers set an example of progressive
business enterprise, on the plan of joint interest, which
marks them as pioneers in this regard. Organized into
closely knit communities as early as 1787, they should be
numbered among the first to develop farming, gardening
and manufacturing from a household scale to one marked
by many of the essential factors in combination and mass
production. Their numerous shops were equipped at an
early date to produce on possibly an unprecedented plan,
and the presence of large numbers undertaking communal

life necessitated certain cooperative and inventive practices in which the Shakers were leaders in America. Their pioneering contributions in such occupations as the growing and marketing of garden seeds, the manufacture of brooms and brushes, the growing, preparation and distribution of medicinal herbs and roots, the manufacture of chairs, etc., are especially deserving of recognition and record.

Not only did the Shakers thus initiate new methods and start new businesses, but so intimately related were these secular activities to the religious idealism cherished by the members of the order that they early set a pattern for the most painstaking workmanship in all the productions of shop, garden and field. No organization in America held such an enviable reputation for honest dealing and dependable product as did the Shakers during the long, successful course of their economic career. The spirit with which the Shakers put their "hands to work and hearts to God" is as significant as their actual achievements and early contributions in the utilitarian application of the agricultural and mechanical arts.

The religious phenomena underlying this most successful of all American experiments in communistic living are already well known and will be treated only as they bear directly on the industrial theme. The world which the Shakers renounced already knows much about their creed: that they consecrated themselves and their property to God, holding all their goods in common but owning nothing; that they led celibate lives; that they were the recipients of strange visions and the first spiritualists in America; that their early meetings were characterized by unrestrained emotions and unbridled ecstacies of spirit and body; that they did not vote nor run for public office;

that they were profoundly committed to the cause of peace and would not bear arms. It is likewise common knowledge that the Believers considered themselves a body of saints, whose mission it was to redeem themselves and others from the sins of worldliness and carnal nature. This rigid religious organization was accompanied, however, by a healthy and vigorous occupational life, a factor which has seldom been present in other communistic schemes. It seems evident, therefore, that the *sine qua non* of success in the sustaining of a religious system based on communistic principles, no matter how seemingly fantastic the theological doctrines involved, is an accompanying organization based on practical economics and unselfish cooperation. These factors have rarely been found in such systems, a fact which gives added historical value and interest to the Shaker experiment.

The society at New Lebanon (N. Y.), called Mount Lebanon after the post office was installed in 1861, is taken as the setting for the present study. This was the first society to be organized; for many decades it was the largest society, having eight families; it served as a pattern when other societies were established; it was the home of the central ministry or religious government; in fact, it was the "fountainhead" of Shakerism. A study of the organization of this commune is therefore in effect a study of each of the other 17 societies and 51 families. Each of the Shaker villages was like the others, not only in the organization of its religious and temporal affairs, but in its architecture, in its customs and folk ways, in its dress and the speech of its inhabitants, and in the general nature of its agricultural, horticultural and industrial art activities. Such similarities were brought about and augmented by the rigid regulations of the central ministry, the periodical visitation of this ministry to the several societies, the cooperation of different communities in constructional enterprises, the frequent movement of members from one village to another, and the interchange of goods. Although each family (and each community) was economically an independent unit with its own business managers or trustees, and although circumstances of location and native talent led to some differentiation in occupations and economic well-being, such variations were accidental rather than fundamental. The entire range of occupations may be gauged only by a survey of all the societies, but an examination of the important community at New Lebanon will serve to give an accurate basis for appraising the entire field. In the same manner the affairs of one family typify those of others in the same or other communities; in this study the Church family at New Lebanon receives focal emphasis, not only because this group carried on the traditional industries, but also because it was the earliest and most influential of the families and doubtless initiated certain secular as well as religious practices which later affected other families and societies.

The author has known the Shakers for a number of years. Many friendships have grown from these contacts and an ever-increasing interest in and respect for their ideas and ideals, those in particular which found expression in their occupational and craft life. No claim is made, however, that this is the last word on the subject; the theme is a broad one, with many ramifications. The study is based largely upon the known literature by and about the Shakers and upon such manuscript material as the author has collected in the course of his various sojourns among this people. The large amount of manuscript data in the hands of others—such institutions as the New York State Library at Albany and the Western Reserve Historical Society—undoubtedly would add greatly to our knowledge of the Shakers' industrial activities. Effort is directed mainly to an exposition, as complete as our material will permit, of the occupations at the one society at New Lebanon, with the hope that this will lead to fuller studies in the future.

Grateful acknowledgment is made for the generous cooperation of the several Shaker sisters who have felt the importance of a clearer revelation of their society's historical past; and to Dr Charles C. Adams, Director of the New York State Museum, whose far-sighted recognition of the importance of the subject matter was the initial stimulus to this research, I am also under the deepest obligation.

THE RISE OF SHAKERISM

The United Society of Believers had its origin in the English Quaker Church and in the sect of French Prophets known on the continent as the Camisards. Because of the unusual physical manifestations of their worship they were sometimes referred to as "Shaking Quakers"; the name "Shakers" appears as early as 1774 in the records of the constables of Manchester (The Manifesto, September '92, p. 193). The Shaker society was an outgrowth of a religious order founded in this English industrial center about 1747 by James and Jane Wardley. Ann Lee, the daughter of a blacksmith, joined the order in 1758, and soon, by the vigor of her personality and professedly inspired utterances, became the accepted leader of a new movement. It had been revealed

16

to her from divine sources, she preached, that God possessed "two natures, the masculine, the feminine, each distinct in function yet one in being, Co-equals in Deity" (White and Taylor, '05, p. 19). The secret of man's sin lay in "the premature and self-indulgent use of sexual-union . . . The natural function, which was intended in each individual to subserve its purpose and then to be left behind as higher spiritual development was attained, became, in fact, for all humanity, a constant curse, the source of crimes of all degrees of hideousness, of wars and sufferings untold. Woman, under its sway became in all lands and among all races, the abject slave, burdened not only with the weight of her lord's cruelties and

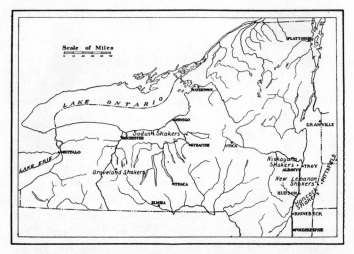

FIGURE 2 Map of New York State, showing location of three Shaker societies at Groveland, Niskeyuna and New Lebanon. Hancock lies just over the line in Massachusetts. Trade centers at Albany, Troy, Hudson and Poughkeepsie furnished early markets for Shaker goods.

passions, but with her own vile passions as well" (Note 1).[1]

This vision brought with it "the command to abstain from such indulgence. Jesus, the Revealer, was in his human life pure and undefiled; such were his early followers. Such must all become, said Ann Lee, after this revelation and anointing, who would be true followers of Jesus Christ" (White and Taylor, '05, p. 19).

In response to divine inspiration and to further the plan of advancing her doctrine, Ann set sail for New York on May 19, 1774, with eight followers. Landing on August 6, 1774, the group separated for the time being in order to earn their living. John Hocknell, the only member possessed of means, purchased a piece of land about seven miles northwest of Albany, at a place then known as Niskeyuna. The small company assembled herein the spring of 1776, and through the summer they cleared the land and erected buildings for a permanent home. The first gathering was in September of that year, in a log cabin.

For three years the vicissitudes of war and want frustrated the carrying out of their plans. In the winter of 1779 a religious revival, chiefly among the Baptists, took place in the town of New Lebanon, N. Y., and the surrounding country. Through the medium of Talmage Bishop and others, people there heard of the strange group at Niskeyuna, and in the spring of 1780 sent Calvin Harlow to investigate. Harlow returned, "but neither the people nor himself being fully satisfied," he went again, accompanied this time by Joseph Meacham and Amos Hammond, both Baptist preachers, and Aaron Kibbee

---

[1] See Notes, Supplementary to the Text, p. 266.

(Note 2). These men became fully convinced "that what they had seen and heard was the work and truth of God," and "the people at large were also encouraged to go and examine for themselves." By the middle of 1780 visitors were coming to Niskeyuna in crowds and many were converted to the Shaker faith. Among the first of these converts was the above Joseph Meacham, who became the leader in the organization and development of the order after the deaths of Ann Lee and James Whitaker, her first successor. David Meacham, Joseph's brother, a wealthy resident of Enfield, Conn., was also an early convert.

The encouragement attending this enthusiastic reception of her gospel soon ripened into missionary enterprise, and in May 1781, Ann Lee, accompanied by the elders of the church, started eastward to spread their faith. In the next two years they visited some 36 towns and villages in Massachusetts and Connecticut, their journeying attended always by hardship, opposition and severe persecution. In August 1783, almost at the end of their mission, the group was driven from New Lebanon after having held a meeting at the house of John Bishop, the site of the present South family.

Mother Ann, as she was lovingly called by her followers, died September 8, 1784, and Father James Whitaker, one of her original companions in Manchester, succeeded her as head of the order. In 1785 this leader directed the Believers at New Lebanon to build a house for public worship. The meeting-house illustrated in figure 3 was completed as a joint enterprise early in 1786, and on January 29th the first assembly was held. Father James died July 20, 1787. Of the three most prominent elders who survived him, the two Meachams and Calvin Harlow,

Joseph Meacham was selected to assume active leadership of the society.

From this date New Lebanon came to be considered the central home of the sect, the site of the first church to be established. In September 1787 all who had accepted the faith were notified by the elders "that those living in the vicinity of New Lebanon, if they so desired, could on application, be gathered into the Church" (Note 3). Before the close of the year the membership had exceeded 100 persons.

FIGURE 3 The first Shaker church at New Lebanon, built in 1786. (After Nordhoff, '75.) When the second meeting-house was built in 1822–24, the original church was moved a few rods to the north. Subsequently it was remodeled and used as a seed-house.

The society was further organized in 1788. Hezekiah Hammond, Jonathan Walker, David Darrow and other residents of New Lebanon had consecrated their lands and homes to the welfare of the order, but more land and buildings were required. A frame dwelling was erected in the later months of the year and occupied by Christmas time. Elder Joseph had organized the church on a carefully conceived plan. An order of ministry, consisting of two brethren and two sisters, was appointed to preside over the whole church, "wherever they might be located" (The Manifesto, August '89, p. 170). It was further planned to have an order of elders in each family, or household group, in every society which might be established, their function being to direct the spiritual affairs of their particular group. A third order, the trustees, were to take charge of the temporal interests and duties of the society, the buying, the selling, the holding of deeds and so on.

In 1790 the society began to expand to other places in New England. Mother Ann's journey early in the preceding decade had prepared the way for the formation of these new branches of the society. In that year the community at Hancock, Mass., was organized in "gospel order," and in 1791 one at Harvard, Mass.; in 1792 three societies were "gathered," at East Canterbury, N. H., at Enfield, Conn., and at Tyringham, Mass.; in 1793 three more, at Alfred, Maine, at Enfield, N. H., and at Shirley, Mass.; the society at New Gloucester, 25 miles northwest of Portland, Maine, was founded in 1794, the last of the New England settlements to be organized. In each case "the senior minister for the Brethren as well as for the Sisters was sent from the Society of New Lebanon, and the others were chosen from the place where

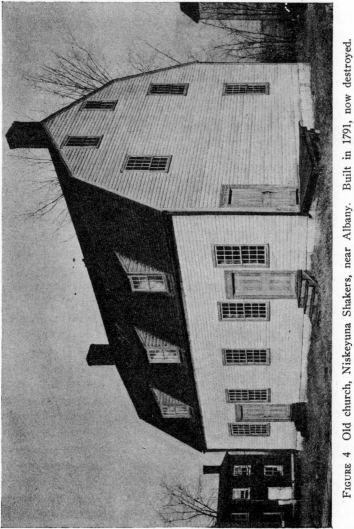

FIGURE 4 Old church, Niskeyuna Shakers, near Albany. Built in 1791, now destroyed.

the Community was formed" (The Manifesto, August '89, p. 171).

As in the case of the New Lebanon society, several of these New England communities arose out of regional religious revivals, chiefly among the Baptists, and often their original properties were a consecrated bequest. This was true of Alfred, Canterbury and Enfield, N. H. The societies at Shirley, Harvard, Hancock and Enfield, Conn., had received an initial stimulus from the earlier visits of Mother Ann and the elders, and in certain cases, notably at Hancock and Shirley, as well as at other societies not included in this missionary tour, meeting-houses had been erected before the communities were actually organized. The pioneer group at Niskeyuna, or Watervliet, N. Y., had been organized "in gospel relation" after the death of James Whitaker in 1787, and was included in the New Lebanon bishopric (Note 4). The early church at this society, built in 1791, is illustrated in figure 4.

The organization of the society begun in 1787 and 1788 by Joseph Meacham was gradually perfected. By 1791 two more dwellings had been built at New Lebanon, and members of this society had been sent to assist in erecting a dwelling at Hancock and meeting-houses at Watervliet, Harvard and Enfield, Conn. The same year Elder David Meacham (Note 5) was appointed senior trustee at New Lebanon, with the responsibility of directing all business transactions. An order of family deacons was also established to oversee the temporal affairs of each family.

In 1793 several farms adjoining the original properties at New Lebanon were purchased, and we find the early small gardening activities of the Believers expanding into more extensive agricultural pursuits. A start had earlier been made along industrial lines, prominent among which were blacksmithing and the tanning of leather.

Although the communal idea had not originally entered into Ann Lee's social and religious doctrines, an oral agreement on basic principles of property rights was made soon after the organization of the New Lebanon society. It had been agreed that no member should hold private property, and that no one should buy or sell in the church, "nor trade with those not of the Church, except by the union of the Trustees" (The Manifesto, September '89, p. 194). In business management it had been from the start assumed that the sisters should have equal privileges and equal responsibilities with the brethren, and union meetings for consultation were frequently held. The first covenant to commit to writing such agreements and the rules for membership was signed in 1795. The extracts given below indicate the religious basis of the "Joint Interest" idea. This document (MS. No. 1)[1] illuminates the principles of communism as they first developed in the Shaker order:

The following is the Covenant of the Church of Christ, in New Lebanon, relating to the possession and use of a Joint Interest

In the year of our Lord 1788, the year in which most of the members of the Church were Gathered. The following order and Covenant was then, and from time to time after, made known and understood, received and entered into by us as members of the Church, agreeable to an understanding of the order and Covenant of a Church in Gospel order.

For it was and is still our Faith, and confirmed by our experience, that there could be no Church in Complete

---

[1] See Manuscripts in the Andrews Collection, p. 301.

order, according to the Law of Christ, without being
Gathered into one Joint Interest and union, that all the
members might have an equal right and privilege, according to their Calling and needs, in things both Spirritual
& temporal. . . .

Thirdly, All that should be received as members, being
of age, that had any substance or property that was free
from debt, or any Just demand of any that were without,
either as Credittors or Heirs, were allowed to bring in their
Substance, being their natural and Lawful right, and give
it as a part of the Joint Interest of the Church, agreeable
to their own faith and desire, to be under the order and
Government of the Deacons, And overseers of the Temporal Interest of the Church, and any other use that the
Gospel requires, according to the understanding and dis-
cression of those members with whoom it was Intrusted,
and that were appointed to that office and care.

Fourthly, All the members that should be received into
the Church, should possess one Joint Interest, as a Religious right, that is, that all should have Just and Equal
rights and Priviledges, according to their needs, in the
use of all things in the Church, without Any difference
being made on account of what any of us brought in, so
long as we remained in Obedience to the order and Government of the Church, and are holden in relation as members. All the members are likewise Equally holden,
according to their abilities, to maintain and support one
Joint Interest in union, in Conformity to the order &
Government of the Church.

Fifthly, As it was not the duty or purpose of the
Church, in uniting into Church order, to gather and lay
up an Interest of this Worlds goods; But what we become
possessed of by Honest Industry, more Than for our
own support, to bestow to Charitable uses, for the relief
of the poor, and otherwise as the Gospel might Require.
Therefore it is our Faith never to bring Debt or blame
against the Church, or each other, for any Interest or
Services we should bestow to the Joint Interest of the
Church, but Covenanted to freely give and Contribute
our time and Tallents, as Brethren and Sisters, for the

mutual good one of another, and other Charitable uses, according to the order of the Church.

The foregoing is the true Sense of the Covenant of the Church, in relation to the order and manner of the Possession and use of a Joint Interest, understood and supported by us the members. . . . We believed we were debtors to God in relation to Each other, and all men, to improve our time and Tallents in this Life, in that manner in which we might be most useful. Experience of Seven years Travel and Labour, and Received a greater Confirmation and Establishment in our faith, that the order and Covenant in which we have gathered, and Solemnly entered into, is a greater privilege, and Enables us to be more useful to ourselves, and others, than any other State in our Knowledge, and is that, that was Required, and is accepted of God. . . . In Testamony whereof, we have, both Bretheren and Sisters, hereunto subscribed our names in the year of our Lord 1795 (Note 6).

It was the conviction of the early Believers that the true Christian principle called for equal rights and privileges "in things both Spiritual and temporal" and that no difference should be made on account of the original contribution of the members. The phrase—"We believed we were debtors to God in relation to Each other, and all men, to improve our time and Tallents in this Life, in that manner in which we might be most useful"—summarizes what is meant by the term "consecrated industry" so often used in Shaker literature. During their long history the members of the Shaker community system have labored for the support and advancement of their church alone. Both their temporal and spiritual interests are united in a church relationship.

It was largely through the executive genius of Joseph Meacham that the scattered, disorganized members of the Shaker faith were finally bound together in such a carefully ordered union. Through his instrumentation the Believers were gathered "into a body religious, not a body politic, or a body corporate. . . . Their real and personal estate could not be treated as a joint tenancy, nor a tenancy in common, therefore it was made a consecration— a consecrated whole" (Robinson, '93, p. 28). Because the institution of Shakerism was thus believed to be a derivative from Divine rather than civil or political authority, the society could not "connect itself with the world; from this it must ever remain in isolation" (Robinson, '93, p. 29).

By 1795 not only had the general plan of organization been thus perfected, but the basic beliefs of the sect had become clarified. Later historians rightly regard the principles of Christian communism and separation from the world as among the fundamentals of Shakerism. Separation from the world was further a safeguard from that worldliness which interceded between the individual committed to the life of the spirit and the heavenly kingdom he sought. The virgin life, which Ann Lee so strongly felt was an unalterable principle in this higher life, and the confessional, which signalized the novitiate's advent into this life, were also necessary commitments in the Shaker faith.

ECONOMIC ASPECTS OF SHAKER COMMUNISM

In the organization of an institution which represented itself as an advance in social welfare, and in the pursuit of whose aims separation from the life of the world and from an imperfectly constituted society was deemed necessary, one of the chief tasks lay in the development of an economic system efficient enough to maintain this institution and make its ideals attainable. One of the chief distinctions between Shakerism and the many short-lived communistic enterprises in the United States lies in the thorough organization of the Believers on the material side, and it is to their success in agriculture and industry as much as to their spiritual sincerity that the long life of this society must be attributed. In the course of developing a sound agricultural and industrial foundation, there evolved a complex occupational economy. Although the basis of the social system was agriculture, many industries were instituted from an early period, carefully organized and energetically prosecuted. There was no place in Shakerism for an idler or a "slut," and the reputation of the Believers for industriousness was as broad and well-founded as that for cleanliness, order and earnestness of purpose.

Shaker industries are readily divided into two classes—those pursued for the sake of supplying the needs of the society itself and those "undertaken with an eye to the demands of the world outside." Both the farm and the shop functioned for each of these ends, and the products of each were as necessary to the temporal well-being of the Believers as they were useful in the world which lay beyond their sequestered domains. In a report to the New York State Senate in 1850, attention was called to the fact "That the faith and principles of the society . . . tolerate only such branches of industry as are useful to the public, instead of those which tend to superfluity and extravagance . . . " (State of New York, No. 89, In Senate, Mar. 19, 1850, p. 8). Under such conditions there was no inconsistency in receiving and putting to good use the products of the shop. Brooms and medicinal extracts found a ready domestic use as well as a ready sale. The famous Shaker garden seeds distributed through New England, New York and the South were used by the Believers themselves in their unexcelled gardens. The products of the tannery were sold in quantity, but the tanning house also provided leather for Shaker shoes, hat linings, harnesses and bookbindings. The Shakers wove cloth and made garments and hats for sale, but they also made their own clothes and bonnets and stockings. On the other hand, the primary purpose of their industrial activities was the acquisition of sufficient income to cover expenses and to provide for necessary construction and expansion; and an examination of their accounts from year to year indicates that as a rule their credit balances were small. From this point of view it is legitimate to make the distinction between industries for home maintenance and industries for profit, although it should be remembered that in many cases, in the chair-making industry for example, this distinction is difficult to make.

The Shakers believed that in practising the principle of community of goods they followed the example of the primitive Christian church. In their original covenant the conviction was solemnly recorded "that there could be no Church in Complete order, according to the Law of Christ, without being gathered into one Joint Interest and union, that all the members might have an equal right and privilege, according to their Calling and needs, in things both Spiritual and temporal. . . ." This joint interest was held as a consecration, and although the Shakers shared their goods in common, these temporal properties were dedicated to God and what they believed to be His plan in this world.

The relinquishment of all personal and private property and of the right to receive wages for their services was the accompaniment of the individual's reception into church or "covenant relationship." It was customary for the prospective member to remain for a time in what was known as the novitiate order, where one might still live with his or her family (Note 7). While maintaining this partial relationship to the society the individual retained full control of any property possessed and the freedom to withdraw at any time. Entrance into "church relation" involved not only freedom from all involvements, but a full dedication of all personal property (Note 8). A covenant member was still free to withdraw at any time from the society. Although in this case no claim could later be made on property once dedicated, the trustees of the temporal interests of the Shaker church invariably exercised justice by making "donations to the full amount of property that such persons have brought in, or become heir to, on their withdrawal." (Note 9)

An illustration of such a dedication of goods has recently come into the possession of the writer. It is entitled, "A Memorandam of Things carried to the North-House (New Lebanon) by Samuel and Elisabeth Johnson in the year 1793 for the use of the Famaly." (MS. No. 5) The memorandum follows:

	£		
Two Cows	10—	0—	0
Four Swine	2—	8—	0
one Barrel one half Pork	5—	0—	0
one Case of Draws	1—	10—	0
Two old Chery Tables	0—	12—	0
Two Fether Beads bolsters and Pillows	5—	10—	0
Two under Do and two Pillows	0—	9—	0
Six pares of Sheets	4—	0—	0
five Pairs of Pillow Cases	1—	5—	0
Nine Towels	0—	9—	0

one Flowered Coverlet	1—10—0
one toe Do one Duck Blanket	1— 6—0
one old brass kittle	1— 0—0
one Iron Pot one Tea Kittle	0—13—0
two Small Do and one Skillet	0—12—0
one Pair of Hand Irons	0—16—0
Shovel and Tongs	0— 8—0
An ax	0— 8—0
A warming Pan	0— 8—0
a frying Do and two pails	0— 5—0
one Pair of Iron Flats	0— 4—0
Puter Plate 23½ a 1/6	1—15—3
three Pounds of Feathers	0— 9—0
one bead Quilt	0—10—0
A Tosting Iron	0— 4—0
An old Horse	3— 4—0
Money which had been lent to the town of West Stockbridge was collected and brought back here and delivered to Amos Hammond	2—12—0
also a lot of Land which I sold to Daniel Goodrich for	73— 6—8
and collected the Money and delivered it to Amos by the Liberty and Priviledge I had	
Elizabeth Johnson the Second hath had	
A Bead and Beading	5— 0—0
A New Chest	0—12—0

Lebanon January 25th 1803
I have made a Statement for Distribution of my Estate according to a Rule of the Church viz. (a Daughter one Part, a Son two Parts, their Mother four Parts, and the Father Eight) One Part is 53 Dollars 29½ Cents

The same dedicatory spirit in which men and women entered into this great adventure of consecrated living exalted their attitude towards the daily task. Here dwelt the same inspiration as in the old monastic orders: *laborare est orare,* "to work is to worship." Mother Ann's injunction to the early Believers that they should "put their hands to work and their hearts to God" was sacred doctrine. Dixon calls theirs a "celestial industry," and notes their regret at the necessity of hiring help from the world, "this throwing of the saint and sinner into a common society for the sake of gain . . ." (Dixon, '69, p. 313).

Every incoming member was assigned to the work which he or she could most profitably accomplish. The indenture agreements between the society and the parent or guardian of a minor taken into the sect stipulated among other terms that the Shakers should provide "such manual occupation or branch of business as shall be found best adapted" to the said minor's "genius and capacity" (Note 10). The young men and women were apprenticed to responsible "caretakers" in the home, shop or field. If a man were engaged in a particular trade, he usually found the opportunity to continue in this same occupation. Some of the brethren had two or more trades; the Shakers believed in "variety of labor, for variety of occupation is a source of pleasure" (Dixon, '69, p. 315). The daily journals kept by many a brother or sister testify to the variety of chores and tasks which were often a part of the daily routine, and expressions of satisfaction or relief were common when the diarist was about to enter or leave some particular occupation in which a system of rotation of labor was practised.

The actual business affairs of the society were under the direction of trustees, who held and managed "the temporalities in trust" (Green and Wells, '46, p. 35). There were two of these officers in each order, who could be removed at any time by the ministry. Each of the trustees was to keep an account of all disbursements and receipts, and the two registers were compared by the ministry at the close of each year. The duties of the trustees, or deacons and deaconesses as they were often called, are thus further specified in the Millenial Laws (MS. No. 4):

1 Those called as Deacons or Trustees, shall stand as stewards in the house of God, and their dwelling place should be at the outer court.

2 It is the duty of the Deacons and Deaconesses or Trustees, to see to the domestic concerns of the family in which they reside, and to perform all business transactions, either with the world, or with believers in other families or societies. All trade and traffic, buying and selling, changing and swapping, must be done by them or by their immediate knowledge and consent.

3 No new fashions in manufacture, clothing, or wares of any kind, may be introduced among Believers, without the sanction of the Ministry, thro' the medium of the Elders of each family thereof.

4 All monies, book accounts, deeds, bonds, notes, etc., which belong to the family, must be kept at the office, unless some other suitable place be provided therefor, by the proper authorities. Exceptions with regard to spending money are sometimes necessary, which must always be directed by the Elders, in union with the Ministry.

5 Those appointed to transact business of a temporal nature, should keep all their accounts booked down regular and exact, and as far as possible avoid controversies with the world.

6 Believers must not run in *debt* to the world.

7 The purchase of needful articles that appear substantial and good, and suitable for Believers to use, should not be neglected to purchase those which are needlessly adorned, even if they are a little cheaper.

8 Neither Trustees, nor any one in their employ should be gone from home among the world, on trading business, more than four weeks, at one and the same time.

9 Three brethren who shall be appointed by the Ministry, two of which if consistent, should be Deacons or Trustees, are sufficient to go to the great and wicked cities to trade for any one family.

10 Believers should have no connection in trade or barter with those who have turned their backs to the way of God. Neither should they sojourn with them at night, nor keep company with them in the day, if possibly consistent to avoid it. But if it be necessary to hold conver-

sation with them, do it in such a manner, that when you return home, you can give a correct account of it to your Elders, which should always be done.

11 When you resort to taverns, and to public places, you shall not in any wise blend and gather with the wicked, by uniting in unnecessary conversation, jesting and joking, talking upon politics with them, or disputing or enquiring into things which will serve to draw your sense from the pure way of God.

12 All who go out among the world, should observe as far as possible, the order of kneeling, and should always kneel in prayer twice each day, if they have to do it by the road side, or in the waggon while driving along.

13 Trustees desiring the help of members, not in the Trustees order, to do business for them, or to perform any of their official duties, at home or abroad, must apply to the Elders for the same.

14 Members employed by the Deacons or Trustees to do business at home or abroad, must render a full and explicit account to them, of all their transactions and expenditures, when such duties are performed, specifying particularly every article for which such expenses were made.

15 When two or more are out together, they should as far as possibly consistent, all eat at one tavern, and lodge in one room, and when you walk in the streets, you should keep so close together that there would not be room for even as much as a dog to run between you and your companion.

16 Those who go out on business for the Deacons or Trustees, have no more right to buy, sell, barter or trade in any way, than any other member in the family, save by the authority of those who send them.

17 It is contrary to good order for any persons except the Ministry and Elders, to have correspondence with the Deacons or Trustees, relative to their official lot and calling, such as their bargains and contracts in general, except in cases wherein they are by them employed to do

2

business, in union with the Elders, and in such a manner as the nature of the case may require. But is reasonable and consistent for members to know the *market prices* of articles bought or sold, as groceries, dry goods, provisions, hard ware and other ware if they desire to. But it should be understood that the Deacons are under no obligation to tell *common members just what they paid* for articles sold; but they should be free to tell the *market prices*.

18 The order of God forbids that Believers should lend money upon usury, (or interest) to their brethren of the household of faith, neither should Believers accept interest (or usury) from their brethren, should it be offered.

19 As the Deacons or Trustees are called to be examples of godliness, gospel plainness, prudence and good economy in temporal things, they may not purchase for themselves, or receive as a gift, to be kept by them, or at their place of residence, any article or articles that are superfluous, unnecessary or such as are disowned in the family where they reside.

20 Those appointed to transact business are required to keep all their transactions plain and open to their visible Lead, and when they sustain lapses, whether in money or other things, to lay it open before the Lead in its true light. They are also required before making any heavy purchases to ask counsel and obtain union of the leading influence of the family in which they reside.

21 Those appointed to transact business abroad are required to attend meetings with the family, as far as their circumstances will possibly admit, as they need the union and strength of the body of the family. They should also attend meals with the family as much as possible, that they may know how to feel for their temporal needs and circumstances, in the line of provisions.

22 When brethren or sisters want any thing bought, or brought in from among the world, or from other families of Believers, or wish for any article or articles which it is the duty of the Deacons and Deaconesses to provide,

they must apply to them for whatever they desire, those of each sex in their own order.

23 A supply of such small tools and articles as sisters need, which brethren make, should be made by order of the Deacons, and delivered to the Deaconesses, to whom the sisters should apply for the same, when desired.

24 If sisters desire tools, conveniences, or articles of manufacture which come in the brethren's line of business, and which it would require much time to make, they must apply to the Deaconesses, but if it be small chores, they may apply to either Deacons or Deaconesses for the same.

25 When brethren need help of the sisters in their line of business, that will require much time, they must make application to the Deacons, but if it be small chores, they may apply to either Deacons or Deaconesses, as the case may require.

26 No work done in the family for sale, shall go out of the family save by the knowledge and direction of the Deacons & Deaconesses, except in some uncommon emergency, and then a correct account should be rendered as soon as may be.

27 The Deacons & Deaconesses are required by the orders of the gospel, to give to the Elders from time to time a correct account of all matters of importance that have come within their knowledge, concerning the temporal business of the family, and of things that have been called for, and of all they have given out.

28 It is the duty of the Deacons & Deaconesses to see that suitable furniture for rooms, and suitable food for the family are provided, (as far as lies in their power,) and to see that the food is cooked with good economy.

29 Brethren and sisters have no liberty to make for themselves or for others, accommodations or conveniences without the union and consent of the Deacons and Deaconesses, each sex in their own order.

30 It is the duty of members to render due respect to the Trustees, Deacons, and Deaconesses.

It is well at this point to clear up a common misconception of Shaker internal organization. A society was not "one great Community of temporal interests," but was divided into several communities or families, each of which was separately organized. "Families [might] differ in their temporal conditions, from fortuitous circumstances, such as location, the business they chose to adopt, the ability to conduct affairs, the number of members, and from many other causes of a temporal or spiritual nature—the same contingencies as those to which Societies are subject" (Note 11). One reason for such division lay in the belief that the management of property was facilitated, and "that in case of great loss by one Family the others help bear the burden" (Hinds, '78, p. 109). The industrial unit, then, was the family. Each family had its trustees, who could buy from and sell to the trustees of other families or carry on business with outside individuals or concerns. Sometimes it happened that several families would unite in an industry or business venture, or 'maintain a common store as a clearing house for manufactured articles.

As families were large, such an arrangement did not lessen the advantages of the principle of combination. The laundries, dairies and bakeries were models of cooperative efficiency. Farming was a well-organized joint enterprise in which many operations were reduced to an almost regimental precision. In every industry—tanning, coopering, broom making, the cultivation of garden seeds, the extraction of juices from barks and plants, the manufacture of boxes, sieves, horsewhips, tubs, pails and pipes, the preparation of wines, preserves and apple-sauce, the drying of sweet corn and the manufacture of hats, gloves, fans and baskets—in these, as in many other occupations, the principle of a careful division of labor was carried out. Every member had his or her appointed task at an appointed time. In these early group activities of the Shakers one recognizes a formative chapter in large scale or "mass production" enterprise, an anticipation of the corporate businesses which rose in the later machine age in this country.

The more one dwells upon the subject, the more surprising it seems that a people who had segregated themselves from the world and who held spiritual blessedness as the *summum bonum* should have developed such an amazingly progressive economic system. They were as practical in their "temporalities" as they were idealists in their religious convictions. The secret lies in part in the advantages of combination to which reference has been made. Their progressiveness in the applied sciences and success in business were due in large measure to the great drive and motivation furnished by the consciousness of a spiritual destiny. They worked for ends more stimulating and significant than mere personal advancement. It was Dixon's conviction that the common saying "about the Shakers giving their minds to the culture of land may be used as a key to unlock nearly all the secrets of Mount Lebanon" (Dixon, '69, p. 302). And back of all this earnestness of purpose was a great organization built up by unusual leaders and made binding by the powerful sanctions of religion.

It is impossible to evaluate the industrial life of this sect without a just consideration of the effect of the religious influence. It was part and parcel of their everyday life and work. "What are goods worth," a writer in The Shaker asks, "unless they are full of genuine religion?" (The Shaker, November '72, p. 83.) They catered, as we have seen, not to the frailities of human nature, but to the genuine needs of society; their goods were meant to serve some real use. The result was that the Shakers early achieved an enviable reputation for reliability and honesty, and the quality of their products was uniformly high—so high that "Scarcely a branch of business (was) taken up, and succeeded with, ere they were confronted by counterfeits in market, that looked like their goods before being used, but which came to an end of their usefulness much sooner" (The Shaker, November '72, p. 82).

In setting up such a high standard of honest and progressive industrial and agricultural practice the Shakers exercised a wide and beneficial influence in their neighborhoods. Charles F. Wingate reported that "When the farmers in the vicinity want to buy new implements or machinery they usually call and see what the Shakers are using, and what they think will serve best for the purpose. To have gained the endorsement of the Shakers for his wares is a great card for a manufacturer or dealer, and one man remarked that 'he would rather do a piece of work for them for nothing than make a bad job of it, as their good will was not to be despised'" (The Manifesto, May '89, p. 114).

A survey of literature about this communistic sect reveals many similar tributes to their progressive methods. A correspondent in The Manifesto (to quote a single instance) notes after a visit to Mount Lebanon in 1880 that "the society has kept pace with the age of progress in agriculture, horticulture, fruit growing, improved implements, machinery, buildings etc., also in hygiene and the best methods of attaining to and preserving healthy bodies with all the appliances for cleanliness, plenty of pure water applied inwardly and outwardly; also a system of drainage and ventilation to insure breathing pure air, practical industry is also habitual . . ." (The Manifesto, December '80, p. 272).

The most graphic proof of the Shakers' genius for efficiency and improvement over common practices lies in the many inventions and labor-saving devices with which they are credited. As Arthur Baker, an English editor, pointed out, "The list of their [Shaker] inventions is a standing refutation of the theory that Communism would reduce production to a dead level; it shows rather, that nothing so much stimulates the inventive genius of a group as a system which enables them to reap the benefits of their own talent, and to save their own labour by whatever labour-saving devices they introduce" (Baker, '96, p. 16).

Their contribution in this field was far from negligible. The Shaker historians Anna White and Leila Taylor state that the "list of inventions and devices of Shaker wit and wisdom is a long one, and if extended into little labor-saving contrivances about the dwellings, shops and barns would seem almost endless" (Note 12). Many of these implements were the outcome of necessity. Removed from the main paths of progress, these people often had to resort to their own ingenuity. Moreover, they engaged in activities not always commonly practised elsewhere, activities which were prosecuted on an unprecedented scale, and it was necessary to create instruments to solve their own peculiar problems. The list of inventions and improvements submitted below makes no claim to absolute reliability. In some cases a particular machine or article may be wrongly attributed; in other cases it is almost impossible to prove whether the Shakers had precedence over some outsider. It is merely a list of credits, which indicates nevertheless that the society numbered among its members many unusually alert and gifted mechanics. The list is an amplification of those compiled by D. A. Buckingham (The Shaker, August '77, p. 59) and by White and Taylor ('05, p. 311–16).

1 *Screw propeller*. Invention of Thomas Wells of Watervliet.

2 *Babbitt metal*. Invention of Daniel W. Baird of North Union, Ohio. (Erroneously credited as original Shaker invention.)

3 *Rotary or revolving harrow*. Invention of Daniel W. Baird of North Union, Ohio.

4 *Automatic spring*. Invention of Daniel W. Baird of North Union, Ohio.

5 *Sash balance (for ventilation)*. Invention of Sanford J. Russell of South Union, Ky.

6 *Governor of an over-shot water wheel*. Invention of Elder Matthew B. Carter of Ohio.

7 *Turbine water wheel*. Invention of George Wickersham of New Lebanon.

8 *Threshing machine* (1815).

9 *Machinery for matching boards* (Tongue-and-groove machine). Invention of Henry Bennett and Amos Bishop of New Lebanon (1828).

10 *Planing machine* (Note 13).

11 *Fertilizing machine*. Invention of Charles Greaves of Mount Lebanon.

12 *Machinery for splint making, basket working and box cutting*. Invention of Elders Daniel Boler and Daniel Crossman.

FIGURE 5 "Self-acting" cheese press from New Lebanon, showing cheese-hoop and block. The lever raises the circular plate, automatically exerting pressure on the curds within the hoop. From South family, New Lebanon. New York State Museum.

13 *Cut nails* (Note 14). ⎱ Inventions of Sarah Babbitt
14 *Circular saw.*   ⎰   of Harvard.

15 *Improved washing machine or wash mill* (Note. 15).

16 *Improved windmill.* Invented at Canterbury.

17 *Summer covering for a flat-iron stove.* Invented by George W. Wickersham.

18 *Stove-cover lifter.* Invented by Sewell G. Thayer of North Union, Ohio.

19 *Shaker wood stoves.*

20 *Machinery for twisting the handles of "sopus whips."* Invented at Watervliet.

21 *A pipe machine.* Invented at Watervliet.

22 *Pea-sheller.* Invented at Watervliet.

23 *Butter-worker.* Invented at Watervliet.

24 *"Self-acting" cheese press.* Invented at New Lebanon (figure 5). Patent "cheese vats" were being sold at Canterbury just before the Civil War.

25 *First one-horse wagon used in this country* (Enfield, Conn.).

26 *The common clothes pin* (North Union, Ohio).

27 *Loom for weaving palm-leaf bonnets.* Invented by Abner Bedell of Union Village, Ohio.

28 *Silk-reeling machine.* Invented by Abner Bedell, 1837. (Iron vessel and furnace for this machine invented by Thomas Taylor of Union Village.)

29 *Apple-parer "which quartered and cored the fruit."* Invented by Sanford J. Russell.

30 *Revolving oven.* Invented by Eldress Emeline Hart, Canterbury.

FIGURE 6 Model of wash mill or washing machine patented, sold and used by the Shakers. The model is operated by a handle causing the dashers to move back and forth in the six tubs. Wires or cables attached to the scaffolding reduced friction on the sliding frame to which the dashers were attached. In use, the "mill" was run by water power. Andrews Collection.

[43]

31 *Metal pens*. Invented by Isaac Youngs, New Lebanon. First pens were made of brass and silver, 1819. "Machinery for rolling the brass and silver plate and shears for cutting the pens were home inventions."

32 *Machine "for cutting and bending machine card teeth and punching the leather for setting."* Invented at New Lebanon by Benjamin Bruce.

33 *The first flat broom.* "Invented" at Watervliet by Theodore Bates.

34 *Improved lathe with "screw feeder," for turning broom handles.* Invented at New Lebanon by Jesse Wells (Note 16).

35 *Machine for sizing broom-corn brush.* Invented at Harvard.

36 *Improved kiln for drying corn.*

37 *Machine for filling seed bags.* Invented at Watervliet.

38 *"Printing presses for printing seed bags and herb packages."* Invented at Watervliet and "improved" at New Lebanon.

39 *Machine for filling herb packages.* Used and probably invented at New Lebanon.

In seeking for the most efficient means of carrying on certain industrial operations the Shakers often bought concessions from the patentees of various mechanical devices. The purchase of a washing machine in 1811 and a planing machine in 1831 has elsewhere been referred to (see Notes 15 and 13). The original model of the Canterbury "wash-mill" is pictured in figure 6. In a letter to Jonathan Wood in 1843, W. Willard of Shaker Village (Canterbury), N. H., ordered a planing machine from the New Lebanon Church to be built "on the most approved plan" and to be paid for in part by "a few rolls of fine flannel" (MS. No. 49). Wood may have made other such machines for sale. As early as 1797, one Ebenezer Kellogg, who had secured a patent for clothing shears "adapted to Shearing Machines," granted to David Meacham "full Liberty or License to use, vend, & Make s^d Shears"—the compensation to be conditioned by Kellogg's payment of a certain note (MS. No. 40). In 1808 Stephen Munson paid a Cornelius Young (?) $65 for the right to make and use a "bark mill for the grinding of Bark exclusively for himself in that town [Canaan]" (MS. No. 41). In 1810 the same Shaker trustee paid $12 to Benjamin Tyler jr and John Tyler of Claremont, N. H., for the right to build, use or vend a wheel for grinding tanner's bark; this wheel was on the model of Benjamin Tyler's Patent Wry-Fly Wheel which had been patented in 1793 (MS. No. 42). In 1814 Munson purchased for $16 the rights to an "improvement in Looms" from a certain Ebenezer Jones (MS. No. 44); and in 1816 manufacturing rights to a machine called "a Roller for compressing & extending sole (?) leather" were sold to the same trustee by William Edwards, "late of Northampton" (MS. No. 45). "A ten spindled . . . Spinner," and the right to use the same for fourteen years from the date of August 11, 1821, was purchased by Munson from a man by the name of Wilkes Hyde (MS. No. 46). In 1830 rights to patent door and window springs were obtained from a native of Southboro, Mass. (MS. No. 47).

No better measure of the remarkable agricultural and industrial development of the Shaker society during the first half-century of its existence may be obtained than by comparing their living conditions and properties at the time the society at New Lebanon was organized in 1786–88 with the properties reported under the New York State Trust Act of 1837.

The first buildings at New Lebanon were made of logs. The first frame dwelling was erected in 1788 (Note 17). That year a drought practically destroyed the grain crop and great hardships resulted. In a record handed down by Calvin Green, living conditions of that period were thus described:

We had very little bread, not much milk, scarcely any pie, butter or cheese. We had to live on meat, such fish as we could get, porridge, salt meat, broth and potatoes. For a time potatoes were our chief food. In short, we labored hard, lived poor and had crowded, poor accommodations for shelter. They tried to do as well by the children as their knowledge and means would permit. The children in general partook of the same zeal in support of the cause as the grown members. They worked hard and were not overfed. I was hungry all the time. Mother Lucy possessed great love for children and did much to improve their condition and give them comfortable support. It was several years before the Church were well accommodated and had plenty of food and clothing. (White and Taylor, '05, p. 75).

And fifty years later? On April 15, 1839, the assessors' returns on the real estate of the Shakers at New Lebanon showed that they owned 2292¼ acres, valued (including buildings) at $68,225. Not a miraculous performance, but certainly a progression and enough worldly success to instigate a state inquiry into their yearly income and accumulation of land (Note 18). The number and size of the buildings owned by the Shakers in 1839, given here, not only show what a complete and self-sufficient little world had been developed in this comparatively short time, but afford a broad perspective of the scene in which the varied occupational activities of the society at New Lebanon were carried on.

One meeting house of wood 80 × 65 feet, with a porch 35 × 27.
Nine dwelling houses of wood, 2 stories, averaging 56 × 35.
Two school houses,   do   do one 36 × 28, one 34 × 24.
One office for trustees and store, brick, 2 stories, 80 × 40 and basement.
One office for trustees and store, wood 1½ stories 30 × 24.
One work shop, stone, 3 stories, 70 × 40.
One   do   do   2 do   55 × 30.
One   do   brick, 3 do   70 × 40.
One work shop, brick, ⎞
Eighteen do wood, ⎠ 2 stories, and for storage av'age size 47 × 27.
One   do do   3 do   65 × 38, dairy, etc.
One   do do   2 do   40 × 30, spin.
Two   do do   2 do   37 × 28.
Two   do do   2 do   37 × 28.
One   do do   2 do   28 × 28 and for storage.
One tannery, wood,   2 do   84 × 46.
One grist mill, stone, 2 do   50 × 35.
Six saw mills, wood, average   45 × 25.
One carding house, wood, 2 stories, 40 × 30.
One clothier's shop, do 2 do   38 × 28.
One blacksmith's shop, stone, ⎞ about 28 × 25.
One   do   do wood, ⎠
One granary, wood, 2 stories, 50 × 38.
One do   do 2 do   40 × 25.
One do   and cider mill, wood, 2 stories, 50 × 46.
One garden house,   do 2 do   36 × 30.
Seven barns, wood, averaging, 70 × 35.
One   do   70 × 52.
One   do   60 × 50.
Two   do   60 × 40.
Three   do   50 × 40.
Three   do   40 × 30.
One   do   36 × 28.
Four   do averaging, 36 × 24.
One cow barn, wood,   80 × 36.
One   do   40 × 20.
One barn and shed, wood, 90 × 30.
One wash house, wood, 24 × 20.
One carriage shed, wood, 30 × 20.
One wagon   do   100 × 22.
Eight wood   do average size, 48 × 25.
Two   do   do   50 × 24.
Two   do   do   30 × 20.
One teazle   do   40 × 30.
Three   do   for farming tools.

| One | do | 60 × 28. |
| One | do | 80 × 50. |

Twenty out buildings of wood, of various sizes for storage and different purposes. (State of New York. [Document] No. 89, In Senate, Mar. 19, 1850, p. 1–3.)

Several different methods of conducting business were adopted by the early Shakers: the consignment of goods to be sold on commission by established agencies, a practice at first applying to many kinds of commodities and later employed particularly in the seed business; the establishment of regular routes for the purpose of soliciting orders and delivering goods; the retailing of manufactures at the local community store; the wholesaling of products through the medium of distributing houses in larger business centers; and barter or exchange.

At first such businesses as blacksmithing and tanning were with farmers and small tradesmen in the immediate neighborhood. Joseph Bennet jr, who conducted the business affairs of the Church family at New Lebanon before the appointment of David Meacham as senior trustee, had conducted a store at Cheshire, Mass. It was at this latter village that he first heard the preaching of Ann Lee. His "Day Book, Begun July 29th, A. D. 1776" (MS. No. 6) is made up of miscellaneous items indicating that he sold general merchandise ranging from coffee and molasses to candlesticks, needles, shoes and brads. The account was transferred to New Lebanon on May 6, 1788. Apparently Bennet continued to conduct his business as a private venture for a few more months. Entries to the credit of the Shaker society first appear on January 1, 1789, and in 1789 and 1790 various accounts were settled or "discharged" between Bennet, acting as trustee for the Church family, and sundry persons doing business with the early sect. Most of the entries in 1789 and 1790 covered transactions between the Church family and private individuals in New Lebanon or early adherents to the Shaker faith in New Lebanon, Hancock and Watervliet. The relationship between the societies at New Lebanon and Watervliet was a close one, and journeys back and forth took the Believers to the busy industrial center at Albany. This place provided one of the first large markets for Shaker goods, and from here business was extended to Hudson, the shire town of Columbia county, and up and down the Hudson River valley. Thus in a few short years the market for the society's products expanded from a limited local area to a much larger range.

The business affairs at the Hancock settlement similarly developed out of private occupations. In 1776 Jehiel Markham, a native of Enfield, Conn., and one of the early converts to Shakerism, kept a "Minnit Book" containing accounts with 38 individuals (MS. No. 59). Markham was evidently a blacksmith, as the bulk of the items deal with horseshoeing and the making of nails, brads, spikes and other ironware. He also sold salt, "rie," wood, beef, mutton and veal, earthen pots and pans, milk, indigo and New England rum. By 1787–88, according to his Minnit Book No. 7 (MS. No. 60), he was distributing such miscellaneous products as "puter buttens," broom corn (in some quantity), "candels" and "sope grease," and charges were entered for spinning "yearn," knitting "woosted stockins" and dressing cloth. Ironware still predominated in the entries, but apparently by 1787 Markham was acting for a larger group. Shakerism had by this time become fairly well established in this section; the foundation of the first meetinghouse is recorded as having been laid on August 30, 1786; and although Calvin Harlow was not sent from New Lebanon until 1790 to organize the society at Hancock, converts had gathered much earlier and probably were carrying on a more or less well-defined community life.

The earliest illustration of selling on commission occurs in the "Church Book of Accompts Kept by Benj^m. Bruce & Nich^s. Lougy. Lebanon 25th, March A D 1789" (MS. No. 73.) It seems likely that Bruce and Lougy kept independent accounts in the name of the Church. Most of the entries for 1789 and 1790 deal with blacksmithing, sharpening and mending plow irons, "ironing a Brick mold," ironing cart wheels, mending chains, etc., and with the manufacture of such ironware as horseshoes, hoes, staples, "sythe tacklin," hinges and the like. On January 3, 1791, however, occurs a five-page account "of the Articles delivered William Naughton to Sell for us on Six P. C. Commissions, or Return." Naughton was a storekeeper somewhere in the neighborhood. The account totals £274:14:11 and includes such articles as sleigh whips, felt hats, whip lashes, pails, tubs, "soal" leather, shoes and boots, saddles and saddlebags, nails and brads, jacket buttons, shoe and harness buckles, leather mittens and sheep skins. These were all Shaker manufactures. On March 10, 1792, Naughton made a settlement with Amos Hammond, who represented the Church. The settlement shows that by this date the storekeeper had disposed of most of the consignment, the balance being valued at £79:11:11. With the development of the seed business late in the century and in the early 1800's, the practice of placing consignments in widely separated districts was commonly pursued.

New Lebanon has always been a country village. The Shakers had to seek out markets for their ever-increasing quantities of farm products and manufactures. A lucrative business could not have been developed by confining their sales to a local store or jobbing house. For this reason the sect early evolved simple methods of carrying their products to large town and city consumers. The route system antedated the establishment of stores by several decades. Nathan Slosson and other delivery men started out on their regular trips to Albany, Hudson and elsewhere early in the 1790's, driving wagons loaded with such articles as those consigned to Naughton, and returning with their collections from "dubils" and with various necessities of life not produced by the Believers. The trustees' office illustrated in figure 7 acted as a depot for such outgoing and incoming commodities, and articles

FIGURE 7 Trustees' office and store at the New Lebanon Church family. Used also as the Shaker post office after 1861. (After Nordhoff, '75.) An earlier office was in operation by 1812 at least. (See Thomas Brown's "An Account of the People called Shakers." Troy, N. Y., 1812, p. 361.)

could be purchased there by other Shaker families and by outsiders if desired. Regular "store" accounts do not appear, however, until the third decade of the nineteenth century.

Many articles manufactured by the Shakers soon gained a wide reputation and the wholesaling of such goods became an established practice by the middle of the last century. Prominent among such products were the far famed Shaker garden seeds, brooms, medicinal extracts, and later, Shaker chairs and foot benches (Note 19). The latter were handled in quantity by such concerns as Marshall Field in Chicago, Lewis and Conger in New York, and leading Boston houses.

Few references have been found regarding the practice of exchange. Most goods were sold and bought for cash, a business habit which was encouraged by Shaker regulations. In his catalog of chairs issued in 1875, Robert Wagan warned prospective customers that "The principles as well as the rules of the Society forbid the Trustees or any of their assistants doing business on the credit system, either in the purchase or sale of merchandise, or in making bargains or contracts" (Note 20). Although it is true that the Shakers paid promptly, they often accommodated themselves to worldly practices in the sale of goods, insisting, however, that accounts be promptly "discharged." In some few cases, nevertheless, the possession of articles for which there was a ready demand led to the practice of exchange as a convenient and direct method of reciprocity. Thus, on September 15, 1805, the Church at New Lebanon exchanged 12 chairs with one John Tryon for "1 Gall. Sherry Wine, 1 Do Malaga Do, 6 lb. Rasons, 3 Chambers, 8 milkpans" and a small cash balance; on January 12, 1848, the Hancock Shakers paid in brooms for a quantity of garden seed paper, tea and a lantern, and two days later "received in barter for brooms 4 lbs. tea at 50 c., 4 lbs. Tobacco, 45½ yds. Cotton Cloth," a lot of leather and their expenses to North Adams.

Before this chapter is closed, a word should be said about the worldly wealth of the United Society. This has been variously estimated at different times. In 1878 Hinds stated that the wealth of all the Shaker societies approximated twelve million dollars (Hinds, '78, p. 83), but in 1902, when his book was reissued, he implied that this previous estimate was exaggerated, and wrote "that the Shaker Societies are not nearly so rich as they are generally supposed to be, nor as rich as they formerly were, they having sustained considerable losses from fire and other causes (Note 21), and their large land-holdings having greatly diminished in market value." (Hinds, '02, p. 28). Nordhoff declared in 1875 that "nearly all the Shaker societies have the reputation of being wealthy" (Nordhoff, '75, p. 163), but quoted Elder Frederic Evans of New Lebanon as saying, "If every out-farm were sold, the society would be better off. They are of no real advantage to us, and I believe of no pecuniary advantage either. . . . We ought to make no more than a moderate surplus over our usual living, so as to lay by something for hard times. In fact, we do not do much more than that" (Nordhoff, '75, p. 162–63).

The various accounts examined in the course of this study bear out the last declaration. During the last decade of the eighteenth century and the first half of the nineteenth, the credit sides of the Church ledgers show negligible excesses over the debits. The following reported balance of the society account at New Lebanon between February 1849, and March 1850, is typical of a later period (State of New York, [Document] No. 89, In Senate, Mar. 19, 1850, p. 8) :

Amount of sales for the above time................	$38,405 35
Amount of money and other property expended.....	37,810 07
	$595 28

Seldom was money speculated. Moreover, the society supported its own poor, bore its share in contributing to the support of the county poor, and daily extended "such other deeds of charity to our fellow men, the yearly amount of which would be more than $2,000." (Senate No. 89, p. 8.) Taxes on the extensive farms and wood lots of the society were heavy.

It should be remembered that each society, and each family within a society, was a distinct commune "for all pecuniary and property ends," and great differences existed, and exist today, in the accumulated resources of the several units. Certain families—the Canaan branch of the New Lebanon society, for instance—found it exceedingly difficult to prosper, while others, through circumstances elsewhere related, increased their holdings and reaped the rewards of successful industry.

Before entering upon a detailed description of the industrial activities and manufactures of the Shakers, it would be well to outline the family organization at New Lebanon, which is taken in this study as a specific model of the economic life of the whole society. This community consisted at first of only one organized family, called the Church or First family, or sometimes the Church order. The other groups in the settlement were rather loosely organized under the name and leadership of some dominant figure. Thus, between 1787 and 1790.

according to an old manuscript (MS. No. 62. Note 22), there were "seven separate families" at New Lebanon, "known and distinguished by the names of the First Family, Rufus Clark's Family, the Walker or West Family, John Bishop's Family, the North Family, Benjamin Ellice's Family, and Elisha Wood's Family." Some order must have prevailed, however, for each of these was "under the Superintendence and Care of separate heads or ruling Elders who held and managed the Estates of each Family, to which he or they belonged separate from the rest."

The group referred to in the above account as the First family was the Church. Rufus Clark's family was organized "under his care and government" in 1790; and Clark was signing deeds for the Shaker society as late as 1804. Apparently this group, and possibly those known as John Bishop's, Benjamin Ellice's, and Elisha Wood's families, formed the beginning of the Second family, the first covenant for which was probably drawn up in 1815 (Andrews MS. No. 69). The names of John Bishop and several other members of the Bishop family, as well as that of "Benjamin Allis" (sometimes spelled Ellis) are annexed to a subsequent covenant signed in 1827 (Andrews MS. No. 70) and it seems likely that these families, formerly semi-independent, were in due time united under one head. At this date Amos Stower and Chauncey Chapman were the leading family elders, and Daniel J. Hawkins and John Mantle the leading deacons or trustees. Subsequent to 1827, the group first known as John Bishop's family was organized as the South family; this family throughout the century and up to the present has been closely associated in its industrial enterprises with the older Second family. The

Walker family was located on land owned by Jonathan Walker and dedicated by him to the society. This group may later have become merged with the Church. None of the above names appears in the list of signers of the Church covenant, however, and these men apparently laid the foundations for families distinct from but closely related to the Church.

The general outline of the early family organization at New Lebanon as reported by the Shaker historians White and Taylor differs in certain details from the above account. According to these authors, the Church order first became known as the First family or First order in 1811, at which time those groups which had entered the society since the first "gathering" were constituted into a Second family or Second order. "A covenant was drawn up adapted to that circle of families and signed March 27th, 1814." The same year, the family at the north of the village, known as the Gathering or Novitiate order, whose temporal interests had up to that time been under the supervision of the Church deacons, was given control of their own affairs and a separate covenant drawn up for their use. "In after years," according to these historians, the various groups became known as the Second, Center, South and East families.

The group known as the Center family originated in the Office family of the Church, which was called the Second order in 1814. This order was closely affiliated with the Church until the late 1870's, or early in the next decade, when its members, desiring to be recognized as an independent family, changed the name to the Center family, the buildings being located in the center of the Shaker village. When the trustees' office at the

Church was erected in 1827, the occupants of this dwelling became known as the Office family; the main group at the Church, living in the central dwelling were distinguished as the First order or First family. The East or Hill family at an early date also became a branch of the Church order. At the time of the establishment of the Shaker society, the East family property was owned by Jabez Spenser and Richard Spiers. Some of it was willed by Spenser to the Church, some of it bought from Spiers. By 1792 there were two Shaker families living there consisting of 40 persons, mostly young people; the principal occupation was brick-making, the brick yard being rented at an annual rate of ten dollars. In 1806 the two families united, forming a single group of over a hundred people (Andrews MS. No. 71). The North family at New Lebanon had two branches in the neighboring town of Canaan, called the Upper and Lower Canaan families, which were started in 1813 and fully organized in 1821. Thus, when completely established, the New Lebanon Society consisted of eight families, whose final designations were the Church, the Second, the North, the East, the South, the Center, the Upper Canaan and the Lower Canaan.

The East family dissolved in 1872, the Center family was absorbed by the Church family in 1896, the Lower Canaan family disbanded in 1884, and the Upper Canaan family moved to Enfield, Conn., in 1897. At present there are four families at Mount Lebanon, each a distinct organization, managing its own affairs and promulgating its own industries—the Church, the South, the Second and the North.

New Lebanon, Watervliet and Groveland composed what was known as the central bishopric, a bishopric being a group of societies operating under the supervision of a single ministry. Hancock, Tyringham and Enfield, Conn., formed another bishopric, the New Hampshire societies another, and the Maine communities still another. The first ministerial order was established at New Lebanon, however, and this society remained the "center of union" for all Believers.

Little space in this handbook can be devoted to a comparison of the industrial life of the Shakers with that of other successful communities, such as the Rappists or Harmony society at Economy, the Baumelers or Separatists at Zoar, the Eben-Ezer society or True Inspiration Congregations at Amana and the Perfectionists at Oneida and Wallingford (Note 23). Suffice it to say that almost every experiment in communistic organization in this country has had its basis in agriculture. This was true of the Shakers, although they have shown, in Nordhoff's words, "more skill in contriving new trades than any of the other societies," and certain important industries, like the garden seed and medicinal herb, although based on soil culture, can as correctly be classified as shop activities. The Perfectionists, the only other important sect in New York State besides the Shakers, are a lone exception to this rule of agrarian communism; this group depended primarily on manufacturing, although shopwork was supplemented by some attention to farming and fruit growing.

Most of the communistic societies in the United States endeavored as far as possible to produce what they needed themselves. Gristmills and sawmills were established not only by the Shaker societies, but by such sects as those at Amana, Harmony, Zoar, Bethel, Aurora and Icaria. The first four also operated woolen mills and tanneries.

Various shops for supplying home needs, and sometimes for manufacturing articles for sale, were also built by these various societies. Thus the Rappists at Harmony had shops for blacksmiths, carpenters, hatters, tailors, shoemakers, tinsmiths, saddlers, weavers, and watch and clock repairers. Besides a planing mill, a machine shop and a dye house, the Zoarites built for their own use a wagon shop, blacksmith and carpenter shops, a cider mill, a tailoring shop, a dressmaking shop and a cobbler's shop. The Perfectionists had mills and shops for manufacturing woven goods, machine and sewing silk, silk-measuring machines, silk-strength testers, traps, chucks, gate hinges and foundry castings. The communists at Bethel possessed small shops for their carpenters, blacksmiths, coopers, tinners, tailors, shoemakers and hatters. The Aurora commune constructed a cabinet-maker's shop, a blacksmith's shop, a carpentry shop and a tin shop. It also possessed a carding-mill and a fruit-drying house. The Bishop Hill Colony had a sawmill and shops for carpenters, blacksmiths and wagon-makers. The Icarians were provided with carpentry, blacksmith, wagon-making and shoemaking shops. The early Ephratans operated paper, flouring, oil and fulling mills. And so on. These were basic industries with these communists, as with the Shakers. It was in the range and complexity of industrial organization that the Shakers excelled, as well as in the high quality of craftsmanship maintained in their manufactures over a long period. To the utilitarian arts they made a special contribution; their fine craftsmanship in furniture in particular warrants their recognition as a people whose religious culture attained such a vitality and high quality as to be directly impressed on all their workmanship.

BASIC FUNCTION OF AGRICULTURE—
FARMING AND GARDENING

The industrial foundations of the Shaker communes were agriculture and horticulture. The societies at New Lebanon and elsewhere were established in regions devoted to farming, and the first bequests were of land well adapted to husbandry. It was natural that a people intent on leading an independent existence should pay particular attention at first to the cultivation of the soil, and all available land was put to use as rapidly as possible. What was at first the result of necessity became thought of in time "as a settled principle of their political economy" (The Manifesto, July '87, p. 166), and the later leaders of the sect became more and more convinced that the prosperity of a community life was dependent upon an agricultural foundation. "Only the simple labors and manners of a farming people," Frederick Evans once remarked, "can hold a community together" (Nordhoff, '75, p. 161).

The early history of farming at New Lebanon is briefly recorded in the issue of The Manifesto for March 1890. From this source we learn that wheat, oats, rye, barley, corn, flax and potatoes were the first crops cultivated. As early as 1789, 3000 bushels of potatoes were harvested. In 1797 or earlier, a garden for the use of the family, called a kitchen garden, was laid out and kept separate from the botanical and seed gardens. Fruit trees were planted at an early date, and in 1848 strawberries were first raised in quantity. Threshing machines were first used in 1815, "a side-hill plough" in 1825, a hay rake in 1827, and a mowing machine in 1856. The farms were managed by certain persons, called "farm deacons," "orchard deacons" and so on, "who were appointed specially to that calling." At certain busy times of the year, during the planting, haying and harvesting season, the farm work required extra help, and brethren engaged in other occupations were drafted into agricultural labors. The cutting of firewood in the extensive wood lots of the order required the services of many laborers.

The careful study of agriculture was exalted by the Shakers into a kind of religious ritual. They looked upon the soil as something to be redeemed from "rugged barrenness into smiling fertility and beauty" (Note 24). This thought is expressed in many ways. Dixon (p. 321) found the Shakers believing that "if you would have a lovely garden, you should live a lovely life," and in the introduction to the Gardener's Manual published in 1843, the writer insists that the garden is "an index of the owner's mind." Dixon's conversation (p. 322) with Elder Frederick Evans illuminates this attitude of spiritual devotion to husbandry.

This morning [he writes] I have spent an hour with Frederick in the new orchard, listening to the story of how he planted it, as to a tale by some Arabian poet. "A tree has its wants and wishes," said the Elder; "and a man should study them as a teacher watches a child, to see what he can do. If you love the plant, and take heed of what it likes, you will be well repaid by it. I don't know if a tree ever comes to know you; and I think it may; but I am sure it feels when you care for it and tend it; as a child does, as a woman does. Now, when we planted this orchard, we first got the very best cuttings in our reach; we then built a house for every plant to live in, that is to say, we dug a deep hole for each; we drained it well; we laid down tiles and rubble, and then filled in a bed of suitable manure and mould; we put the

plant into its nest gently, and pressed up the earth about
it, and protected the infant tree by this metal fence."
"You take a world of pains," I said. "Ah, Brother Hepworth," he rejoined, "thee sees we love our garden."

According to this writer, the difference between the
Shaker and the Gentile farmer lay in the fact that while
the latter was "watching for his returns," the former
was "intent upon his service. One tries for large profits,
the other strives for good work."

The conduct of the farmer was not, however, beyond
the realm of detailed regulation. It was required, for
instance, that "when brethren and sisters are about the
farm and pass through bars, or gates, they should always
leave them closed, unless they find them evidently left
open on purpose. And when brethren are about the
farm, and find gates open, bars down, or fences broken
down, they should put them in order if consistent, if not,
inform those set in order to take care of them, on their
return home. All implements of labor, carts, waggons,
sleighs, sleds, etc. should be put in their proper places,
on Saturday night, and as far as consistent every night,
and all of these things should be done in season to retire
at the time appointed if possible" (MS. No. 4, p. 77).

The stock, consisting of horses, cows, oxen and sheep,
were well housed in large, clean, well-equipped barns
(figure 8). Elkins (p. 130) reported that the Shakers took
"great pains to improve their breeds of domestic animals,
particularly cattle and sheep." The Enfield (N. H.)
society, about which he was writing, transported Durham
cattle from Kentucky for this purpose, and a superior
strain of sheep from France, the latter costing "from two
to five hundred dollars per head." Poultry and turkeys
were also raised at New Lebanon, and at one time several

FIGURE 8 Large barn and wagon sheds at North family, New Lebanon. When Nordhoff visited this community just previous to 1875, he noticed this "enormous" barn, which was said to be the largest, and "in its interior arrangements . . . one of the most complete" in the three or four states "which near here come together." The dimensions are given as 296 feet long by 50 feet wide, and 5 stories high.

colonies of bees were kept. No dogs were allowed, and "no kind of beasts, birds, fowls or fishes" were permitted "merely for the sake of show or fancy." Special orders regarding the care of beasts, "the natural creation," were likewise enforced. They were never to be neglected, nor "chastened or corrected in a passion."

Some of these orders have a quaint interest. For instance: "Different species of trees, or plants may not be engrafted or budded upon each other, as apples upon pears, quince, etc. peaches upon cherries, or contrawise." "The different species of animals, should also, be kept distinct, each in their own order." "No fowls, may be set on the eggs of fowls of different kinds" (MS. No. 4).

The scope of agricultural activities at the Church family in New Lebanon a few years before the Civil War may be judged by the following account of produce and stock in 1858 (MS. No. 20):

Produce Raised on the Farm.

Hay, tuns 118. Barley, 100 bushels. Oats, 375 bush. Corn & Cob, 219 bushels. Cucumber seed, 265 lbs. Onion seed, 747 lbs. Potatoes, 320 bushel. Wool unwashed, 380 lbs.

Stock Kept.

Oxen, 3 yoke. Steers, 2 yoke. Fatten oxen, 1 yoke. Fatten cows, 6 all butchered. Cows Milch, 20. Young Cattle, 15. Sheep, 80. Horses, 3.

Produce of Orchards and Nurserys.

Apples, 300 bushels. Pears, 12 bushels. Quinces, 24 bushels. Cherries, 18 bushels. Currants, 16 bushels. Grapes, 12 bushels. Strawberries, 21 bushels. Plumbs, 10 bushels.

Fruit Sold.

Apples, 67 bushels, 5 bbls. of sauce. Tomato, 72 gallons. 24 gls. Maple (?) Currants, 8 do. Quinces, 13 bushels.

Preserves Made.

Apples dried, none. Tomatoes, 100 gallons. Strawberries, 18 gallons. Cherries, 7 gallons preserved, 7 dried. Blackberries, 11 gals. Whortleberries, 3 gals. Grape jelly, 3 gals. Pears, 6 gals. Plums, 36 glls. Quince, 30 glls.

Produce of Dairy.

Cheese, 1131 lbs. Butter, 2538 lbs.

In 1860 more than 800 bushels of oats, 515 bushels of corn on the cob, and six tons of fodder corn were grown. In that year the crop of eating apples amounted to 1200 bushels, and cider apples to 400 bushels. Ten bushels of gooseberries and 84 bushels of pears were picked. In 1863, 40 bushels of currants were sold. Some mutton was marketed as early as 1810. In 1866 more than 5200 pounds of beef were sold and more than 500 pounds of "fried tallow." Most of the butter and cheese at this time was consumed at home; in 1860 only 380 pounds of cheese were marketed, and in 1863 only 50 pounds of butter.

It will be noted that grain was not raised on a large scale even as late as 1858, and from the first the Shakers were obliged to buy corn, wheat, rye, barley and oats in great quantity from outside the limits of their own domains. Neither could the relatively small number of sheep supply the Believers with sufficient wool, nor their own cattle with sufficient hides or beef. When one considers how extensive were such industries as tanning, cloth manufacture and the drying of sweet corn, it will readily be seen that the society could not supply sufficient raw materials for its own demands, and the oft-repeated opinion that the Shakers were sufficient unto themselves must be radically revised in this regard. Nevertheless they utilized their own resources as far as they were able, and hired "world's people" when labor shortage became acute.

3

THE GARDEN SEED INDUSTRY

In the numerous catalogs and posters advertising the garden seeds produced at New Lebanon, the date of the establishment of this business is given as 1794. The Manifesto states that the raising of garden seeds became "a prominent industry" in 1800. As a matter of fact, garden seeds were sold in small quantities as early as 1789, although there is no record to prove that these seeds were produced in the community's own gardens. A few early items indicate how modest was the beginning of this flourishing occupation (MS. No. 8):

1789.	May 1.	(To David Shapley) An oz. Onion seed 1/ Cucumber seed 6 d	1s — 6 d
	May 10.	(To Constant Moseley) Sundy Garden Seeds	5s — 0 d
	May 10.	(To Nathan Cummins) ½ bushel seed Corn	2s — 4 d
	May 23.	(To Alpheus Rood) Sundy Garden seeds	4s — 2 d
	July 20.	(To Oliver Smith) 3 oz. Turnip seed	1s — 6 d
	Oct. 27.	(To John Truesdal) Nails & Garden Seeds	4s — 7 d
	Oct. 30.	(To Rufus Clark) Garden seeds Rec'd last spring	4s — 6 d
	Oct. 30.	(To Daniel Goodrich Sr.) Garden seeds rec'd last spring	1s — 0 d
1790.	April 20.	To Sundry Garden Seeds	6s — 0 d
1791.	Mar. 22.	To Garden Seeds to Amt. of	£4 –7s — 10d
	Jan. 12.	To Garden Seeds	13s — 0 d

The next decade saw a gradual increase of activity in this industry. The period 1790–1800 marks the initial steps in the growing and marketing of seeds not only at New Lebanon, but in such other settlements as Watervliet, Hancock and Enfield, N. H. It is purely conjectural whether the seed business originated at New Lebanon or at Watervliet. In his "Epitomic History of the Watervliet Shakers" (The Shaker, July '77, p. 49-50), D. A. Buckingham states, "In the year 1790, Believers in this place had a family garden, occupying about two acres of land. Joseph Turner supervised it, and began to raise a few seeds for sale." After "a few years" the seed business was run by Ebenezer Alden, who invented a "printing-box" for hand printing the seed bags. Later David Osborn of the New Lebanon Shakers took over the management and "did much to advance the seed business." In 1811 the Watervliet Shakers raised about three hundred dollars' worth of seeds; from 1811 to 1840, the seed business was the chief industry at this colony, sales amounting to thousands of dollars a year.

In an old account book, "Seeds Raised at the Shaker Gardens" (MS. No. 17), 1795 is given as the first year in which garden seeds were systematically grown at New Lebanon. Onion seed was the largest item, 201 pounds for that year. Blood beet amounted to 120 pounds, while scarcity beet, carrot, cucumber and summer squash brought the year's total to 44 pounds, priced at $406. The following year radish seed, two varieties of turnip and three of cabbage were raised. The head gardener or seedsman in these early years was one Artemas Markham.

The record shows a slowly increasing business in these and other varieties of seeds. By 1800 the sales had passed the $1000 mark. In 1805, 1385¾ pounds of seeds were raised, selling for $1240. In September of that year Nathan Slosson received among other commodities consigned to Albany dealers, "23 B. & 12 Quarts flax Seeds @ 14/3," amounting to £16:13:1. On October 26th, "Wm. & John Radcliff Spake for a Quantity of Garden Seeds." On November 13th, eight boxes of seeds were sent to this concern (located in Rhinebeck) by way of Reuben Folger. This consignment amounted to $133.33, but a "reduction" of 25 per cent brought the bill to an even $100. The same discounts were applied to two boxes of seeds sent to Tyron & Clark on December 28th; one box was valued at $30.03, the other at $20.42. On November 2d, the Church expended £1–4s for 300 "Bills for Seeds." Two weeks later seeds were purchased from Israel Talcott at Hancock as follows:

1 lb. 11 ounces	Onion Sead at 8/				£	0:13:6
4 lb. 2	do	Cucumber	Seads at 6/			1:4:4
1 lb. 6	do	musk melleon	do	at 4/		0:5:6
1 lb. 12	do	Watermillion	do	at 4/		0:7:0

Early in January 1806, Nathan was receiving consignments of garden seeds "for the Northward." A list of 20 different orders was entered in the account, the consignment being valued at $460.86 after reductions of 20 and 25 per cent. One "box for sale" was entered at $16.04, another "for Retailing" at $31.42. The same month Stephen ————— received boxes of seeds for 14 customers valued, after the subtraction of discounts, at $346.40. On March 6, 1807, Nathan delivered four boxes to "Northamton." On the tenth of this month "Nathan Rindal Delivered to Elam Tilden One Box of Garden Seed which am't, as pr. Bil, to twenty dollers & Ninety four Cents. To be Sold Commissions of fifteen pr. Cent"; and another box valued at $20.30 was sent to Reuben Swift under similar conditions. Flax seed, which is not mentioned in the early garden seed book, was an important, perhaps the largest selling commodity during the first decade or so of the century. The following memorandum gives a few prevailing prices about the year 1807 (MS. No. 18):

40	Bags of	Red Onion Seed	@ 12	$	4	80¢
2	do	White do	14			28
20		Blood Beet	8		1	60
1		Yorkshire Cabbage	10			10
4		Winter do	8			32
12		Lettuce	8			96
4		Scarcity	8			32
26		Cucumber	6		1	56
8		Turnip	8			64
2		French do	6			12
2		Sage	8			16
12		Carrot	6			72
12		Parsnip	6			72
14		Radish	6			84
6		Sum^r Squash	4			24
2		Winter do	4			8
8		Watermelon	4			32
8		Musk do	4			32
4		Asparagus	6			24
2		Celery	4			8
2		Parsley	4			8
2		Peppergrass	4			8

The above records indicate that the seed business was at first confined to a local area. As time went on, the trips of Nathan and Stephen, and of seedmen (Note 25) from other communes, became more extended, not only to the "Northward," but to the "Eastward," the "Southward" and the "Westward," "until in all parts of the country the Shaker Seed wagon and the shrewd, honest sedate but kindly Shaker Brother, who sold the seeds, were familiar as the spring-time" (White and Taylor, p. 315). The important westward route through eastern and central New York state was inaugurated by 1812 or earlier. In that year 1313 pounds of seeds were sold for $1198. With the exception of the year 1818, the annual production after 1814 was in excess of 2000 pounds, which provided an income of well over $2000. In the first 25 years of the seed business at the Church family, 37,242 pounds of seeds were raised at a market value of $33,901. Seeds were first put up in bags by the Center family at Union Village. This was in 1816. The Shakers are said to have been the first to put up seeds in small paper envelops, such as those shown in figure 9.

For a while a certain amount of seeds were regularly purchased from outside sources, but it was not long before Shaker seeds gained a wide reputation for quality, and the society considered it not only poor business but unethical to distribute any but Shaker grown seeds. On April 13, 1819, certain deacons, gardeners and trustees from Hancock, New Lebanon and Watervliet entered into the following covenant:

We, the undersigned, having for sometime past felt a concern, lest there should come loss upon the joint interest, and dishonor upon the gospel, by purchasing seeds of the world, and mixing them with ours for sale; and having duly considered the matter, we are confident that it is best to leave off the practice, and we do hereby covenant and agree that we will not, hereafter, put up, or sell, any seeds to the world which are not raised among believers (excepting melon seeds).

New Lebanon, April 13, 1819. (Note 26.)

Some difficulty was caused by the fact that almost every New York and New England society became engaged in this business, and as it prospered each seed company extended its field of operations. As a result societies naturally encroached upon one another's territory. In a letter dated Watervliet, December 26, 1822 (MS. No. 61), Brother Morrell thus voices his complaint to Daniel Goodrich of Hancock:

. . . Being placed in this poor condition, we were obliged to seek ways and means to get our livelihood and prety soon commenced the business of raising garden-

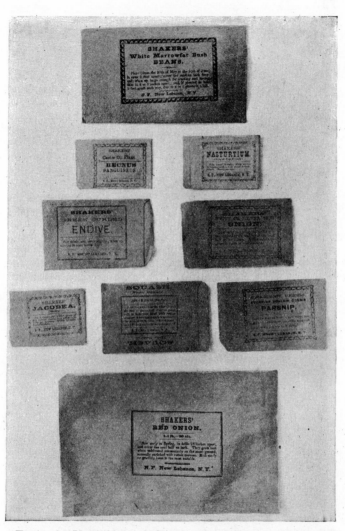

Figure 9 Vegetable and flower seed packages. "S.F." and "N.F." stand for Second family and North family, New Lebanon. The envelops were often printed in colors.

seeds. There being none among the other societys of believers at that time who thought it worth commencing,
or at least were not under the necessity to do it. All this
time we vended our Seeds throughout the State we live
in. But our Lebanon Brethren in a few years perceiving
it was becoming profitable and that we were not able to
supply the call for Seeds commenced the business. This
we had no objection too, because they first entered into
this agreement not to sell any Seeds this side of the North
river. But soon our Brethren at Hancock followed, and
not only they but still our Brethren towards the east did
likewise, so that in a short time the business become so
extensive, that our Lebanon Brethren were under the
necessity to cross the river (but not without our consent
and full union first) The Brethren at Hancock soon
followed, so that now through our liberality of giving in
we are almost compeled to give ells and some prety long
ones too. Our Lebanon Brethren, on the north, on the
South, on the east and on the west of us. And our
Hancock Brethren a breadth through our whole state
more than three hundred miles long so that at present
we are confined to less than one fifth part of the state
we live in and have no right to sell one seed in the state
you live in nor any other state to the east of us. For the
correctness of the above statement, see the limits proscribed to us. Begining from this to White Hall, 72
miles north, Also from this to New Hartford 92 miles.
a little south of northwest, from there to the east end of
Lake Ontario, then down the St. Larance to Ogdens-
burg. A little patch in the northwest corner of our state,
Look also at the number of inhabitants residing in those
countrys limited to us to sell seeds in. Excepting we sell
as many seeds in Albany and Troy as we can, and our
Lebanon Brethren do so too at both of those places, we
also sell a few at New York and some at Brooklyn and
our Lebanon Brethren do likewise. I had almost like
to forgot to state that we sold all the seeds we could in
our limits proscribed to us, and you and our Lebanon
Brethren sell 5 times as many seeds as we do and I believe it would not be much out of the way to say 7......

The gardeners often kept a journal of their daily occupations, and from these interesting sources much may be learned regarding the various problems and rewards of this important industry. One such "garden account" begins with miscellaneous remarks and observations on such matters as "cureing" corn, preserving beets and growing onion seeds. A "trial of the vegetation of seeds" from 1829 to 1840 is carefully recorded. The following varieties were included: scarcity, scarlet radish, orange carrot, squash, ice top lettuce, mammoth lettuce, "parsnep," "hybrid turnep," "turnep beet," mangel beet, "E. C. cucumber," "D. W. cabbage," "E. D. lettuce," watermelon, Savoy cabbage, marrow-fat peas, rutabaga and sage. In 1836, 150,000 seed bags were printed at New Lebanon, and in the five-year period 1836–40, 930,400. These were printed on home presses in eight sizes known as pound bag size, bean size, beet size, onion size, cucumber size, cucumber long size, radish size and lettuce size. Onion, lettuce and cucumber seeds seem to have been the most popular at this time.

In 1836 gardeners' manuals were issued for the first time (figure 10). These were edited by Charles F. Crosman and sold for six cents apiece. According to the foreword, which was inscribed "To Gardeners and Dealers in Garden Seeds," the purpose of the manual was "to enable our trading customers, while furnishing their assortment of Garden Seeds, to afford instructions, at a trifling expense, to such of their customers as may wish to obtain some practical information relative to the raising and management of those valuable kitchen vegetables which are considered the most useful and important in a family." The manuals, 16,000 of which were printed, were sold to dealers for three or four cents apiece (Note 27).

According to the catalog which prefaces the manual, the following kinds of seeds were being raised and put up in 1836:

Asparagus (Giant), Bean (six varieties), Beet (six varieties), Cabbage (five varieties), Cauliflower (Early),

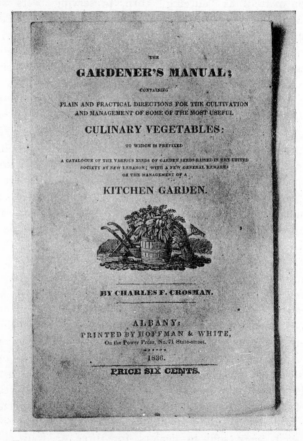

THE

GARDENER'S MANUAL;

CONTAINING

PLAIN AND PRACTICAL DIRECTIONS FOR THE CULTIVATION
AND MANAGEMENT OF SOME OF THE MOST USEFUL

CULINARY VEGETABLES:

TO WHICH IS PREFIXED

A CATALOGUE OF THE VARIOUS KINDS OF GARDEN SEEDS RAISED IN THE UNITED
SOCIETY AT NEW LEBANON; WITH A FEW GENERAL REMARKS
ON THE MANAGEMENT OF A

KITCHEN GARDEN.

BY CHARLES F. CROSMAN.

ALBANY:
PRINTED BY HOFFMAN & WHITE,
On the Power Press, No. 71 State-street.

1836.

PRICE SIX CENTS.

FIGURE 10   Cover page on first gardeners' manual issued by the New Lebanon Shakers in 1836

Carrot (two varieties), Celery (White Solid), Corn (two varieties), Cucumber (four varieties), Lettuce (six varieties), Melon (three varieties), Mustard (two varieties), Onion (three varieties), Parsley (Curled or double), Parsnip (two varieties), Peas (four varieties), Pepper (two varieties), Pepper Grass (Double), Radish (four varieties), Saffron (American), Sage (English), Salsify (or Vegetable Oyster), Savory (Summer), Spinage (Roundleaf), Squash (four varieties), Turnip (five varieties).

In 1843 a more complete manual was issued containing "Plain Instructions for the Selection, Preparation and Management of a Kitchen Garden." The chapters deal with

  I   Directions for the selection of a garden spot and implements.
 II   Of preparing the ground, and putting in crops.
III   Of Cultivation.
 IV   Directions for making and managing a hot-bed.
  V   Of insects injurious to the gardener.
 VI   A catalogue of garden seeds.
VII   Particular treatment of the different varieties of culinary vegetables.
VIII   Field culture of garden vegetables.
 IX   Preservation of vegetables in winter.
  X   Of the uses of vegetables.
 XI   Recipes for cookery, etc.
XII   Pickling

The following entries are culled from a gardener's journal covering the period from 1840 to 1849 (MS. No. 19). The head gardeners or foremen during this time were in succession: John Allen, Franklin Barber, George Allen and Philemon Stewart (Note 28). It will be noted that the seed bags were cut, folded, pasted and printed by the Shakers themselves in their own seed shops. Certain devices were used to save labor, but the ever-present task of sorting over and throwing out old seeds that were returned by various consignees was a manual operation with no alleviation.

1841. January   11. Thrash the celery.

12. Put up two cash orders for Poughkeepsie.

14. Put up the seeds for Hudson.

15. Put up the Pine Plain Seeds.

16. Finish off the two loads—plain labil and mark.

February   6. The week past cleaning seeds at the tan house. Repairing the machineary & making a new one for the purpose of shaking our great ridle after altering making braking & having a great deal of trouble we finally succede & our machine works well & we think if carefully used will prove to be a great improvement and save much hard labour.

27. Repairing the cutting block, printing press, etc.

March   13. H. Bennet & John have commenced getting & picking up stuff for a new seed cupboard which is to be 16 feet long 8 high & 2 deep.

26. Franklin sows the hot bed.

June   1. Put up $150 worth of seeds in $5 and $10 boxes.

August   25. 785 Advertisements received from Albany.

1842. January   31. Printed and cut some bags: we cut enough to with those on hand to make a years stock, but the printing is not yet done. The spring to raise the types against the ball broke after useing it about 3 days. . . . Have been lately looking over the types & setting up a new Bill or Catalogue adapted to the Southern demand.

March   5. There has been a new Beet machine made this winter & today we use it. Strip the white & turnip Beett. It works finely.

September 19.   We have sorted the majority of the Old Seeds, torn open the poor papers, etc. they have sold better than for 3 years heretofore I think generally.

October   1.   Finish boxing the Western Load. 224 Boxes am'ting at $3353.67.

4.   Aaron D. Bill starts off alone on the Western Journey intending to be back in 3 weeks. .   .   .   Put up the Newburgh seeds 11 Boxes Amt. at $145.00.

13.   Set out roots in the Cellars.

24.   At boxing the Green Mtn. Load of seeds.

1843.   February   24.   We have concluded to have the prices of all papers of seeds at 6 cents.   .   .   .

March   11.   We have printed 850 Seed Bills the past week for the North Family.   .   .   .

October   27.   Geo. makes a set of Spools for packing-twine for this shop.   F. casts a printing Ball & fixes for a little printing of bags.   .   .   .

November   8.   Smash and wash out the Tomato Seed.

10.   Geo. throws out Old Seed from Cuba.   .   .   .

December 18.   F. & Geo. engaged in makeing a leather band or a belt for carrying the seed mill at the Tan House, weighing seed, etc.

1844.   February   17.   F. C. & S. puts up the Granville & Hudson loads.

23.   Geo. lineing fans for faning seeds.

October   8.   Geo. & Sam finish the Florida Order am't to $53.10.

14.   Geo. & Sml. take up a flooring of old seeds.   C. & Daniel C. tear open bags.   Sml. throws out old Seeds from Pine Plain.   Geo. in the shop.   Daniel C. threshing Onion Seed.

17.   Hurrying times to forward the western load .   .   .   the Sisters offer their service in puting up seeds.

1845. September 24. Geo. Cleaning marking instruments makeing ink, etc.

October 16. Geo. St. & Sml finish Cleaning seeds for the west. . . . Joel Turner an old man almost 70 years old says he papers and paists 400 bags in a day.

31. P. Stewart calls the bill for us from about ½ past 6 oclock P. M. till 1 oclock at night boxing Seeds to a good jog.

November 1. We finish Boxing, nailing and lay-billing the seeds for the *West*.

1846. October 16. Pound out pepper seed. Squeeze and wash out the yellow Tomatoe. . . .

19. The sisters have put 35,000 papers of seeds for this Western load.

21. Commence Boxing for the Western Load. We Gardeners alone box 15 $9.00 and 45, $12 boxes.

22. Box 54 $18 boxes.

23. Box up 13 $21 boxes.

26. We finish packing the western loads of seeds. There is 4 two horse waggon loads.

November 6. Finish threshing the Long Blood Beet, and pick out some Boxes to go to Philadelphia and Baltimore.

7. Finish said Boxes. Though shrined in confusion of business, yet I believe they are done correct. The farmers have been ploughing in the dung with their Teems.

December 3. This afternoon Sml has been cleaning and grinding Onion Seed.

7. We have been puting a heavy Order from the South, North Carolina, between 5 and 6 hundred Dollars, I believe they are sent on commission. But I hope they will never return.

24. We have finished puling up all the Assorted Seeds for the west, and are now ready to commence upon those by the lb, ½ and ¼, etc.

31. We have had to put up the Printing Press, and print about 2000 bags for this Western Package.

1847. January 9. Samuel W. says he has printed 30 Thousand (bags) in one day when the press worked well, and run steady.

25. I have been turning some Mallets, and grinding the knives we cut bags with.

29. Gideon has put up about 6000 papers of Cucumber seeds this week.

February 3. Samuel W. has finished printing the common small baggs; he has Printed 200,000.

10. I have finished cutting the lettuce baggs, cut 45,000.

March 5. We thresh the Beet, Scarcity with the machine. The White with a flail.

June 9. We have finished seting the Cellery, 2 rows east the ally. We have also resowed 4 of the east rows of the Vegetable Oysters, and all of the new Asparagus bed, we have soaked the seed for 4 or 5 minutes in scalding hot water, and for two hours in warm water.

23. We have sold from our Hotbeds this season about 14 dollars worth of plants.

26. The 3 aged brethren work destroying worms upon the parsnips, Gideon Kibbee helps them in the forenoon. The worms appear 10 times worse than ever, we have put tobacco juice, strong soap suds, Guano Juice, Salt and Lime, but it does not kill them or keep them off, therefore we have gone to squshing them with our fingers. . . .

1848. November 2. Jonathan W. and I have been to try grinding of Bones in a plaster mill, twill do nothing to any effect.

4. We have put 2 Orders of seeds for Canada.

6. This afternoon I have made a trial of pounding Bones (for fertilizer) under the Triphammer, it succeeds very well.

The entries above quoted have dealt principally with activities in the fall and winter, when the inside work was done. The gardeners or seedmen were busy all the year, fertilizing, cultivating, hoeing and so on during the spring and summer, and threshing, cleaning, boxing and labeling in the fall and winter. The western load, which covered a good section of New York State, was the important shipment of the year; the journalist uses capital letters for this entry, and in the exclamation marks which follow the actual dispatch of this annual load one can visualize the relief attendant on the consummation of an arduous task.

Doubts of the wisdom of continuing the seed business occur as early as 1841. One "journalist" observes under date of April 26th: "It has generally been thought that for some years past we have extended our seed business far beyond the medium to make it profitable for us and by reason of others as well as ourselves raising and selling so many seeds the market has become clide [?]— appears to be almost useless to try to raise seeds expecting to sell them & get what they are worth. (Onion seed selling at ¢25. per lb. & but little sale for that or any other kinds—we are almost afraid we shall have to fling many of them away, for we have now upon hand I should think $10000 worth.)" (Note 29.) There was talk of reducing the acreage devoted to seed gardens, and turning part of the space at least into kitchen gardens. Nevertheless the seed business continued to show profits. The sisters of the First order made 31,000 paper seed bags in 1845, and the following year they put up 40,000 bags of seeds. If the extent of the business can be measured by the number of cloth and paper bags made, the seed industry showed a perceptible increase rather than a decrease during the next 25 years:

Table of Sisters' Work on Paper Seed Bags

1846................	24 700	1858................	130 000
1847................	6 000	1859................	200 000
1848................	206 000	1860................	260 000
1849................	69 000	1861................	7 900
1850................	6 500	1862................	50 000
1851................	36 000	1863................	52 000
1852................	64 000	1864................	130 000
1853................	102 000	1865................	136 100
1854................	104 000	1866................	75 450
1855................	110 000	1867................	286 200
1856................	101 500	1868................	200 000
1857................	30 000	1869................	32 000
		1870................	255 000

Evidently the seed business at New Lebanon made a good recovery from the Civil War depression and weath-ered for a considerable period the pressure of outside competition. In 1868 the "list" of seeds raised in the Shaker gardens and on "out-farms" amounted to $7196.10, and in 1870 a high total of $7570.15 was recorded. This success may have been due partly to the fact that the Shakers came to resort to "worldly" methods of advertising. Brightly colored posters were distributed, and the seeds were put up in neatly labeled boxes and in gayly tinted little packages. The next decade or so after 1870 saw "many unlooked-for reverses" (The Manifesto, March '90, p. 50) in the seed business, but the industry continued at Mount Lebanon until the late 80's or early 90's (Note 30).

The garden seed business was as important to other families at New Lebanon as to the Church. The herb and seed gardens at the Second family, for instance, covered a considerable acreage, and the large shop at present used for the manufacture of chairs was at one time the site of a thriving seed business. The early seed packages bore the initials or name of Daniel Hawkins and the initials "S. F." for the Second family. A retail office, which served as a clearing house for the products of the brethren's and sisters' shops, was established here at about the same time as that at the Church. The North family also carried on an extensive seed business.

THE DRIED SWEET CORN AND DRIED APPLE INDUSTRIES

The business of drying sweet corn for the wholesale and retail market was started at New Lebanon in 1828 and continued throughout the century. At first the process consisted merely of boiling the cobs in great iron kettles, cutting the kernels off with hand knives, usually three-bladed affairs screwed to a vise (see figure 11), and then drying them in the sun on large boards. A drying house was erected in 1840. Large wheeled platforms ran out of this house so that the corn, spread thinly over them, could be exposed to the sun at will. It was then raked at intervals to insure even drying. This early process was imperfect, however, as the corn was apt to sour if not properly dried and success was largely dependent upon the weather.

At a later period the process was mechanized by the introduction of steam-operated corn-cutting machines. The corn was delivered to the drying house in August and September by neighboring farmers; the Shakers themselves grew only a small portion of what was needed. The husked corn was first weighed, and then the ears were picked into small square baskets, only carefully selected ears being used. The Chatham (N. Y.) Courier thus described the process:

The baskets of corn are closely packed upon an elevator, to the extent of nearly a ton, a rope is pulled, and the engine in the basement lowers them into a steam-box, where they are subjected to about six minutes of rather intense cooking. This accomplished, a bell rings, and they rise, pass the first floor, steaming from their bath, to the second floor. . . . The second floor is devoted to removing the corn from the cob. Here are three machines operated by steam, each capable of removing the corn from forty-five ears per minute. The machines are fed directly from the baskets, while the cobs shoot through an inclined tube into the carts, and are drawn away. . . . The corn falls into larger baskets, which are placed upon a car, and then rolled along a track which connects, by means of a long bridge, the building we have just left with the kiln. The corn is then placed in long shallow pans, and subjected to an even heat from the roaring furnaces below. In this manner two kilns full are dried

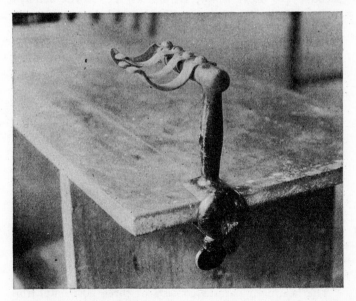

FIGURE 11 Three-bladed device for cutting the kernels from sweet-corn. The upright knife at the end scraped the cob clean. New York State Museum.

in twenty-four hours. The dried corn is then passed through a mill which winnows from it every particle of silk or husk which may be with it, and placed in a large bin. A tube passes from this to the lower story. A barrel is placed on the scales, a slide pulled in the conductor, and the barrel filled to a certain weight. It is then headed, marked, and is ready for shipment. In this manner they expect to fill twelve hundred barrels this season (1879). They also put up a fine shelf package for grocers' retail trade (Note 31).

In 1866 this commodity sold for $20 a barrel and constituted a prosperous industry at the Church and Second families. In October and November of this year, one account (to Levi Shaw, trustee at the North family) amounted to 59 barrels, or $1180. Dried pumpkin was also sold at this time, the price ranging from $9 to $10 a barrel. Pop corn was sold for $4.50 a barrel. In the early 80's the severity of the competition met in the dried sweet corn industry was such that the business was greatly reduced, but it continued to provide an economic return throughout the century (Note 32).

Although it is well known that the Indians knew the art of drying corn for food, the Shakers were said to be the first to engage in the occupation on a considerable scale, building kilns for the purpose and marketing the product, as they did their seeds, in convenient containers. The dry-houses or kilns, which were also used in drying apples, were built of stone or brick (figure 12). One such kiln at New Lebanon is thus described by Mrs Sylvia Campbell ('55, p. 77), a prebellum expert on cookery who lived near the Shaker village:

The heating apparatus consists of three horizontal iron cylinders, somewhat like the flues of a steam engine, running the whole length of the building, near the ground—

FIGURE 12 Apple-drying house or kiln at the Church family, New Lebanon.

the center tube larger than the other two—the former for burning long wood, the latter for conducting and distributing the hot air. On either side of the chamber are shelves made of moveable drawers the bottoms of which are made of woven rattan or willow rods, open-work, like a large riddle sieve.

Apple-paring machines, set on frames, were made in some number, and at a later period purchased from the city and attached to homemade benches or chairs with

FIGURE 13 Device for quartering apples. The hole in the board is fitted with two blades crossed at right angles. The plunger forced the apple down on these knives and through into the receptacle beneath the bench. New York State Museum.

improvised arms.   Figure 13 shows a device for quartering apples and the type of bucket used for dried apples or apple sauce.

THE MEDICINAL HERB INDUSTRY

The medicinal herb industry was as natural an outgrowth of the Shakers' early interest in gardening and agriculture as was the seed business.   Each was a semi-agricultural occupation, a combination of garden and shop activity.   It was only a step from farming to kitchen gardening, and but another step to herb gardening and the growing of select vegetables for their seeds.   The Shakers were among the first in this country to see more than the obvious possibilities of gardening, and here, as in many other fields, their habitual genius for recognizing and developing economic opportunities is apparent (Note 33).

The passion of the people composing this sect for being useful, for doing useful things and for making things useful is evidenced in these soil culture activities.   It was consistent with their pragmatic philosophy that plants should be utilized in every way possible.   Some were useful for food, some for their medicinal qualities, some for seed production; in their roots and leaves, in their flowers and fruits, one or the other useful quality was present.   This was true of larger shrubs and trees as well, and certain barks and leaves were sought not only for their value in medicinal preparations, but also for their usefulness in making dyes and in tanning leather.

In a catalog of "medicinal plants, barks, roots, seeds, flowers and select powders" issued by the New Lebanon society about the middle of the last century, the claim is made that this industry was first established in 1800, "being the oldest of the kind in the country."   Eldresses

White and Taylor (p. 315) also state that the Shakers were "the first in this country to introduce botanical medical practice, the first roots, herbs and vegetable extracts for medicinal purposes placed on the market having borne the Shaker stamp." The date, 1800, is substantially correct. It should be noted, however, that although the gathering of herbs was practiced "from the first of the organization for the use of the physicians at home . . . (only) very few were sold except for the purpose of purchasing medicine to be used instead of the herbs." According to The Manifesto the Believers did not begin to prepare herbs and roots for sale until 1820.

A careful examination of a collection of early ledgers kept by the trustees at New Lebanon bears out this statement. With the exception of rose-water (Note 34), no record of the sale of herbs or extracts occurs until the year 1821, when, on November 21st, an entry under "Articles Sold" (MS. No. 9) reads: "for herbs . . . $1.15." On February 12, 1823, an entry of $21.50 is made "for Herbs & oils," and on April 2, one of $2.34 for "herbs & Extract."

The Manifesto statement is further supported by an interview in 1852 between Edward Fowler of the New Lebanon society and a representative of The American Journal of Pharmacy (1852). Fowler is here (p. 89) quoted as saying: "It is about fifty years . . . since our Society first originated as a trade in this country the business of cultivating and preparing medicinal plants for the supply and convenience of apothecaries and druggists, and for about twenty years conducted it on a limited scale" (The American Journal of Pharmacy, Vol. 18, p. 89). According to this source, the business was not conducted on a very serious scale until about 1820, when "Drs. E. (Eliab) Harlow and G. (Garrett) K. Lawrence, of our society, the latter an excellent botanist, gave their attention to the business, and induced a more systematic arrangement, and scientific manner of conducting it, especially as to the seasons for collection, varieties, and methods of preparation."[1]

Two general account books, one covering the period 1817–29 and the other 1823–28, reveal not a single item relating to this business, which seems to have been conducted by these physicians independently from the other village industries. In the writer's possession is a slim herb account book styled on its flyleaf as "Ledger No. 1, 1827," but presenting items from 1825 to 1827; there is little reason to doubt that this was Harlow's and Lawrence's first sales record (MS. No. 22). A selection of items will indicate the character of the products at that period, and current prices. The names of buyers are omitted.

1825 items:	Medicines	$ 3 75
	One box Bilious Pills	37½
	(Note 35)	
1826 items:	1 lb. Cow Parsnip Ext.	2 00
	1 Dozen Digestive Pills	3 00

Late in 1826 and early in 1827 an order amounting to $24 was sent to Thomas Corbett of Canterbury, N. H., the originator of the famous Corbett's Shaker Syrup of Sarsaparilla, Corbett's Wild Cherry Pectoral Syrup etc. The order included 30 pounds of Balm, 10 pounds of sweet marjoram, 2¾ pounds of poppy capsules, 2½ pounds of sassafras bark, 8 pounds of pleurisy root, and 1 pound of red rose. Later in 1827, 1 pound of extract

---

[1] For their plant names the Shakers at that time used the various manuals of botany (1817–40) by Amos Eaton of Rensselaer Institute, Troy, N. Y., the leading authority on the botany of the northeastern states prior to the publication of Torrey and Gray's Flora of North America, 1838–43.

"Gentiana Quin." (at $3) and 10 pounds of white root, priced at 50 cents a pound, were added to the order.

1827 items:

2 lb. Skunk Cabbage Root	$ 75
1 lb. Lycopus Virginicus	50
¼ lb. Cicuta Extract & Jar	37½
10 lbs. Herbs at 30 cents	3 00
40 lbs. Herbs "for vapour Bath"	12 00
1 Barrel of green Texas	4 00
1 Box Herbs as pr. Invoice	46 50
1 Box Herbs & Extracts	34 80
1 Jar Violet Blossoms	50
2 doz. Bottles Syrrup Liverwort	18 00
Herbs and Pills	158 00
1 lb. Sweet Marjoram	75
15 lb. Marsh Mallows	4 50
Liatris Roots	37½
2 oz. Peppermint oil & Phial	56
6 lb. White root @ 50 cents	3 00
6 lb. Foxglove @ 30 cents	1 80
6 lbs. Barks	1 80

Other 1827 items entered but not priced included saffron, strammonium leaves, bittersweet, elder flowers, coltsfoot, bugle, mugwort, "Heabane" (fleabane?), basil, elm bark, horehound, sage, scull cap, spearmint, thyme, boneset, *"lobelia syplitica"* (*Lobelia syphilitica*), *"lobelia inflata,"* mallow roots fresh, wild lettuce extract, borage, maiden hair and hyssop.

1828 items:

5 quarts Rose water (no price)	
50 lbs. unpressed Elder flowers @ 14¢	$7 00
50 lbs. Pressed Elder flowers @ 30 cts	10 00
6 lbs. Borage unpressed @ 30 cts.	1 80
2 lbs. Inspissated Juice Cicuta	3 00
10 lbs. Peony root @ 30 cts.	3 00
22 lbs. "Sarsaparilla" (no price)	
3 lbs. Flour of elm @ 50 cts.	1 50
3 lbs. Princesspine	1 14
3 lbs. Ext. Butternut	3 00
4 oz. Oil Goldenrod	4 00
15 lbs. Catnep, and 4 lbs. Balm Lemon (no price)	
½ lb. Button Snake root	25
1 oz. Henbane Ext.	25
1 lb. Parsley tops	40
½ lb. Ext. Dandelion	56

3 lbs. Rue	1 50
Thorn Apple leaves	56
4 lb. Ext. Cow Parsnip "bonafide"	8 00
1 lb. Ext. "Hyoseyamus"	3 00
1 lb. Crawley Root	2 00
6 lb. Belladona Ext.	15 00
2 lb. Ext. Strammonium	2 50
5 lb. Bayberry	1 87½

In 1828 we find the first evidence of herbs, syrups etc. These were sent out to dealers to be sold, as were garden seeds, on a commission basis of 25 per cent.

1829 and 1830 items not heretofore mentioned:

1 Bottle Yellow Root Syrup		$ 50
12 lb. Scullcap		
7 lb. Spikenard	29 pr. Ct. off	9 59
3 lb. Blue Cardinal		
3½ lb. Cleavers		
7 lb. Rad. Cohosh Black		3 50
1 lb. Ext. Hops		2 00
½ oz. Lettuce Opium		25
1 oz. Oil Fleabane		1 00
1 Bottle of Atropa roots		75
2 lb. Oak Jerusalem		1 13
4 lb. Peppermint (small papers)		1 50
1 lb. Ground Ivy		62
1 lb. Blackberry root		25
1 lb. Mountain mint		38
3 lb. Golden Seal		4 50
1 lb. Wild Celandine		15
2 lb. Wormwood		80

The quotations listed above indicate how varied the industry was even in its earliest stages. By 1830 herb catalogs were being issued (Note 36), and the same year $2.50 was paid to Phineas Allen, a Pittsfield (Mass.) printer, for 4700 labels. On October 18, 1831, a box of herbs valued at $30.68¾ ("subject to 25 pr. ct. dis.") was sent to Paris, and on October 25th, 13 boxes of medicinal herbs were delivered "on board Ship Hannibal in the port of New York" consigned to Charles Whitlaw, "Botanist of London, England." This order amounted to $895.65 (Note 37). In this year (1831) "about 4000 lbs. of roots and herbs were sent to the market" (The Manifesto, vol. XX, p. 195). By 1836 production had increased to 6000 pounds, and in 1849 to 16,500 pounds.

In the early years of the industry wild herbs constituted the main sources of supply. With its serious development arose the cultivation of medicinal plants. It is difficult to state just what plants or herbs were first grown. The gradually increasing demand for Shaker herbs and extracts made it necessary to rely upon outside growers for large quantities of different herbs, roots etc., and certain kinds which could not be produced in the "physic gardens" at New Lebanon were imported from various parts of the country and even from abroad. As early as 1826 we find the Shakers buying from outside sources such items as red rose, sweet marjoram, cicuta extract, saffron and lobelia. On the last page of the journal from which early herbs and herb prices have just been quoted occurs the following list of "Prices that we give for root & Herbs":

	D	C			D	C
Angelica root		10	Sassafras Bark			14
Avens root		6	Malefern root			10
Bloodroot		18	Pennyroyal			5
Boxwood bark		5	Princespine			4
Burdock root		6	Red Rosleaves			20
Black Cherry Bark		5	Sage			20
Bethroot		10	Sarsaparilla			6
Bitter root		15	Scrofula plant			6
Crawley		37	Skunk Cabbage			6
Cohosh of all kinds		6	Solomon Seal			10
Comfrey		6	Spiknard			10
Cranesbill		12	Sweetflag			6
Culvers root		37	Southren wood			10
Dandolion		6	Wild Turnip			15
Elm Slippers from 5 to 7 cts.			White root			15
Gold thread		37	Wintergreen			6
Ground Ivy		6	Yellow Dock			6
Horehound		10	Mandrake root			10
Ladies Sliper		20	Indigo root			10
Liverwort		20	Wild Coltsfoot			10
Lobelia		5				
Lovage Seed		10				

FIGURE 14 Original herb house at the Church family, New Lebanon. Destroyed by fire in 1875. (After Nordhoff, '75.)

In 1832 "a large building was demanded" for the industry (figure 14), and about this time more attention was paid to the preparation of extracts. Between April 1 and December 31, 1834, an herb account book mentions the following extracts: cicuta, henbane, stramonium, hops, belladonna, butternut, dandelion, boneset and garden lettuce. Wine bitters and honey, lavender, cologne and peach waters were also being prepared. Buckthorn and sarsaparilla syrups are mentioned, as well as cephalic and "Veg. Bil." pills and the popular elm composition. Ointments were also being manufactured of sambucus, althea, savin and elder. The barks from cherry, bayberry, boxwood, oak, ash, alder, hemlock and elm were stripped, ground and papered. Various roots were included: angelica root, avens root, burdock, bethroot, bloodroot, blackberry root, dandelion, garget, mandrake, peony, poke, pleurisy root, parsley, slippery root, stoneroot and yarrow. The leaves of burdock, hardhack, rose, raspberry and thornapple are frequently listed, and coriander, fennel and larkspur seed were sold in some quantity. Other herb items were bugle, balsam, boneset, bittersweet, borage, balm, catnip, coltsfoot, comfrey, wild and garden celandine, cranesbill, cicuta, cohosh, carduus, "cazenna" (cassena or the yaupon) clary, cleavers, Centaurea, camomile, digitalis, yellow dock, elder flowers, "elacampane," ergot (pulverized), foxglove, fleabane, frostwort, feverfew, goldthread, golden seal, hyocyamus, hops, horehound, hyssop, henbane, hollyhock, Indian hemp, ivy, Johnswort, liverwort, lobelia, lavender, yellow pond lily, life everlasting, marshmallow, motherwort, mullein, maidenhair, myrrh, malefern, mountain mint, mayweed, mugwort, marjoram, low mallows, nervin (pulverized), Jerusalem oak, pennyroyal, peppermint, prince's pine, poppy flowers, parsnip, rue, sage, spearmint, skunk cabbage, snakehead, sweet flag, scullcap, Solomon's-seal, sarsaparilla, sweet-fern, southernwood, sweet basil, spikenard, scorfula plant, savin, scurvy grass, senna, summer savory, saffron, "squareweed," stoneroot, sweet scabious or scabish, tansy, thyme, wild turnip (pulverized), vervain, wintergreen, rose willow and wormwood.

That all these plants were not indigenous to New York State is apparent. In the short period of ten years the industry had grown to such an extent that herbs were being purchased from far and near. Garrett Lawrence was a prominent figure in the industry until his death in 1837. Harlow's name is not found after 1834, but the name of Jonathan Wood enters prominently into the records in the 40's. In 1844, the herb business was confined strictly to the Second order of the Church family, and the broom and seed business exclusively to the First order. The Second order was really a distinct family before this time, and the Church deacons did business with this family (where Lawrence was located) as with any other concern.

The large ledger covering the period 1844–48 indicates that the herb industry was developing rapidly during these years. Most of the plants and herbs used in the 1830's were still being prepared, and the ointment and extract business had greatly extended its scope. Many new items appear in 1844, such as hellebore, deadly nightshade, lemon balm, witch hazel, wild indigo, pile wort, green meadow root, white sanicle root, star flower, water pepper, "poppoose root" (papoose-root), gravel-plant, lady's-slipper and cankerweed. Many orders appear for such miscellaneous products as poppy capsules, inspissated conium and lovage seed. Small bottles, each containing two dozen capsules of "Pearls of ether" and "Pearls of turpentine," were sold about this time. Rose water had become nearly as important a preparation as peach water.

The herb industry at New Lebanon received an impetus in 1850 by the addition of such machinery as a steam boiler and a globular-shaped copper vacuum pan for drying the herbs. Three double-presses, similar, no doubt, to the one used at Niskeyuna (figure 15) and capable of pressing 100 pounds daily, were then being used. These power presses had supplanted the earlier type shown in figure 16. The Manifesto records the amount of herbs pressed in 1850 as being "not less than 21,000 lbs.," besides about 7000 lbs. of extract (Note 38). In 1852 a new steam engine and other additional machinery was bought; the next year 42,000 pounds of roots, herbs and barks were pressed, and 7500 pounds of extracts produced. The comprehensive nature of the industry is evidenced by the declaration on the cover page of an undated catalog issued about this time: "Catalogue of Medicinal Plants, Barks, Roots, Seeds, Flowers and Select Powders; With their Therapeutic Qualities and Botanical Names; also Pure Vegetable Extracts, Prepared in Vacuo, Ointments, Inspissated Juices, Essential Oils, Double Distilled and Fragrant Waters, Etc. Etc. Raised, Prepared and Put Up in the Most Careful Manner, by the United Society of Shakers at New Lebanon, N. Y." The title concludes with the verse:

> A blade of grass—a simple flower
> Culled from the dewy lea;
> These, these shall speak with touching power,
> Of change and health to thee.

The "physics gardens" at New Lebanon occupied at this period about 50 acres, which were given over chiefly to the cultivation of hyoscyamus, belladonna, taraxacum,

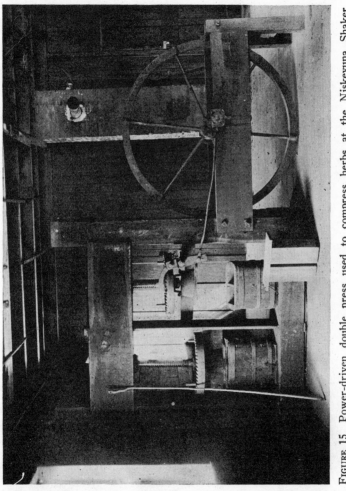

FIGURE 15 Power-driven double press used to compress herbs at the Niskeyuna Shaker community. New York State Museum.

FIGURE 16 Objects illustrating the medicinal herb industry at the Niskeyuna Shakers. At the right is a double press worked by hand levers. An herb cutter, showing knife and chute, stands in the center. The printing press was probably used for seed as well as herb labels. In the background is a storage case with herb packages. New York State Museum.

aconite, poppy, lettuce, sage, summer savory, marjoram, dock, burdock, valerian and horehound (Note 39). Extract of taraxacum was the chief product. Conium, hyoscyamus and belladonna classed next. About 50 minor varieties of plants were also raised, including rue, borage, carduus, hyssop, marshmallow, feverfew and pennyroyal. "Nearly 200 varieties of indigenous plants were collected, and 30 or 40 other varieties were brought from the South and West and from Europe" (Andrews, '30, p. 6).

Fowler thus described the method of preparing plants for the market in the middle of the century (The American Journal of Pharmacy, '52, p. 89):

The drying and storing of so many plants requires much space, and several buildings are occupied wholly or in part for this purpose; the principal and central one of which is a neat structure about 120 feet long by 38 feet wide, two stories high with a well-lighted basement and airy garret. The basement is devoted to the pressing, grinding and other heavy work, whilst at one end the steam boiler is placed. The first story is used for packing, papering, sorting, printing and storing the products, whilst the second story and loft are used exclusively for drying and storing. Being well-lighted and airy, these rooms are well fitted for the purpose. Racks of hurdles are conveniently placed along the center on which the herbs previously garbled are put to dry, which is rapidly accomplished by the free circulation of air that is maintained throughout. The sides of the second story room are arranged with large and tight bins, in which the plants are put as soon as they are properly desiccated, until removed for pressing.

The extract business in particular was stimulated by such reorganization and improvements, and in the period 1861–62 more than 100 different varieties, both solid and fluid, were being manufactured. These were usually put up in five-pound or one-pound bottles, but in some cases one-half-pound, one-fourth-pound and one-eighth-pound and ounce sizes were used. Total production in 1861 amounted to 3588 pounds of solid extract and 5544 gallons of fluid extract. In 1862, 6478 pounds of solid extract were prepared, and in 1864, 16,450 pounds of extracts were "dressed." Between 1860 and 1867 the yearly output of powders or pulverized roots and herbs averaged over 7000 pounds. Ointments and such preparations as oil of wormwood, rose water and Norwood's Tincture also showed an increased production. According to Johnston ('51, p. 266) the sale of Shaker herbs was promoted by the popularity of the so-called Thomsonian medical system, which "makes use of herbs only." Samuel Thomson was an itinerant herb doctor from New Hampshire, the author of "A New Guide to Health," which was once widely read.

Conium maculatum, or the poison hemlock, must have been a particularly important extract at one time. Engaged on one of the countless expeditions of discovery at Mount Lebanon, the author picked up recently a lithographer's stone used in transferring labels. On its surface was engraved the following:

PREPARED IN THE UNITED SOCIETY
D. M.
NEW LEBANON, N. Y.
EXT. CONII MAC.

This is the only such stone known, and presumably there were few others. On its side is painted in red the numbers "06.," which may or may not represent a date. The "D. M." is David Meacham, whose name, by the way, was included on herb and seed labels for some time after his death in 1826. Many of the first extracts prepared "in vacuo," such as sarsaparilla, rhatany and *"lupulus humulus"* or hops, were put up in small cylindrical boxes of green pasteboard (figure 17).

FIGURE 17 Green cardboard boxes or containers for dry extracts prepared "in vacuo." New Lebanon Church family. "D.M." stands for David Meacham, the first official trustee at this family.

A fragmentary but intimate glimpse of the herb business at New Lebanon at about the Civil War era is presented by one of the Shaker sisters, Sister Marcia Bullard, who wrote as follows:

Forty years ago it was contrary to the "orders" which governed our lives to cultivate useless flowers, but, fortunately for those of us who loved them, there are many plants which are beautiful as well as useful. We always had extensive poppy beds and early in the morning, before the sun had risen, the white-capped sisters could be seen stooping among the scarlet blossoms to slit those pods from which the petals had just fallen. Again after sundown they came out with little knives to scrape off the dried juice. This crude opium was sold at a large price and its production was one of the most lucrative as well as the most picturesque of our industries.

The rose bushes were planted along the sides of the road which ran through our village and were greatly admired by the passersby, but it was strongly impressed upon us that a rose was useful, not ornamental. It was not intended to please us by its color or its odor, its mission was to be made into rose-water, and if we thought of it in any other way we were making an idol of it and thereby imperiling our souls. In order that we might not be tempted to fasten a rose upon our dress or to put it into water to keep, the rule was that the flower should be plucked with no stem at all. We had only crimson roses, as they were supposed to make stronger rosewater than the paler varieties. This rosewater was sold, of course, and was used in the community to flavor apple pies. It was also kept in store at the infirmary, and although in those days no sick person was allowed to have a fresh flower to cheer him, he was welcome to a liberal supply of rosewater with which to bathe his aching head.

Then there were the herbs of many kinds. Lobelia, pennyroyal, spearmint, peppermint, catnip, wintergreen, thoroughwort, sarsaparilla and dandelion grew wild in the surrounding fields. When it was time to gather them an elderly brother would take a great wagonload of children, armed with tow sheets, to the pastures. Here they would pick the appointed herb—each one had its own day, that there might be no danger of mixing—and, when their sheets were full, drive solemnly home again. In addition to that which grew wild we cultivated an immense amount of dandelion, dried the root and sold it as "chicory." The witch hazel branches were too tough for women and children to handle, so the brethren cut them and brought them into the herb shop where the sisters made them into hamamelis. We had big beds of sage, thorn apple, belladonna, marigolds and camomile, as well as of yellow dock, of which we raised great quantities to sell to the manufacturers of a well-known "sarsaparilla." We also made a sarsaparilla of our own and various ointments. In the herb shop the herbs were dried and then pressed into packages by machinery, labeled and sold outside. Lovage root we exported both plain and sugared and the wild flagroot we gathered and sugared too. On the whole there was no pleasanter work than that in the "medical garden" and "herb shop." (Good Housekeeping, July '06, p. 37.)

As late as 1890 the services of six brethren and about as many sisters were required in the herb industry. Such extracts as mandrake and colocynth were made until as late as 1900, and the industry survives today in the preparation of the famous Norwood's Tincture of Veratrum Viride.

Herb growing and the preparation of herbs for pharmaceutical use were also important industries at the Second family in New Lebanon as well as at Watervliet (Note 40), Harvard (Note 41), Canterbury, Enfield, N. H., and New Gloucester. In Ohio the largest medicinal herb and extract industry was located at Union Village.

BOTTLES, JARS AND LABELS

The reputation of the Shakers for self-sufficiency has been such that they have been credited with making almost every article found in their homes and shops. This is true in particular regarding the fine glassware and earthenware found in their "nurse-shops," dwelling houses and herb buildings. This ware was never manufactured by the New Lebanon Shakers, however, nor as far as the writer has learned, by any other Shaker society. The quantities of bottles, jugs, jars, vials and demijohns needed for the herb industry and other uses were purchased from a variety of sources. A book of invoices covering the period 1856–61 and posted by Edward Fowler and Benjamin Gates, trustees at the Church, contains several entries in support of this fact. In 1856 the Boston and Sandwich Glass Company of Boston supplied an order of several dozen half-gallon, three-pint and quart "blown Bbl. Jugs ptd." Flint vials were purchased in 1857 from Dexter & Nellegar in Albany; covered jars in 1858, from Schieffelin Bros. & Co., New York City; "Sand bottles" in 1860, from A. B. Sands & Co., Wholesale Druggists, New York City; bottles of various kinds the same year from Penfold, Parker & Mower, New York City; and "self-sealing preserve cans" from Nathan Clark jr, Athens, N. Y. Pottery butter pots were obtained from E. & L. P. Norton, Bennington, Vt., in 1858 and at earlier dates; jugs were also bought from the Norton concern as well as from the Fort Edward (N. Y.) Stone Ware Potteries. Covered jars were purchased in 1861 from M'Kesson & Robbins, New York City, and "flat-top" crockery jars in 1858 from A. Gilbert & Co. of Bennington.

As in the seed business, the labels required for the papers and jars of herbs and extracts were at first printed on presses constructed by some ingenious Shaker mechanic (see figures 18 and 19). As time went on and the fame of Shaker medicines became widespread, the business managers of the industry found it expedient to have the printing done by regular commercial printers and electrotypists. In 1856 Albert H. Jocelyn, of New York City, submitted a bill of $50 "To composition & 55 electrotypes of labels." Hoffman, Knickerbocker & Co. printed and transferred 15,000 labels in 1856 and 40,000 in 1857. In 1859, $42 was paid to the aforesaid Jocelyn for "setting type with rules, and for 56 Electrotypes of do Herb Labels." Lewis & Goodwin of Albany also printed and engraved labels for the Shakers. Their 1861 bill was itemized as follows: "11,200 Ext. taraxacum, 4000 Ext. Hyocyamus, 4000 Ext. Belladonna, 4000 Ext.

FIGURE 18 Label printing press from Niskeyuna settlement.
New York State Museum.

Gentina, 2400 Ext. Conium, 2400 Ext. Aconiti, 2400 Ext. Sarsaparilla, 2400 Ext. Sarsaparilla Comp., 2400 Ext. Jugland [Juglans?] and 2400 Ext. Stramoni." In 1862 the bill was for printing 20,000 labels and for "transfer labels." Paper used in the herb and seed industries was

FIGURE 19   Labels for extract and ointment bottles and containers.   New Lebanon Church family.   These were printed in various colors.

obtained from the Crane company in Dalton, Mass., as well as from other sources. Paper boxes were bought in 1859 from Sturmwald Muller, New York City; manila bags in 1860 from L. Whitney & Co., Watertown; and twilled and plain seed bags in 1861 from H. R. David, New York City. Spruce barrels were supplied to the Shakers at this time by the Dean's Company of Cheshire, Mass.

SISTERS' WORK IN THE HERB INDUSTRY

The major part of the laborious and routine labor connected with the medicinal herb industry, such work as cleaning roots, picking and "picking over" flowers and plants, cutting sage, cleaning bottles, cutting and printing labels, papering powders and herbs, and "dressing" or putting up extracts and ointments, was done by the sisters. They also made the ointments. The herb houses were situated in the Second order section of the Church family, and most of this work was done by the Second order sisters, who sat at long tables such as the one pictured in figure 20. The deaconesses assigned certain sisters to the occupation of picking and cleaning herbs, flowers and roots; a record was kept of the number of days so spent, and the order was reimbursed by the family deacons at the rate of 20 cents a day.

The first record of the sisters' part in this important industry occurs in 1841 (MS. No. 30). In 1847 the Second order sisters cleaned 4500 pounds of roots, and in 1848, 9327 pounds. By 1850 they were engaged in putting up "elm flour" (Note 42) and "composition flour" in two-ounce packages; in the 20-year period 1850–69 more than 30,000 pounds of these preparations were papered. The manufacture of ointments by the sisters dates from

Figure 20 Room in an herb shop at the Center family in New Lebanon, as it appears today. The Shakers still put up the medicine known as "Veratrum Viride."

1852. In the next 20 years 5550 pounds were made and dressed. The various extracts made by the Shaker chemists or "botanists" were being put up for the market by the sisters in 1855, and in the next 15 years a total of more than 75,000 pounds was prepared. Norwood's Tincture of Veratrum (Note 43), one of the principal medicines produced, was first put up in 1859, when 143 bottles were dressed. The next year a thousand bottles were prepared, and in the six years between 1866 and 1871, when the record ends, 1349 gross (bottles?) were dressed by the Second order sisterhood for the pharmaceutic market. The deaconesses' accounts show several miscellaneous activities in which the sisters were at one time or another engaged. In 1853, 576 bottles of "sweet herbs" were dressed, and in 1860 three gross of verbena. Rose water was distilled from 1861 on, 35 gallons in that year, 20 in 1862, 25 in 1864, 82 in 1865, 55 in 1866 and so on. In 1861, 118 herb sheets, used in the collection of herbs, were made, and these were supplied as needed. The picking and drying of poppies and marigolds occupied much time. In 1870, 12,564 bottles were cleaned to be filled with Norwood's Tincture, and in 1871, 14,079 bottles. The extent of the herb or extract business at this time may be gauged by the fact that in 1870 the Second order sisters cut more than a million labels.

THE MEDICAL DEPARTMENT

It has been noted that herbs were first used as medicines or in exchange for medicines. The progress of the society soon necessitated the organization of a medical department or "order of physicians," two of each sex. The first nurse shops were constructed soon after the organization of the society; the present building at the

Church was built in 1858. Harlow and Isaac Crouch were the first physicians at New Lebanon; later, as we have noted, Garrett Lawrence served with Harlow in this capacity, and at a still later period the medical responsibilities were undertaken by one Barnybus Hinckly. Sisters were assigned to the infirmary as nurses.

The Shakers at New Lebanon, Canterbury and elsewhere made early use of the electric current for therapeutic purposes. Sometime in the 1820's, if not earlier, several "static" machines were invented. These consisted of large glass cylinders which revolved against a chamois rubbing pad producing a frictional electricity, which was applied for curative purposes to afflicted parts of the body (Note 44). The first reference to such machines is found in the old medical register (MS. No. 22), under date of April 17, 1827, when five dollars was charged to Olivar and William Hull for the use of "an electrical cylinder" (Note 45). In Elizabeth Lovegrove's journal (MS. No. 33) the following entry occurs on March 31, 1837: "Elder Sister remains feeble but is relieved some of her cough by the vaper bath and electricity." On April 2d of the same year it is recorded that "Elder Sister . . . is not much better, we keep her in and continue shocking her." On June 9th one of the elder sisters fell down and hurt her side. Skunk cabbage leaves were applied and tea was prepared made of Johnswort and peppergrass seed. The nurses also resorted to "shocking rubing and bleeding her."

In such large communities as those developed by the Shakers there was naturally a certain amount of sickness, especially among the older members, as well as the expected quota of accidents in the shops and on the farms. In the main, however, they were a healthy, temperate people, leading out-of-door lives, subject to few of the worries that harassed the usual wage-earners, maintaining regular hours in sleeping, eating and working, living under the most sanitary conditions, and achieving as a group an enviable record for longevity.

BLACKSMITHING AND THE MECHANICAL TRADES

From the earliest years of the order the Shakers have had the reputation of being highly versed in the mechanical arts. Mechanics and blacksmiths were drawn into the various societies in no small numbers, and there they became imbued with that progressive spirit which characterized the whole system of Shakerism during these early decades of vitality and development. Seldom did the visitor fail to notice how farming and industrial operations were accelerated by all manner of skilful means and devices, how the labor of the household was lightened by labor-saving machinery fashioned in the Shaker shops, and how efficiently sanitary systems had been constructed. In the water power that drove all the shop machinery, in the machines themselves, in the many farming and manufacturing operations and in the constant constructive activity which permeated the material life of the sect, the hand of the skilled mechanic is ever amazingly apparent.

It is sometimes difficult to distinguish between the blacksmith and the mechanist. Except possibly for a few years before the society at New Lebanon was organized, the blacksmith's shop was more akin to a machine shop, and with the institution of power-driven machinery became even less like the "smithies" of popular fancy. The contribution of these workers in metal to the revenues of the embryonic order was second to none. Their skill was constantly being drafted into the service of the farm and shop, their products were sold in the early trustees' offices, and they did jobbing for the farmers and gentry of the surrounding country.

The versatility of these early smiths was remarkable. They could turn their hands to almost anything required in hardware or wagon-making, and were called upon to repair all sorts of tools and machinery. They forged and mended chains; made saddle nails, sheathing nails, wagon nails, spikes, brads and copper nails, wrought and cut nails; set horseshoes; shod sleighs; made knife blades and all kinds of shop and garden tools; mended "chizzels," augers, frying pans, ox-yokes, shovels, plow-irons; made rings, staples, hasps, picks, bails, iron and steel candlesticks, gate hangings, latches, "ketches," chest hinges, keys, axes, saws, scythes and butcher knives; constructed wagons and wagon boxes; sharpened drag teeth; "ironed" neck-yokes; made clothiers' shears; and turned out "sundry brass ware." Hoes were manufactured in some quantity as early as 1789 and sold for five shillings and four pence apiece. In 1806 there was still a demand for these tools, the price at this time having advanced to eight shillings. Turning tools were also made in 1789. A set of wagon boxes sold at this date for 12 shillings. Cut nails, ten penny, sold in 1790 for a shilling a pound, wrought nails for slightly more. A pair of "nailers shears" was sold July 17, 1790, for three pounds, 12 shillings. Two pairs of grinding shears were sold in 1806 for 24 pounds. "Taylor's shears" were marketed at this date for 16 and 18 shillings; in 1810, two pair of tailor shears sold for $3.24. The first kitchen "arches" may have been made at outside furnaces (the Church paid $12.70 in 1807 for arch irons at the Dalton "furnice"), but these were also made at the Shaker blacksmith shops, and we find such items listed as a frying arch which was sold in 1824 to the North family for the sum of $12. A few early charges are given below (MS. No. 8):

1788.	Sept.	To 18 lb. 4d Nails	£ 1:4:0
1789.	July	To Ironing Whippletrees	0:1:2
	July	To Sharpening plow irons	0:1:0
	Nov.	To 3 Pair of Hinges	0:10:0
		To one Door Latch	0:5:8
		To 2 Door handles and Latches	0:8:0
	May	To setting 2 Shoes	0:1:0
		To Shoing Horse	0:3:9
	Dec.	To Mending Chain	0:2:6
	May	To Hinges & Buttons to...Clock door	0:4:0
	Apr.	To Sundry Tools of Smith work	1:1:3
	Sept.	To Sundr Brass Ware	4:16:0
	May	To ½ Sett Waggon Boxes	0:6:0
	Sept.	To 3 Sett of gate Hanging	0:14:0
	Dec.	To a plain Iron	0:2:6
		To one Shaving Knive	0:5:6
	Aug.	To 4 large Staples, @ 1/6	0:6:0
	March	To a Pair Hinges for Chest	0:1:6
	March	To one Scythe	0:8:0
	July	To one Scythe Sneath	0:1:0
	Oct.	To Ironing Cart Wheels	0:16:0
	Apr.	To 1½ Saddle Nails @ 2/8	0:4:0
	Oct.	To Making a Butcher Knife and Mending one	0:1:0
	May	To a Knife Blade	0:0:8
	Nov.	To 3 Pair large HL @ 3/6	0:10:6
		To a half Inch bit	0:1:9
	Oct.	To Sundr Turning tools	1:5:0
	Aug.	To a Pair hand Iron 24¾ lbs. @ 1/	1:4:9
	Dec.	To a Pair Hand Irons	2:8:0
	Nov.	To 35½ lb. Sheathing Nails @ 9d.	1:6:7
1790.	Jan.	To a Door Latch	0:5:4
	Mar.	To an Ax	0:8:0
	Jan.	To 4 lb. Cut 8d Nails @ 13d	0:4:4
	Apr.	To Ironing a Neck Yoke	0:4:0
	Mar.	To 2 lb Cut 10d Nails @ 1/	0:2:0
	July	To a Draught Chain	0:16:0
	Jan.	To ½ lb. 6d Nails (Hammer'd)	0:0:7
	April	To a Stone drill	0:5:0
		To a Smoaking Iron Pipe	0:2:8
	April	To Bailing Bake Kettle	0:1:4
	July	To a Narrow Chizzel	0:2:6
		To Mill Saw	2:0:0

A certain amount of farm and shop machinery was also manufactured by the Shaker blacksmiths and machinists, the whole process, pattern making, casting, framing and so on being carried through as an independent project.[1] In 1793 Benjamin Bruce invented and made a machine for setting card-teeth. A trip hammer was made in 1800, and in 1828 the first foot lathe for turning and drilling. Machines for mortising and dovetailing, for making wooden shoe-pegs in quantity, for filling herb packages, for gumming saws, and for facilitating numbers of other operations formerly done by hand, were also devised at an early date (see pages 40–45).

Hundreds of knives were used in the herb business for cutting roots, stems and barks. At first these were all made in the blacksmith's and wood-turner's shops; at a later date the blades were purchased and fitted into the homemade handles. Countless tools, a few of which are selected for figure 21, were also produced. The business of making wrought and cut nails was "for several years . . . a source of considerable income. These wrought nails were used in the coarser work while building, until the year 1812 when they were superseded by the cut nails. Wrought nails were also used as early as 1780 for shingling and lathing, but on the introduction of cut nails, soon after the organization of the Community the wrought nails passed out of use. The machinery for cut nails and the work of forming the heads by a hand hammer, employed not less than twelve persons and yielded a very profitable income" (The Manifesto, April '90, p. 74–75). The manufacture of cut nails was "closed" in 1830.

---

[1]Plows may at one time have been made for sale. Although no further reference to such an industry can be found, the notation is made on certain early extract labels used by one Rufus F. Hibbard, 96 John street, New York, that this "general agent for the Shakers" could supply "a full assortment of Fresh Shaker Herbs, Roots, Extracts, Ointments, Garden Seeds, Syrups, Thomsonian Medicines and Compositions, Brooms, Seives, Ploughs, and all other articles manufactured by the Shakers."

Figure 21 Collection of small tools used in various occupations. The two chisel-edged instruments at the left were used in making buttonholes in brethren's garments. At the left and right are two awl-like bodkins. To the right of the curly-maple mallet is an L-shaped tool used in pressing bonnet pleats. Paring knives and knives for cutting herbs and roots were made in quantity. A sister's hammer, a gimlet and a molding plane complete the lot.

MACHINE SHOP WORK

The machine shop at the Church was equipped with several machine lathes propelled by water power over a huge wheel. The shop was located on the mountain side, and considerable energy was generated by this method. Iron work of all kinds was turned out at this factory. Here the pattern makers worked, and here were constructed many of the mechanical devices used by the Shakers in their manifold activities. Also, wagon-making and the manufacture of wagon parts presumably were carried on at this place. One of the blacksmith's shops was reorganized in 1846 by the instalment of water power for driving the great trip hammer made earlier in this century; this shop was equipped also with machine lathes and various mechanical devices for making machine parts.

Jobbing was done for other Shaker families and for outsiders. In 1838 "Work done at Machine Shop for others" was reported by the trustees to amount to $164.81 (MS. No. 14)—not a large revenue, but one of the many contributions advancing the common fund. A few entries for 1839 in "A Journal of Domestic Events Kept by Benjamin Lyon" (MS. No. 28) will illustrate some of the activities at the machine shop. Lyon was a capable mechanic, and we must overlook his literary shortcomings (Note 46).

January 1. Tuesday work to the Mashine shop at boreing waggon hubs for the Second faimely.

January 5. Saterday go to the Mashine Shop saw some timber for a fraim to drive spoks.

January 25. Friday . . . doe a little in the shop make some patruns to cast Waggon boxes. . . .

February 1. Friday work some at mortising hubs for the First Orders one horse waggon help Amos Bishop some about sawing waggon fellews (fellies).

February 23. Saterday work some in the shop go to the Mill & get some Iron Staves for the Plaster Mill cary them to the Smith shop to repare go to the Second famely get some molding sand to cast a scrue box for the mill.

May 24. Friday work in the shop at a pare of Thils (thills) for a one horse Waggon etc.

July 11. Thursday go to the mashine shop saw out dipper rims.

December 3. Tuesday I go to the Mashine Shop & grind some joiner tools.

December 8. Saterday I do chores take the Candle mashine & wheal it down to the first Order. . . .

December 13. Friday I doe chores to the Mashine Shop & grind axes & knives to be in radeness to kill the hogs next week.

Miscellaneous activities are also recorded in the trustee's accounts. In 1835, for instance, a charge to Daniel Hawkins included work in turning gudgeons, boring segments and hanging and chucking balance wheels. Iron castings formed an appreciable item.

Lyon's record of "domestic events" illustrates well the variety of occupations to which a mechanic, or any other workman for that matter, was obliged under the Shaker system to devote his time and talents. The machine shop occupied only a portion of this brother's schedule. He carried grists to the mill, put up corn for the hogs, mended floors, drove merchandise in from surrounding towns, cut and split wood and sawed boards, helped the sisters pick over apples and "put up" apple sauce, worked occasionally at the tanhouse and "gardening house," plowed and harrowed, hauled manure, assisted in the cooper's shop, periodically drove the "coalts" to turn the washmill and did endless cleaning up chores. Giles Avery, whose manual employment consisted of repairing buildings, digging cellar foundations, sawing stone, plumbing, carpentering, plastering, wagon-making, cabinetmaking, making wooden dippers, constructing liquid manure cisterns, and orcharding, notes in his autobiography (p. 6) "how similar to colonization in a new country, communal association necessarily is; that members of a community should be willing to turn a hand in any needed direction in order to render their best service in building up and sustaining the cause." It was the widespread application of this spirit that more than anything else was responsible for the long continued success of the Shaker experiment in communistic living.

MISCELLANEOUS TRADES — MILLING, CARPENTRY JOBBING, SHINGLE AND BRICKMAKING

At first, in 1789, the New Lebanon Shakers carried their grain to one William Norton's to be ground "without taking Tole and the Tole to be paid for in Leather and Nails." The old stone gristmill of the Church family was erected in 1824; the date appears in end-irons under the north gable. Before this the gristing was probably done in a smaller mill. The first record found of this industry appears on September 14, 1824, when a charge of $64.44 was made to Joseph Allen for grinding grain. Grain was sold to farmers and dealers direct from the mill after this date, and several entries in the trustee's accounts testify to a steady income from this source. On

April 15, 1839, for instance, appears the entry, "Grain from the mill, $24.98," and on July 30th, "Rec'd from the mill, $13.00" (MS. No. 14). The mill was at first run by water power on an over-shot wheel. After a time, however, even with the artificial diversion of several streams of water, this method was found to be inadequate to furnish power during dry seasons, and one of the first turbine devices used in this section was installed.

The sawmills and carpentry shops were among the busiest places in the industrious village. The fact that the society at New Lebanon boasted of six such mills by 1839 is evidence of a particularly active occupation. These mills were equipped with buzz or circular saws (said to be a Shaker invention) as early as 1813. From an early date the Church family did a large business in wood-turning and in planing and matching timber. In another chapter (p. 137 and Note 53) several items in turning such materials as broom, brush and mop handles, bannisters, bedsteads etc. are listed. In 1835 work done for one Thomas Bowman in "plaining and matching 7482 feet floor plank" amounted to $56.11½, and the same year similar work was done for families in the same society.

Shingle and brick-making and stone-sawing were at one time active industries, and shingles and bricks were often made on orders from the world's people. As early as 1789 (December 22) we find an item of 5000 shingles sold at 13/4 for £3:6:8, and as late as 1834, when "4M. shingles @ 18/" were sold for $9, items of this kind appear. Numbers of old shingle-benches (figure 22) attest to the labors of the early carpenters. Bricks were also manufactured at the East family brickyard as early as 1789, although they were seldom employed in the Shakers'

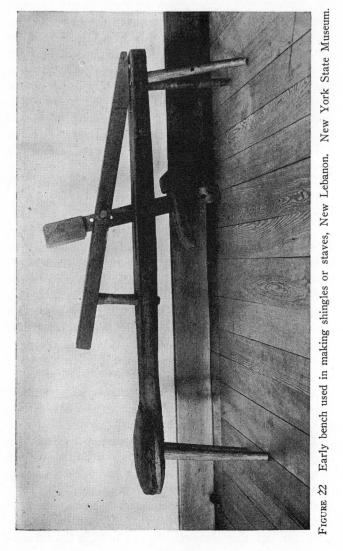

FIGURE 22 Early bench used in making shingles or staves, New Lebanon. New York State Museum.

own buildings until later. On October 10th of this year, "2½ Hund^ed Common Brick @ 2/8" were sold for 6s, 8d.; on December 3, "450 Weather Brick . . . @ 3/" for 13s, 6d.; on March 26, 1790, "5560 bricks @ 26/8" for £7, 8s., 3d.; and on Feb. 4, 1790, 1150 Bricks for £1, 10s., 8d. (MS. No. 8). Operations at the brickyard continued until 1840 or after.

TANNING

One of the most prosperous industries at the community of New Lebanon was the tanning of leather and such affiliated occupations as saddle, harness and shoemaking. In the first year of the community's organized existence a small building was utilized for finishing leather. Here Root, the tanner, ground his hemlock bark by horse power on a simple circular stone. This primitive method was employed until after the turn of the century.

The industry's development after 1800 is thus briefly described in The Manifesto's historical sketch of the New Lebanon Church family (The Manifesto, May '90, p. 97):

In 1807 more additions were made to the buildings, and machines added for rolling the leather. In 1813 a machine was added for splitting leather. The business had so much increased by the year 1834 that still larger buildings were needed and more ample provisions made to meet the growing demand. By this change the vats were placed in the basement of the building and numbered not less than thirty-two. . . . The hides at this date were softened in a common fulling mill, but in 1840 a wheel or cylinder was used and considered a great improvement. As the sales increased, the old process of tanning leather in cold vats was by far too slow to suit the sellers and buyers of this fast age, and a steam boiler was introduced in 1850 for heating the vats and leaches, in order to force the hides more expeditiously through the process of making leather. . . . (Note 47).

The nature of the business at this early period is revealed in the following random selection of sales records (MS. No. 8):

1789.

Novr	2:	To Taning a piece of a Horse Hide 3¾ lb @ 8d	£ 0:2:6
Sepr	22:	To 20¾ lbs. Sole Leather @ 1/10	1:18:0
Oct.	26:	To ½ Side upper Leather	0:11:8
Feb.	17:	To Making and finding Sole Leather a Pr. Shoes	0:6:0
Novr	2:	To 7¼ lb. Sole Leather @ 1/10d	0:13:3
April	17:	To Leather for a Pair Womens Shoes	0:4:0
Octr	10:	To Taning and Currying a Calf Skin	0:8:0
Novr	25:	To 2 Calf Skins	1:6:8
		To 3 Sheep Skins Ready Tan'd and Currying	
		2 Do	0:13:4
Sept.	9:	To Taning & Currying 2 Small sides	0:16:8
Dec.	25:	To Taning a Horse hide	0:14:0
Sept.	17:	To ½ side Neats Leather	0:12:0
1790.	July 14:	To 2 Pair Inner Soals	0:1:8
	Feby. 15:	To a Side Harness Leather 11¼ lbs. @ 2/2	1:4:4

The introduction of improved apparatus for tanning, rolling and splitting the leather soon resulted in a more productive industry. Between 1805 and 1810 shipments of calfskins, "sheap" skins, "lam" skins, foxskins, horsehides, sole leather, "ruffuse" [refuse] leather, white leather, upper leather, harness leather etc. were being sent to neighboring and distant markets. The business was of such dimensions that the Shakers were not able to raise all the hides they needed, and these were bought from farmers and cattle dealers in the neighborhood or near-by towns and cities. Ledgers covering the period from 1810 to 1830 are crammed with leather sales, and the conclusion is self-evident that at this time tanning was among the most active occupations at the Church family. The total account of stock work in 1835 was as follows (MS. No. 27):

 199 Sole leather hides
  95 Upper leather hides
  12 Harness leather hides
  25 Horse hides
 468 Calfskins
 452 Sheepskins
  90 Woodchuck and Cat skins
  26 Deer skins (dressed wash leather)

In 1836 the account was as follows:

 82 Slaughter Sole leather hides
 38 Spanish Sole leather hides
 69 Slaughter Upper leather hides
 55 Patany Upper leather hides
  5 Harness leather hides
 22 Horse hides dressed whip leather
  3 Horse hides tand
Total 274 hides

 600 Calfskins tand
 280 Sheepskins tand
  22 Do dressed white
  20 Do dressed wash leather
  4 Do tand with wool on
Total 326 Sheepskins
  5 Dog skins tand with the hair on
  59 Woodchuckskins tand
  5 Calfskins tand
  20 Deerskins dressed

The year 1837 contains several items of coonskins. Sheepskins were tanned as dressed wash leather, tanned with the wool on, and tanned in "parchment." Small lambskins were "alum dressed" with the wool on. The year 1838 adds a "hogskin" and a "coltskin" to the list, and in 1841, 82 African Upper leather hides are listed.

In 1844, a total of 539 hides and 1010 skins were prepared.

The tannery at the Church family did a steady amount of business for the other families, and this was charged on a yearly account. Yearly bills for tanning in 1833 were: to Charles Bushnell, $91; to Daniel J. Hawkins, $77.75; to Aaron Bill, $25; and to Joseph Allen, $49.25 (MS. No. 12).

An insight into the Shaker tanning business may be gained by following the daily operations of the workmen. A tanner's diary (MS. No. 27) was kept for the year 1846, from which we quote the entries for the month of January: (See Note 48 for explanation of terms.)

1846: We now commence keeping journal for the year 1846.

Jan. 1. Whitened patnays blacked and finish patnays healed up the leach unloaded 128 feet hemlock bark hold the limes and handlers and chores of various kinds, set out sheepskins on the grane side.

2. We took up 1 pack of sole leather cleand the bark out and run in new liquor, hold up a pack of handlers and spred them out for laying down pump of the old and run in new liquor shaved 2 sides belting leather finish patnays trim and board and set patnays pump up the leach grind some oak bark.

3. Lay away 2 packs sole leather Vat. No. 1. has 32 sides in it, to lay six weeks No 2 has 50 sides to lay 30 days brake and grind bark. glass of three dozen patnays and roll up two dozen of them to go to watervliet haul the lime

5. J. S cleans out the leach and fill it up with new bark unloaded 128 feet of hemlock bark.

6. brake and grind bark and various chores in the yard.

7. Unhear 56 slaughter sides and washed the hiar.

8. Beem 56 sides on the flesh side, unloaded 128 bark.

9. trimed and boarded Calfskins and finish sheepskins.

10. Ground bark and various chores.

12. J. S. and F S works a pack of hides on the grane side and put them in the water and wheel 30 upper leather sides and trim them and put them in the graner and blacked 21 Calfskins and scoured shavens and sheepskins.

13. Worked into the handler 26 slaughter sole leather sides and handle them and haul up 100 African sides and wheel and scour 50 of them on the flesh side black 3 Calfskins and past set and size 2 dozen.

14. Whitened 25 patnay sides slicked 2 dozen Calfskins ruff stuf 50 African sides haul the handlers and shave sheepkins turned some beeming knifs handles.

15. Whitened 6 patnays shaved 12 sheepskins 1 Calfskin barked down 50 African sides, beemed 30 Upper leather sides on the flesh in the graner beemed 2 Horse hides and hang them up washed a belt.

16. Whitened 13 Calfskins with the French slicker trimd and boarded them up, scoured some sheepskins and tacked them out on boards for hat lineing hauld up a pack of sheepskins and put them under the press, handle the handlers, and chores of various kinds.

17. We beem 30 Upper leather sides on the grain, blackd 13 Calfskins trim and board paynays, strengthen the sole leather and sheepskin handlers and haul them and raise the upright sharft and put some copper under the end of the spindle and oil it.

19. We black and finish Calfskins. . . .

20. Shave six dozen sheepskins black and past Calfskins.

21. We shave sheepskins today 75 skins, work 30 Upper leather sides on the grain past and finish Calfskins roll up 23 patnas and 1 dozen Calfskins to go to Houdson.

22. We put upper leather sides in the handler and blacked 12 patnas and finished them of and took them to the office to go to Albany, shaved 50 sheepskins ball'd 9 sheepskins for hat linings. James Wilson got a small iron wheel waggon and fixed it up for the use of the taners.

23. We scour a pack of sheepskins in the wheel and pack them up on the bricks strengthened and hauld the handlers, blacked 2 dozen patnas and whitened 14 sides and rubed the stuffin from 3 dozen. finish some Alum dressed sheepskins.

24. . . . We haul all the handlers, the rest of the day We work in the shop. We past set and size 3 dozen patna sides and whiten 22 patna sides.

26. We haul up 4 packs of sole leather and make the liquors for 3 of them, haul 2 packs of handlers. We go to the washhouse and cut up a hog for soap greas, one that died at the grist mill.

27. We clean out a leach vat, make 1 liquor lay way 4 packs of sole leather in vats No. 17..14..10..6.. and hauled up 30 side of Upper leather and beemed it on the flesh and scoured it in the wheel and packed it under the press.

28. We split 30 sides Upper leather and got them into the handler scoured sheepskins and finished white leather for hat binding, made a handler, pump up the leach.

29. Scoured and oil'd sheepskins and hung them up to freeze finish White leather strengthened and hauld the handlers.

30. We rub of stuffin and whiten 25 patnay sides trim and board patnas, haul the handlers and put a pack of sheep skins under the press.

31. rub of stuffin whiten trim and board pay-nays. . . .

There were many by-products and "by-activities" connected with the tan-yard. On February 4th, for instance, a 54-gallon cask of neat's-foot oil was prepared. On the 6th, "F. S." made a pair of mittens and tapped and heeled a pair of "spatter dashers." On the 12th, "J. W. made a new leather apron and fixed his old beeming apron;" and Peter Long bought 62 deerskins for 57 cents apiece. After the skins were shaved the hair was sold; on August 19th, it is recorded that 89 bushels of hair were loaded "into sacks for Anderson the hair merchant." "Sig" [urine] was extensively employed in blackening leather, and the surplus was sold. In Benjamin Lyon's journal, elsewhere quoted, there are many references to the sale of this tanning ingredient: December 26, 1839, seven barrels were sold in Pittsfield for $5.83—one item among many.

The tanning business was continued at New Lebanon almost uninterruptedly until late in the century. Tanneries were also maintained in other Shaker communities, notably those at Watervliet, Canterbury, Alfred and Hancock.

MANUFACTURES IN LEATHER

The manufacture of cloth and leather shoes, leather mittens, bridles, saddles and saddlebags was begun at an early date in the history of Shakerism. The business in saddles and saddlebags was not of long duration, but the extensive use of the one-horse wagon in the early decades of the last century gave an impetus to the occupation of making and repairing harness, and this industry continued over a much longer period. Leather boots and shoes, or shoes with linen cloth tops, were made for the use of the Believers themselves, and often for others, until well into the nineteenth century. An early cobbler's bench is shown in figure 23. Leather was also used in the manufacture of whiplashes, to which reference will later be made; and in most of the societies a certain amount of bookbinding was done, not only for printed publications, but for the manuscript song and copy books commonly used in the early history of the sect. A quotation of early prices (from MS. No. 8) on some of these articles in leather is of interest:

1788.	June	30.	To making one pair Shoes	£ 0 :4 :0
1789.	July	6.	To mend^s Boys Shoes find^s leather	0 :2 :8
			To one und^r Jacket and 2 Pair Leather Mittens	0 :5 :0
	June	9.	To 3 Pair Neats Leather Shoes @ 10/	1 :10 :0
	Nov^r.	24.	To Pair Neats Leather Shoes	0 :10 :0
	Sept.	7.	To one pair Womens leather Shoes	0 :8 :0
	April	17.	To Mak^g a Pair Cloth Shoes, and Rands	0 :4 :6
1790.	July	14.	To Vamps & heels & Rands	0 :1 :9
			To 2 Pair Inner Soals	0 :1 :8
			To a pair Saddle Bags	1 :0 :0
	Feb.	11.	To one Pair Shoes	0 :11 :0
	April	10.	To Vamping a Pair Shoes	0 :6 :0
	June	4.	To a Pair Calfskin Shoes	0 :10 :0
	March	24.	To taping and heeling a Pair Boots	0 :3 :8
1791.	Jan^y.	3.	One mans Saddle	2 :0 :0
			3 Bridles @ 6/6d-6/6d & 6/9d	0 :19 :9
	March	1.	One Pair Boots	1 :16 :0
		22.	One Pair Calfskin Saddle Bags (hair on)	1 :4 :0
1792.	Feb^y.	2.	A Womans Saddle	5 :12 :0
		19.	One Set Harness	5 :0 :0

Shoes were made throughout the first half of the last century, and in some communities even later than this. In early years of the industry the lasts were homemade. About the time of the Civil War, "Shaker lasts" were sold to the society for 25 cents each by George H. Graves & Co. of Albany and other firms.

Figure 23   Early cobbler's bench, with lid of cabinet down, showing drawers and compartments. The equipment includes several heels and lasts.   On the top of the cabinet is a shoemaker's candle-stand.   From Second family, New Lebanon.   Andrews Collection.

BROOM AND BRUSH MAKING

The broom has been referred to as a fitting emblem or symbol of Shakerism. "Its manufacture," writes Elder Goepper's interviewer, "is one of their favorite industries, and they have more ways of making it useful than are known to the outside world. They never disgrace it by making it stand behind the door, as if it were responsible for the untidy litter about the house. The Shaker broom is always hung up against the wall when not in use. They put a clean white cotton hood on some of their brooms, and when thus equipped use them to dry-polish their smooth hard wood floors and to remove the last trace of dust from the hard and shining surface" (The Manifesto, June '87, p. 138).

The Shakers at Watervliet are credited with being the first colony to raise broom corn and manufacture brooms. This was in 1798 (Note 49). It is also claimed that Theodore Bates of this community invented the so-called flat broom as contrasted with the earlier round broom and brush. So little is known of the industrial life of the New Lebanon colony during the last decade of the eighteenth century that it is not yet possible to tell just when brooms were first made at this place; probably about the same time as at Watervliet,—The Manifesto indefinitely states "at the close of the last century" (September '90, p. 193). This seems to have been the time that broom corn was first grown on a serious scale in western New England and New York and the date coincides with that given by Alice Morse Earle ('98, p. 256) for the first systematic raising of broom corn for use in broom manufacture (Note 50).

By 1805 at least the broom industry at New Lebanon was in full swing, and brooms and brushes were being delivered to Albany, Boston and Hudson as well as to such near-by towns as Cheshire and Lanesboro. The business of turning broom handles for other families and societies was also under way by 1805, and probably several years earlier. Current prices may be obtained from the following selected entries in the early accounts of the New Lebanon Church family (MS. No. 9):

Nathan Rec'd for Boston, August 26, 1805:	
8 large Brooms @ 2/8	$2 66½
8 small Do @ 1/9	1 75
6 Brushes	1 08
6 Do Small	96
Nathan Rec'd September 5, 1805:	
3 Brooms	£0 : 7 :6
Nathan Rec'd for Albany, September 12, 1805:	
12 Brooms @ 2/6	1 :10 :0
24 Brooms @ 2/3	2 :14 :0
12 Brooms @ 1/6	0 :18 :0
Oct. 1, 1805:	
4 Brushes @ 1/4	0 : 5 :4
Nathan Rec'd for Albany, Oct. 31, 1805:	
15 Brooms @ 2/5	1 :16 :3
9 Small Do @ 1/6	0 :13 :6
Nathan Rec'd for Albany, January 1, 1806:	
18 Brooms @ 2/7	2 :06 :6
3 Do Small @ 1/9	0 :05 :3

The variation in price indicates that there may have been differences in quality or that both large and small brooms came in different sizes (Note 51). Figure 24 illustrates several early types. On September 15, 1808, Nathan went to Providence with merchandise and returned with a load of broom corn. By this year brooms were selling at from 30 to 50 cents apiece, and brushes at about 20 cents. One lot of 32 brooms was delivered in Albany in September 1809 for about 16 cents apiece. In 1810 five "splinter" brooms sold for a total of 70 cents, and two long-handled brooms for $1.12½ (Note 52). By 1811 both round and flat brooms were being made, as well as a variety of brushes (figures 25 and 26). In September of that year nine horse brushes sold for $8.46, 12 large shoe brushes for $4.86, and 11 small shoe brushes for $3.30. In January of the next year, Nathan's load to Albany included:

8 long brooms	$4 00
6 Flat Do	3 00
6 round Do	2 25
5 Brushes	1 00

A steady business in making brooms and brushes was maintained by several families at New Lebanon throughout the century. The two stores bought from and sold to each other according to the trends of supply and demand. Brushes were made principally in the south of the village, and these, especially the shoe brushes, invariably bore the "D. H." impression on the handle which indicated they had passed the inspection of Daniel J. Hawkins, the senior trustee. In the period 1820–30 brooms listed at a nearly standard price of 30 cents apiece. Thirty dozen round brooms, for instance, were sold on one occasion for $112.50.

A selected list of entries (chiefly from MSS. Nos. 12 and 14) for the next decade indicates the various types of brooms and brushes made at that period, and the interchange that went on in a single society:

1830.	Feb.	19.	(To Daniel J. Hawkins) 2 doz. round Brooms @ 22/	$5 50
	May	3.	(To William Dagwell) 1 Brustle Broom @ 10/	1 25
	July	1.	(To Frederick S. Wicker) 12 Brustle Brooms @ 10/	15 00
	July	5.	1 lather brush @ 2/	25
	Aug.	6.	(To Daniel J. Hawkins) ½ doz. Brustle Brushes @ 48/	3 00
			½ doz. Corn Brushes @ 12/	75

FIGURE 24 Dust-mop, brooms and brush brooms made and used at New Lebanon and other communities. The long brooms were used in cleaning ceilings and high walls. The broom second from the left is a late product of the New Lebanon shops. Every Shaker clothespress used to be provided with a dust-mop, a brush broom, a common broom, a ceiling broom, a dustpan and brush, a broom-corn brush, and a wood-box with shovel and tongs.

FIGURE 25 Various Shaker brushes. The one at the lower right is a dustpan brush. The two at the left are general utility cleaning brushes. The round, broom-corn brush in the center was used for sprinkling clothes, cleaning out pails etc.

FIGURE 26 Scrubbing brush and clothes brush, the latter
bearing in reverse the initials of Daniel Hawkins, trustee
at the Second family, New Lebanon. The slits in the
handle hold the wire to which the bristles are attached.

[135]

1832.	May	25.	(Bought from Joseph Allen)		
			6 small shoe brushes @ 20c.	1	20
			12 large do do @ 2/	3	00
			6 large "close" do @ 4/	3	00
			3 small handle do @ 20c.		60
			6 large Shoe do @ 3/2	2	50
	Dec.	7.	(To William Baily) To Slitting and turning 564 Broomhandles (Note 53)	5	64
		24.	(To Elonzo Chapman) To Slitting and turning 227 Broomhandles	2	27
1833.	April	1.	(Bought from Charles Bushnell) 12 Doz. round Brooms @ 20/	30	00
	Nov.	23.	(To William Moshur) 1 Brass wound round Broom		38
			1 larg Broom Brush		25
		27.	(To Charles Bushnell) 1 Doz. flat Brooms	3	00
1834.	Aug.	13.	(To Daniel J. Hawkins) 1 doz. Round Brooms @ 20/	2	50
			½ doz. flat do @ 24/	1	50
1835.	May	21.	(Bought from Joseph Wicker) 10 doz. Whisk Brushes @ 14/	17	50
	Sept.	19.	(To Aaron Gilbert) ½ doz. fine Brushes @ 16/ per doz.	1	00
			(To Clark S. Dean) 4¼ lbs. Broom Twine @ 3/	1	59
	Oct.	3.	(To Charles Bushnell) 2 Paint Brushes @ 3/3 ea.		81
1839.	April	6.	Sold leather brooms and brushes to the am't.	21	64
	April	13.	Sold 6 Brooms @ 2/2	1	62½
		25.	Sold 4 doz. Brooms @ 24/	12	00
			3 doz. Brushes @ 16/	6	00

The broom and brush industry was still in a prosperous condition at the Church in 1861. In that year 170 dozen brooms were made, and in 1862, 95 dozen brooms and 18 dozen brushes. The manufacture of brushes was discontinued shortly after this period, but brooms were made until quite late in the century. A number of entries occur which reveal that a great deal of the raw material for the broom and brush industry was bought from outside sources. Some broom corn, however, was raised at home, and such items occur as the purchase in 1831 of 96 bushel of broom corn seed for $14.40.

Broom handles were made of soft maple timber and were turned in a common foot-lathe. The first apparatus used for tying the corn on the handle was quite simple, "merely a wheel and shaft," the broom twine being wound around the shaft. "The rim of the wheel was arranged with pins, and operated by the feet" (The Manifesto, September '90, p. 193). The broom was made "by holding the handle in one hand and applying the brush with the other while winding" (Note 54). A few years later the process was improved by "the addition of a bench to the roller, in a frame fastened to the bench, with a rag-

FIGURE 27 Brush vise used at the Church or Center family at New Lebanon. New York State Museum.

wheel to hold the cord, when wound upon the roller with [a] short crank as before. The manufacture of two dozen of brooms per day, well made, was considered an exploit, quite equal to the same of six or eight dozen at the present day" (The Shaker, July '77, p. 50). At first the seed was removed from the brush by a crude machine consisting of a wheel fitted with irregularly projecting spikes and turned by hand. The earliest broom and brush vises were Shaker-made (figures 27 and 28).

FIGURE 28 Late type of broom vise provided with hinged clamps with teeth to hold the broom firm while it is being sewed and bound on the handle; New Lebanon. New York State Museum.

No Shaker industry was perhaps as widespread as the making of brooms. Not only did almost every society engage in this manufacture, but it was common to almost every family within certain societies. This was the case at New Lebanon. The South family, the Canaan families, the North family, the East family, as well as the Church-Center families, all followed this occupation. These groups sold to one another as occasion demanded, but each had its own markets and maintained its own business relationships.

MISCELLANEOUS MANUFACTURES

In addition to the basic industries of farming, gardening, apple and corn drying, blacksmithing, tanning, milling, preparing herbs, raising seeds and making brooms and chairs, the Shakers turned their attention, even at the beginning of their history as an organized society, to the manufacture of many articles needed in the daily tasks of our early national life. While the sisters were occupied with their domestic duties and their own industrial pursuits (see later sections), the shops of the brethren were hives of activity. Besides those manifold products turned out for the immediate use of the community itself, the New Lebanon shops engaged in the manufacture of a long list of articles for the outside market. As early as 1789 the Shakers made whips and whiplashes, pails, tubs and keelers, dippers, cheese-hoops, casks, barrels, churns, firkins, dry measures, hand cards, brass and pewter buttons, shoe buckles, stock and knee buckles, harness buckles, candles, clothiers' shears, hoes and miscellaneous ironware. By the first of the century or soon after, they were also manufacturing spinning wheels and reels, and the famous oval boxes; and by 1810, if not before, such products as smoking pipes, sieves, riddles and various types of baskets. Mops were also made at an early period. If one adds to these basic and secondary or subsidiary industries such trades and occupations as brick-making and bricklaying, shingle-making, fulling, masonry, carpentry, cabinet-making, quarrying and stone-sawing, fence building, wagon-making, hydraulic engineering, wiremaking, toolmaking, tinsmithing, tailoring, carding and clock repairing, besides the many industries carried on in the home, shop and field by the sisters of the order, it can hardly be said, with Nordhoff ('75, p. 149), that the range of their industries was "not great."

Here only the most general survey may be made of those shop manufactures above mentioned. It should be remembered, however, that their contribution to the welfare of the society was considerable, even though production was limited in certain cases and at certain periods.

BUCKLES

At the time the society at New Lebanon was organized it was still the custom of the country to wear stocks, knee breeches and buckled shoes. Steel and brass buckles were manufactured by the Shakers as early as 1789, and for a short period constituted a remunerative industry. With the advent of a different style of dress, the business languished. The following selected items (MS. No. 8) show current prices on these articles:

1789.	Feb.	13.	To Sund^r Buckles etc.	£ 1:7:3
	June	22.	To one Stock Buckle	0:2:0
	Sept.	28.	To a Pair Brass Shoe Buckles	0:3:0
1790.	Jan.	11.	To 6 pair Knee buckles @ ¼	0:8:0
	Feb.	11.	To 2 pair Shoe Buckles @ 6/6	0:6:6
	Mar.	25.	To a pair Old Steel Buckles	0:1:6
1791.	Oct.	26.	To 12 Pair Shoe Buckles @ 3/	1:16:0
			7 Pair ditto at 1/9	0:12:3
			5 Pair ditto @ 1/6	0:7:6
			1 Sett Harness Buckles	1:4:0
1792.	Jan.	5.	To 5 Pair Brass Shoe Buckles @ 3/	0:15:0
			5 Pair ditto @ 1/6	0:7:6

BUTTONS

Jacket, coat and sleeve buttons were also m↓de at the outset of communal organization. Some were of polished brass or pewter, while others were horn molds covered with cloth. The sleeve buttons were made in two parts attached by a chain. These buttons were used for the brethren's garments, but there was also some outside sale. For a number of years after 1825, a small business was also conducted in bone and ivory buttons. Such early prices as these are listed (MS. No. 8):

1789.	Sept.	17.	To 12 Doz. Jacket buttons @ ¼d	£ 0:16:0
	Dec.	22.	To a Doz. Pewter Buttons	0:0:6
1790.	June	1.	To 3 Pair Sleeve Buttons	0:1:9
1791.	Oct.	26.	To 4 Gross Jacket buttons	2:0:0
			To 7 Doz. & 4 Coat ditto ½ 2/8	0:19:6
1792.	Jan.	5.	To 12 Pair Sleeve Buttons @ 5d	0:5:0

COOPERS' WARE—PAILS, TUBS, CHURNS, CASKS, BARRELS AND FIRKINS

Among the first covenanters at New Lebanon there must have been one or more individuals skilled in the trade of coopering, and an active business along these lines was established immediately after the gathering of the community. Entries of "sundry coopers' ware" are not uncommon in 1789; by 1790 the ware was generally listed in more specific terms. For 25 years there was a steady output of pails, tubs, churns, casks, barrels and firkins (figure 29). The Manifesto (May '90, p. 98) reports that this business did not flourish for long, one reason being the scarcity of lumber (Note 55). These products were still being sold in 1820, however, and when a new brethren's shop was built at the Church order in 1826 (figure 30), one room was reserved as a coopers' shop. Pails and tubs were sold in some quantity as late as 1830–32. Production probably did not stop until late in the last century, for the community itself constantly needed such articles as butter and lard firkins, apple barrels, wash and dye tubs, keelers, churns and seed pails. A date on the bottom of one of the latter indicates that seed pails at least were being made as late as 1874.

Tubs and pails were usually made in three sizes, although sometimes odd sizes were produced for special purposes. Tubs were often sold in nests of three. The first pails were manufactured with what were known as "wood-loops." Later they were bound with band-iron, and this type sold for a slightly higher price. The handles and bails were usually of wood. Early prices follow (MSS. Nos. 8, 9, 12 and 13):

For tubs:

				£	
1789.	June	30.	To a die Tub	£ 0:4:8	
	Dec.	26.	To a 2 Barrel Meat Tub	0:8:0	
1790.	Mar.	14.	To a Wash Tub	0:6:0	
	April	8.	To a Sugar Tub	0:4:6	
	May	8.	To a beer Tub	0:4:6	
1791.	Jan.	31.	To 2 large tubs @ 6/	0:12:0	
	April	5.	To 6 Flour barrels @ 4	0:12:0	
	Aug.	26.	To 2 tubs 1 & 3 Size		$3 42
	Sept.	12.	To 1 tub first size	0:10:6	
			To 1 do third "	0:14:0	
			To 1 do fifth "	1:6:0	
1806.	Mar.	1.	To 1 Tub	0:10:8	
	Dec.	11.	To 2 tubs 2 & 3 Size @ 13/6 & 11/6	1:5:0	
		18.	To 4 Nest tubs @ 35/	7:0:0	
1807.	Jan.	13.	To 9 tubs first size 10/	4:10:0	
			To 7 do Second 11/6	4:0:6	
			To 8 do Third 13/6	**5:8:0**	
1809.	July	20.	To 1 neast tubs		$4 50
	May	20.	To 1 tub		1 75
1830.	May	30.	To 1 large Cheese Tub @ 30/		3 75
			To 1 Tub @ 13/		1 62½
	June	1.	To 1 Tub @ 20/		2 50
1831.	April	19.	To 1 1st Size Chease Tub		3 75
			To 1 2nd " " "		3 00
			To 1 1st " Wash "		2 50
			To 1 2nd " " "		2 00
			To 1 3rd " " "		1 38
			To 1 4th Size Wash Tub		1 25
			To 6 Keelers @ 8/		6 00
			To 6 Keelers @ 7/ (Note 56)		5 25
1832.	Feb.	29.	To 1 nest Kelers @ 22		2 75

FIGURE 29 Collection of coopers' ware. The wooden-bound pail on the end of the bench (right) was a milk or "calf" pail. Next to it is a salt or sugar pail; a similar type, but without the cover, was used for water. Leaning against the wall is a shallow tub or keeler, used in washing dishes or small clothes. Two dippers are also shown, one of which is in a spit-box. The handled measure was often used for shavings. On the floor, right to left: apple sauce bucket; flour, meal or grain pail; chopping or mixing bowl; seed pail; and another apple sauce bucket.

FIGURE 30 Brethren's shop at New Lebanon Church family, built in 1826. This building housed several trades, including those of the cooper, clockmaker, tailor, carpenter, toolmaker and cobbler. A physician's office was located on the ground floor, a general repair shop on the third. The view is from the rear.

For pails:

1790.	June	26.	To 3 Pails @ 2/8	£ 0:8:0	
	Jan.	31.	To 14 Pails 2/8	1:17:4	
			To 6 Covered ditto @ 2/	0:12:0	
			To 6 Wooden Bottles 2/8	0:16:0	
1805.	Aug.	26.	To 2 pails	1	12½
	Sept.	12.	To 9 Large pails 6 @ 4/ & 3 @ 4/6	1:17:6	
			To 2 Second Size Pails	0:8:4	
			To 2 Third Size do	0:7:2	
1806.	Jan.	1.	To 255 pails @ 5/	63:15:0	
			To 20 small Do at 4/	4:0:0	
1812.	Feb.	4.	To 3 small pails	1	80
			To 1 iron Bound Do		94
			To 1 wooden Do		75
1830.	Feb.	19.	To 1 doz. Pails @ 56/	7	00
	April	16.	To 1 Pail 6/		75
	May	24.	To 4 Pails 1st size @ 4/8	2	33
			To 2 do 2nd " @ 4/	1	00
1832.	Feb.	29.	To 1½ doz. Pails @ 52/	9	75
1838.	Oct.	19.	To 3 dinner pails @ 4/	1	50
			To 3 " " @ 3/	1	13
	Dec.	29.	To 2 stool pails @ 16/		

Beef barrels, "Pott ash" barrels and meat barrels were sold as early as 1789. Flaxseed casks sold for four shillings apiece at this date, and firkins from four to six shillings. In 1789, a total of 132 such casks were sold to one person—Jeremiah Landon. On May 8, 1790, a churn was sold for five shillings, sixpence; by 1806 the standard price was 13 shillings. In 1809, with the advent of the new coinage, the price was around $2.75.

DIPPERS

The manufacture of wooden dippers was entered upon at the outset, and continued for a half century or more. Two of these are pictured in figure 29. They were made of ash and maple, and were often sold, like tubs, in nests of three. The first dipper item occurs on June 16, 1789; this sold for one shilling, fourpence. Subsequent sample entries follow (MS. No. 9):

1805.	Aug.	26.	To 18 large dippers @ 2/2		$4 87½
			To 12 small do @ 1/8		2 50
			To 2 small Do @ 1/6	£0 :3 :0	
	Sept.	12.	To 18 dippers @ 1/9	1 :11 :6	
1806.	Jan.	1.	To 217 Dippers @ 2/9	21 :14 :0	
1811.	May	20.	To 50 large Dippers		12 50
			To 15 small do		3 15

Little change in price had been made by 1830 (MS. No. 12) :

1830.	Feb.	2.	To 2 doz. large dippers @ 20/	5 00
		10.	To 4 doz. Dippers @ 20/ 1½ doz. @ 16/	13 00
	April	29.	To 14 Nests Dippers @ 20/	35 00
			To 4 do do @ 16/	8 00
	Nov.	19.	To 4 doz. 1st size Dippers @ 20/	10 00
			To 3 doz. 2nd size do @ 20/	7 50
			To 4 doz. 3rd size do @ 16/	8 00
1831.	April	22.	To 12 Nests Dippers	7 00
	Aug.	15.	To 5 Dipper Dishes @ 1/	62½
1835.	June	6.	To 4 Doz. Root Dippers 22/	11 00
		16.	To 4 doz. 2 qt. ash dippers @ 20/	10 00
			To 3 do 1 qt. Maple do @ 20/	7 50
			To 3 do do do @ 16/	6 00

Piggins were also used in the Shaker homes, but apparently this type of dipper was never made for sale.

WHIPS AND WHIPLASHES

The manufacture of horsewhips and whiplashes also dates from the beginning of the settlement. This business was continued at New Lebanon for 40 years or more. Sales were not infrequent in 1830 and after, but the whips and lashes sold at this period were purchased from the Watervliet settlement, which evidently had taken over the industry from its sister colony. The lashes (figure 31) were made of horsehides dressed at the tannery and then cut and braided by the brethren, and often by the younger boys. The stocks were turned in the wood-working shop. William Whiting was one of the chief manufacturers at New Lebanon. The early ledgers offer such entries as these (MSS. Nos. 8, 9 and 12) :

1790.	Aug.	3.	To a Slay Whip	£0: 6:6	
1791.	Dec.	23.	To 6 Sleigh Whips @ 6/	1:16:0	
	Dec.	26.	To 3 Sleigh Whip Lashes @ 1/6	2: 5:0	
1805.	Aug.	26.	To 3 doz. Lashes		6 50
	Oct.	25.	To 2 Whip Lashes @ 2/	0:4:0	
1806.	Jan.	1.	To 12 Doz. Slay Whips @ $12 ($144)	57:12:0	
			5 Do Do @ $11¼ ($56¼)	22:10:0	
			4 Doz. Lashes at 18/	3:12:0	
			1 Do Do @ 19/	0:19:0	
1808.	Nov.	8.	To 18 doz. whip Lashes @ 19/6		42 75
			½ do Long do		2 00
1810.	Sept.	18.	To 2½ doz. common lashes		6 25
			1½ do small do		5 00
			5 Long Lashes		2 60
			7 Six feet do		2 37
1811.	Sept.	24.	To 18 Lashes Snapt @ 20/		10 00
			20 Do 6 feet 30/		6 59
			42 Do tag 13/		5 67
			9 Do long		4 56
1812.	Aug.	24.	To 8 lashes 9 feet		4 25
1821.	Oct.	4.	To 1 Doz. Stage lashes		5 00
1830.	Jan.	7.	To 2 Whip-lashes @ 2/ 1/6		44
	July	13.	By 1 doz. 8 plat Stage Lashes @ 6/		9 00
			1 do 6 do do do @ 4/		6 00
1831.	June	28.	To 1 whiplash		25
	Aug.	3.	To 1 whiplash		63
1833.	Sept.	2.	To 1 whiplash @ 2/6		31

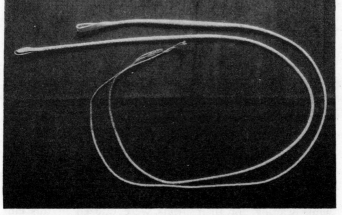

FIGURE 31 Braided whiplashes made at New Lebanon and Niskeyuna. New York State Museum.

CHEESE HOOPS AND DRY MEASURES

A small business was done at an early date in cheese hoops and dry measures (Note 57). The former were sold in 1789 for eight pence. By 1809 the price was about 30 cents. In 1790 a half-bushel measure listed at three shillings, four pence. In 1806 a "Seat of Meashers" could be obtained for ten shillings. Three measures sold for 75 cents in 1809, and two for 37 cents in 1813. By 1833 one could buy four small measures for 50 cents, a peck measure for 40 cents and a half-bushel measure for 56 cents. These were often sold in nests, and at Hancock it was usually specified on the books whether they were "sealed" or "unsealed." Unsealed half-bushels were bought from Hancock for 36 cents apiece, sealed half-bushels for 44 cents apiece. The measure as well as the swift industry (figure 32) was evidently concentrated at this society at this time.

WOOL CARDS, WHEELS AND REELS

Only a few years after the founding of the sect at New Lebanon two industries were established which proved for a time to be sources of considerable revenue. These were the manufacture of hand and machine cards and the making of hair and wire sieves.

Hand cards for carding wool (figure 33) were first made in 1793. The Manifesto (August '90, p. 170) states: "During the continuation of the business, all the available help of the First family was secured. Even the farmers and teamsters would eagerly catch every spare opportunity to assist in the setting of the card teeth. All the family were very much interested in the work, and their mornings and evenings and even the few minutes while waiting for their meals were utilized in this em-

FIGURE 32 Table swift made at Hancock. Colored yellow ochre. When yarn came in skeins, these swifts were used to wind the yarn into a ball, which was placed in the cup at the top of the swift. The swift could be adjusted to handle skeins of any size.

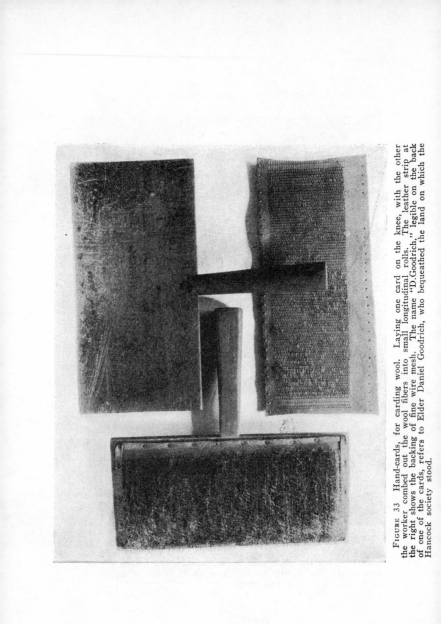

FIGURE 33 Hand-cards, for carding wool. Laying one card on the knee, with the other the worker combed out the wool fibers into small longitudinal rolls. The leather strip at the right shows the backing of fine wire mesh. The name "D.Goodrich," legible on the back of one of the cards, refers to Elder Daniel Goodrich, who bequeathed the land on which the Hancock society stood.

ployment." With the advent of teeth-setting machines about the year 1815, this hand work was necessarily abandoned. The wire used for the teeth was at first "drawn" in the brethren's shops. During the War of 1812 this occupation was again resumed for a short time.

Wool-carding machines were introduced into near-by towns about 1800, and for the next few years the Shakers sent their wool away to be carded into rolls. They soon began to do their own work, however, a carding machine having been purchased from Pittsfield in the year 1809 (Note 58). A page on an old ledger (MS. No. 8) is devoted to "Articles for the Carding Machine." Evidently a special building was proposed to house it. The scheme was thus budgeted:

1809.	April 6.	230 feet of 2 inch Plank	$3 25
	April 19.	8 lbs. of 10d Nails ½	1 17
		18 lb. of 8d Nails ½	2 62½
		38 lb. of 4d Nails ¼	6 33
		8000 Shingles @ 17/	17 00
		3000 Do @ 22/	8 25
		18 Days work Laying & jointing Shingles	
		@ 5/	11 25
		4 lb. of 10d Nails @ ½	58
		55 lb. of Soleleather for Bands	13 75
		Machine & picker and other rolers	312 58
		77⅓ feet of twiled Cards at 2.50	193 33
		bringing the machine from Pittsfield	2 00
		63 gollons of oil @ 81 cents per g.	51 03
		one Basket	1 12

The next year $478.06 was spent for "cards for a Large machine," 10,000 card nails were bought, and $23.84 expended for dyestuff. This or another machine was sold to one Libeas (?) Barton on May 20, 1811, for $280.00, together with 71½ feet of "twiled" cards at $178.75. The Church evidently still possessed a machine, for wool cards were being sold in some quantity from 1810 to 1814, and in lesser quantity for some years afterward. In 1814 appears "a bill of work for carding machine," indicating that the Church order apparently supplied materials and work for another card house at the New Lebanon community. This second machine may have taken over the bulk of the community's business. In 1816, bands were sold, presumably for this same machine.

During the period after the advent of machines and before the society purchased a carding machine of its own, the following prices were paid for carding wool (MS. No. 9):

1805.	August 26, Paid pebody for Carding wool.	
	14 lb. 12 oz. @ 6 cents	$ 90
	8 lbs. @ 6 cents	48
	3¼ lb. mixed @ 10½ cents	33
	2¾ lb. pinans (pina-cloth?) 4 c.	11
	2¼ lb. pinans 4 c.	09
	13½ mixed 10½ c.	1 42
	12 lb. mixed @ 10½¢	1 26

At this time cards were sold as follows:

1805.	Oct. 5.	To 1 pr. No. 8 Cards @ 7/	£0:7:0
	Sept. 23.	To 9 pr. No. 7 Cards @ 4/4	1:19:0
		10 pr. No. 6 Do 4/	2:0:0
		8 pr. No. 5 Do 3/8	1:9:4

On December 19, 1805, the Church received of John Shapley "25 Leafs 5 inch plain Cards 20 feet & 120 inches at ⅔ a foot," amounting to £2:6:10. In February, March and April 1806, several large orders of machine cards were delivered. These were billed by "leafs." On February 13th, four sets of these "meshean" cards were sold to Arthur Scholfield (see Note 58) for 57 pounds and 12 shillings a set, each set containing:

73 Leafs 5 Inch plain Cards 50 5/6 feet @ 16/	£48:13:4
10 Do 4 Do plain Do 6 2/3 feet @ 16/	5:6:8
6 Do 4 Do Twiled Do 4 feet @ 18/	3:12:0

Nearly £900 worth of such cards were sold during this short period. No record exists of such a large quantity

FIGURE 34 Shaker spinning wheel, sometimes called a wool or great wheel; from New Lebanon. Andrews Collection.

having been purchased outside the community, and in spite of the fact that wool was sent out to be carded, the evidence is strong that even before the Believers bought a machine of their own, they adapted themselves to a market demand and engaged in the manufacture of machine cards soon after the machines had been put on the market and the earlier handcards had become less used.

Several orders for "twiled cards," "twiled fancy cards," and "twiled Doffers Cards" appear in the Church's accounts for 1810 and 1811, and in 1814 the orders amounted to more than $3500. Many of these were for "double" machines. Sales appear somewhat intermittently until 1840, but from about 1830 on, the business was apparently not regularly pursued at the Church family.

Spinning wheels (figure 34) and plain and clock reels (figure 35) were made early in the last century if not before. Such items as the following are entered in the records (MS. No. 9):

1805.	Aug.	31.	To one wheele	£1 :2 :0	
	Sept.	12.	To one wheal	1 :4 :0	
1806.	Mar.	22.	To 3 Wheels @ 24/	3 :12 :0	
1807.	Jan.	13.	To 20 wheels @ 22/	22 :0 :0	
1808.	June	8.	To 8 Wheels		$23 75

In 1812 the society purchased a spinning-jenny consisting of 24 spindles, and the home need for spinning wheels was supplied by this machine. Another such spinner was bought in 1821 (see p. 45). Spinning wheels were still manufactured for the market, however, as late as the 1830's. Twenty shillings was the normal price. In 1818, seven wheels were sold for $21 and in 1831 three "great Spinning Wheels" were sold for $7.50. Wheel parts, such as the benches and whorls, were also supplied. Reels were made during the same period. One was sold on September 13, 1805, for 12 shillings. In 1809 the price was $2, a quotation which was standard as late as 1831. A "quilwheel" ($3) is listed under date of April 19, 1819.

FIGURE 35 Shaker reels. The one at the left, from Sabbathday Lake, was known as a "snap-reel." The long wooden trigger makes a snapping sound when the wheel has made 40 revolutions, thereby standardizing at two bouts the length of the yarn wound into the skein. The clock reel at the right measured a single bout at 20 revolutions. Andrews Collection.

SIEVES

For a long period an important industry at New Lebanon consisted of the manufacture of wire and hair sieves and riddles (coarse sieves) (figures 36 and 37). These were designed principally for household use, for sifting flour, straining etc., but they had other uses, and many were said to have been sold for pharmaceutical and chemical purposes. Wheat riddles were also made in some quantity, and seed riddles were a necessity in the garden seed industry. The business at first was not confined to any one family, but about 1830 it was taken over by the South and Second families, and the Church bought from them to redistribute to its own market.

The earliest record falls in the year 1810 (MS. No. 9). On September 18th "sives and brushes" amounting to $18.09 were sold. A sample of account entries for the following year is given below:

1811.	Aug.	8.	To 1 Sive	$ 58
	Sept.	24.	To 12 Small Sives	3 84
			6 Smaller Sives	1 20
			12 large Sives	8 70

By 1821 sieves are specified as being made of either wire or hair. Horses' manes and cows' tails were used for the latter (Note 59) and woven on special looms by the sisters into the round ash frames. This woven mesh was stretched between the two parts of the sieve, tightened and bound, or sewed on the outside, on a "sieve-binder" (see figure 37). On June 4th of that year 16 of these "hare" sieves were sold for $7, and "½ doz. waer sives" for $3.50.

Under the superintendence of Daniel Hawkins, leading trustee of the South and Second families, this business

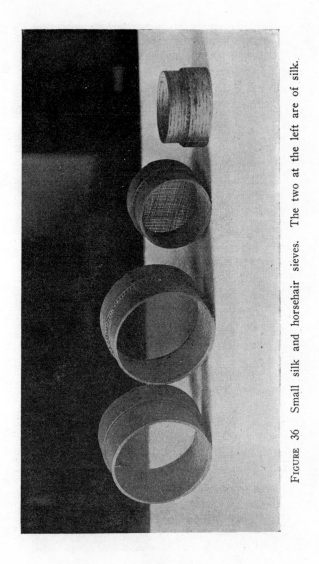

FIGURE 36 Small silk and horsehair sieves. The two at the left are of silk.

FIGURE 37 Three-legged sieve-binder with collection of sieves, sieve rims and riddles. The two large heavy wire sieves or riddles were used in the seed business. The handled cover of the sieve-binder has a lead rim to increase pressure.

had become well established by 1830. Prices current at that time were as follows (MS. No. 12):

1830.	Feb.	8.	By 2 doz. Sieves @ 48.		$12	00
	April	12.	By ½ doz. Sieves @ $6		3	00
	May	3.	By ½ doz. Wire Sieves 2nd size pr. doz.	5	50	
			½ doz. do do 3rd do	5	00	
			½ doz. Hair do 2nd do	5	50	
			6 Nests small Hair Sieves			90
	May	29.	By 1 hair sieve @ 5/			62½
	June	1.	By 12 nests Sieves @ 90 c.		10	80
	Sept.	20.	By 1 doz. 1st size Hair Sieves @ 48.		6	00
1831.	April	18.	By 2½ doz large Hair Sieves @ 48/		15	00
			½ " 2nd do do @ 40/		2	50
			½ Doz. 3rd Size Hair Sieves @ 32/	2	00	
			1 " sink " " @ 26/	3	25	
			3 Nest Sⁿ bolt do @ 9/	3	37½	
			3 do " hair do @ 91c	2	73	
	May	20.	By ½ doz. 2ᵈ size Brass wire Sieves ¼			
			60/		3	75
			2 doz. 1st size Wire Sieves @ 56/		14	00
1832.	Jan	13.	By 1 Cockle Sieve			75

OVAL BOXES

No product of the Shaker wood-working shops possesses greater charm than the multi-sized oval boxes (figures 38 and 39) which were made throughout the last century, and are still made at the Second family at Mount Lebanon and at Sabbathday Lake. All kinds of boxes for all kinds of uses were manufactured, but the oval box was a successful refinement of the more common form, and its novelty and usefulness had a wide appeal.

As with many other products, improved methods of manufacture were adopted as time went on. "At first the rims were cut from the log in a common saw mill. . . . In 1830 a buzz saw did the work of cutting out the rims" (The Manifesto, September '90, p. 193). Two years later the rims and tops, which had been planed by hand, were also planed by machinery. The "fingers" also, which had been hand cut at first, were later machine cut. The automatic element in such early machinery, however, was largely absent, and it is wrong to consider such articles as oval boxes, sieves, tubs, pails etc. as machine-made products. The "machine" was nothing more than a refined

FIGURE 38 Oval boxes of various sizes, from New Lebanon. It was customary to varnish these pieces, although some were painted. These boxes are referred to as early as 1798.

tool, and each box or sieve had to pass through the hands of the individual craftsman, process by process. In figure 40 is shown a group of early oval box forms, showing the pegs by which they were held in the work bench while the workman was shaping and riveting the rims.

FIGURE 39 Oval box, showing details of construction. The top fitted snugly over the base. The "fingered" strips or "lappers" were fastened with copper rivets.

The rims of these boxes were usually made of maple, the tops and bottoms of pine. It was common to sell them in nests, a nest consisting at first of 12 boxes, then of nine, and at a later date of seven and five. In the trustee's accounts they were not referred to as "oval boxes" until 1833.

6

FIGURE 40 Oval box molds and "shapers." Thin strips of seasoned maple, or other wood, were steamed or wet, then wrapped around the mold, which was wedged into a bench, and the rivets hammered and flattened against the narrow strips of iron. The oval discs, shown below, were used to give the correct size to the cover rims.

In 1805 two "neasts" of boxes sold for $3.33. Thirteen shillings was the standard price for a nest. Later prices were as follows (MSS. Nos. 9, 10, 11 and 12) :

1810.	Sept.	18.	To 9 Neasts Boxes	$14 33
	Oct.	21.	To 2 neasts boxes @ 13/	3 25
			4 do @ 10/	5 00
1812.	Feb.	4.	To 4 Neasts boxes	6 66
			4 do of 3 boxes	2 50
			4 do of 2 do	1 64
1824.			To 2 nests of boxes @ 12.	3 00
1830.	Feb.	2.	To 1 Nest Boxes @ 14/	1 75
	Feb.	19.	To 3 Nests Boxes @ 14/ 9 do @ 3.	8 62½
			12 single do @ 10/ 18 do @ 8d	2 70
	April	29.	To 8 Nests Boxes @ 12/	12 00
			24 do do @ 3/	9 00
1831.	April	19.	To 18 Small nests Boxes @ 3/	6 75
			12 " single " @ 8d.	1 00
	April	22.	To 10 large Nests Boxes @ 12/	15 00
			5 small do do @/ 3/	1 87½
1832.	Feb.	29.	To 10 single boxes @ 10c.	1 00
			2 bale boxes (Note 60) @ 5/	1 25
1833.	June	13.	To 1 large single box @ 5	62
1833.	Aug.	14.	To 3 boxes @ 40¢	1 20
			3 boxes @ 30¢	90
			3 " @ 25¢	75

By 1834 oval boxes were sold by number. The largest sizes, Nos. 1, 2, 3, 4 and 5, were the most popular. The introduction of improved methods of manufacture evidently increased the business, for large quantities were being sold by 1834 and 1835. For the next 30 years or more the output was steady. These prices prevailed in 1854 (MS. No. 15) :

March 24.	To 24 nests of oval boxes @ 10/	$30 00
	34 " " small " @ 3/	12 75
	6 doz. small boxes @ 10/	7 50
	6 " " " @ 8/	6 00

It is interesting to note that even at this late date, the computing unit was in the old currency.

"Fancy oval covered wooden boxes" have been made at the Second family from an early period, and a small quantity are still turned out in that section of the society. In an undated leaflet issued about 25 or 35 years ago, a pyramid of 11 boxes graduated in size is illustrated, the whole forming one full nest which sold for $5. The price varied from the smallest boxes (No. 11) which sold for $3 a dozen to the largest (No. 1) which were listed at $9 a dozen.

BASKETS

The weaving of small fancy baskets of poplar wood belongs in the category of the sisters' occupations. The Shakers also made larger baskets of split black ash for the many uses of the farm and home, and a small but consistent business was carried on from early in the last century until about the time of the Civil War, and perhaps for a longer period. In the early days traveling groups of Indians made and sold baskets to the Shakers. Several of these have been found in the settlements, decorated in quaintly formal patterns with berry juice.

Shaker basketware is characterized by an almost unending variety of patterns, some of which are shown in figure 41. Large, shallow ones, sometimes called "conscience baskets" because of their generous size, were used in the weave-rooms and wash-houses. Egg baskets were finely woven, sturdy little affairs, like a deep nest. Special sizes were adapted to cherry, grape or plum picking, larger and stronger ones for heavier fruits. Winnowing baskets were used on the farm. Cheese baskets of large, open weave, whitened by the draining of whey and constant scrubbing, are found in many a Shaker dairy. Immense baskets of varying capacity were used for holding herbs, roots and barks. Chip baskets, often lined with leather, were used by the sisters for carrying chips or fine kindling. Poplar fancy work or knitting baskets were made

FIGURE 41 Collection of Shaker baskets. The large one at the right was used in a weave-room; the one at the left is a winnowing basket. In the center are two open-work cheese baskets. The covered basket at the left end of the bench was sold to the Shakers by the Indians. Next to it is an egg basket. On the basket-mold is a small fancy-work or knitting basket, and to the right of the small cheese basket another made of poplar. In front are two fruit or vegetable baskets, and a rectangular one for general utility purposes. From several Shaker societies.

in all sizes and shapes. Thousands of general utility baskets, difficult to classify, were also woven in the Shaker societies. A few prices will show how cheaply these beautifully constructed articles were placed on the market (MSS. Nos. 9, 12 and 15):

1809.	Nov.	7.	To 4 Baskets	$2 00
1811.	Sept.	23.	To 3 Baskets	1 50
1831.	April	29.	To 1 Basket @ 8/ 1 do @ 4/	1 50
1833.	June	1.	To 1 large Chease Basket	1 00
	July	4.	To 1 Tool Basket	75
1835.	June	6.	To 12 Baskets @ 2/6 ⎫	
			24 " @ 1/ ⎬	
			12 Palm Leaf Baskets ⎭	9 42
1855.	Aug.	6.	To 10 small baskets @ 10¢	1 00
			6 " " @ 16¢	90
			6 long "	1 25
			6 round	2 00

After the Civil War the ministry at Mount Lebanon were wont to "labor at basket-making in the intervals of their travels and ministrations, and [had] a separate little 'shop' for this purpose near the church" (Nordhoff, '75, p. 139).

PIPES

At the East family in New Lebanon there were natural deposits of red clay which were early utilized for making bricks, and this section of the community became commonly known as "the brickyard." It may have been due to the ready supply of such clay that the Shakers became engaged in the manufacture of pipe bowls and stems (figure 42) soon after the beginning of the last century. Smoking was a common habit, even among the Believers themselves in these early days, and there was no moral or hygienic reason why the manufacture of pipes should not have been carried on. The Millenial Laws, revised in 1845, contain many specifications covering the careful use of pipes to prevent fires, and it was not until after

the Civil War that smoking was definitely repudiated as
an obnoxious habit.

The bowls were made of both red and white clay. The
wooden stems were ordinarily made in two lengths, 10
and 15 inches. The first record appears in 1809 (MS.
No. 9), when "some pipes" were sold for $1.62. In 1810
such items appear as "2½ doz. pipes...$1.40," "30 doz.
pipes...$18.73," and "80 doz. pipes...$40.00." In 1814
pipe "boals" were sold in quantity for a penny apiece,
and the stems for three cents each. Pipes were being sold
by the Church as late as 1853; in a gardener's diary (MS.
No. 19), under date of November 23, 1843, is the entry:

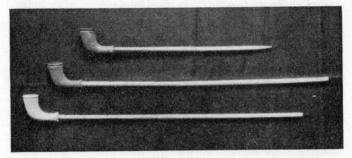

FIGURE 42   Long-stemmed pipes made by the Niskeyuna and
New Lebanon Shakers. Bowls of red or white clay, stems of
wood. New York State Museum.

"B.M. after pipe stem timber below the sap woods." It
is probable, however, that the Watervliet colony was the
chief source of supply at this later period. By 1835 pipe
bowls were being purchased in large orders from Frederick Wicker, the Watervliet trustee, and although the
stems may have been and probably were still made at
New Lebanon, the center of the industry had shifted to
the other settlement. Wicker received $8 a thousand for
both red and white bowls.

PENS

A small industry in making steel, brass and silver pens was carried on by the Shakers at New Lebanon and Watervliet for a number of years, and they have been credited with being the originators of the metal pens. A letter written in 1878 by G. A. Lomas to the editor of the Scientific American (Vol. 39, No. 21, November 23, 1878, p. 325) was claimed by this Watervliet brother to have been written with a silver pen, "one slit," made in that village in 1819. "Two or three years previous to the use of silver for pens," this letter continues, "our people used brass plate for their manufacture, but soon found silver preferable. Some of our people, now living, sold these pens in the year 1820 for 25 cents, and disposed of all that could be made at that price. The machinery for rolling the brass and silver plate was a home invention; also the shears for cutting the pens. . . . At the above date (1819) the inventor writes: 'I now have my new shears, with which I have cut 292 pens in 14 minutes; this is doing it with dispatch!' The metal used was melted silver coins; and at one time the worker says, 'I melted up $55.00 or $60.00 of silver money'" (Note 61). The pen handles were made of wood and tin; the latter were so made that they could close the pen "telescopically."

It is not known who this inventor was. We know, however, that Freegift Wells made pens at Watervliet, and that Isaac Youngs engaged for a time in the same occupation at New Lebanon. In the Church family accounts, the first record of a sale of silver pens is in 1825 (MS. No. 10). On August 27th of that year one was sold for 31 cents. On June 18, 1829, two dozen silver pens (at 14/) were sold for $3.50. In 1831 the price was two shillings, old currency.

Most of the pens sold at New Lebanon were obtained from Watervliet. In 1826 two dozen silver pens were bought from Frederick Wicker for $5; in 1827 six dozen for $15; in 1828, one-half gross of "cased silver pens" for $15 and eight dozen "black handled" silver pens for $14. The Church was purchasing from this source as late as 1835, when four dozen silver pens were bought for $7. Ivory buttons were also made at Watervliet at this time and sold in quantity to New Lebanon and other markets.

'A few other items of small manufacture should be mentioned before this section is closed. Certain ones, like scythe snaths or handles, seem to have been made for a time, and then the industry was left to some other society (Note 62). Round wooden spittoons, or "spit-boxes" as they were called (see figure 29), were made chiefly for the use of the family, but some were sold to other communes or to outside markets. An item in 1839 shows that they brought about 25 cents apiece. Sugar boxes were being sold in nests by 1830, the price varying around 80 cents a nest. Horn combs were sold by Charles Bushnell of the North family in 1835 for $1 a dozen. Horn was also used in the repairing of umbrellas and occasionally in making escutcheons. Spool stands were made in several sizes, and sold in 1838 for from 50 to 80 cents apiece. Spool boxes were bought largely from the Watervliet colony, and swifts from Hancock, where swift-making was a thriving industry about 1830. "Nail dishes" listed in 1835 for a dollar a dozen. Candlewicking was sold in this year for 25 cents a pound.

Floor mops (see figure 24) were made at an early period in many societies besides New Lebanon, where they were sold until well after the middle of the last century. These were made of tow, cotton and wool. In the 1840's the mop industry was concentrated at the Canaan Lower (or South) family. Tow mops sold for about $2.25 a dozen, cotton mops for about $3 a dozen, and "thrum" and wool mops for about $4 a dozen. The handles were turned at the Church family for a penny apiece. As late as 1867 brooms and brushes continued to be the chief industry at this Canaan family.

THE CLOTHIER SHOPS

Joseph Meacham and the first elders of the United Society wisely adopted the policy of maintaining friendly business relationships with the "world." At a time when Shakerism was widely misunderstood and condemned, it would have added to the difficulties of developing a sound institutional life if the Shakers had rigidly cut themselves off from any buying from outside sources. Their asceticism did not go that far. From the outset they bought from and sold freely to the world's markets, and no misunderstanding existed on the economic level such as characterized the world's attitude to the Shakers' religious doctrines. Merchants and tradesmen were glad to have the Shakers' business, and found it was to their advantage to handle Shaker goods.

The Shakers went a long ways nevertheless in supplying their own needs from their own shops. This spirit of self-dependence is nowhere better illustrated than in the complete system of raising their own flax and wool, weaving their own cloth, and making their own clothes. A tailoring shop was instituted at the very beginning of the New Lebanon commune. This was managed by David Slosson, an experienced tailor, who was one of the first converts to the faith. Slosson had several apprentices under his charge, and these in turn became proficient in the art of making clothes; later certain individuals were sent to other societies to help in the organization of similar shops. Few if any printed rules governed the occupation until about 1825, when the clothier's shop was reorganized and a greater measure of standardization was given to the processes.

This early tailoring establishment not only supplied coats, vests, breeches, stocks, surtouts and hats for the brethren of the order, but also made clothes for outsiders.

The nature and extent of this occupation is best illustrated by quoting from the first ledger kept by Joseph Bennet of the Church (MS. No. 8). The buyers' names are omitted.

1789.	Nov.r	27.	To Sund. Taylor Work and Trimings	£ 1 :7 :6
	Dec.r	1.	To Cutting Coat and Breeches for Jon	0 :2 :0
		3.	To Cutting one Coat	0 :1 :4
	June	16.	To Cutting a Surtout for Son Elijh (Talcott)	0 :1 :4
			To Sundr Cutting Surtout & Over Alls for Son Asa (Talcott)	0 :2 :0
	July	6.	To a Round Jacket & Trowzers for Boy	0 :13 :6
			To one undr Jacket and 2 Pair Leather Mittens	0 :5 :0
	Jan.	27.	To making a Suit Cloaths	1 :7 :6
	Nov.r	27.	To Turning Jacket	0 :5 :0
			To Cutting a Pair Overalls	0 :0 :7
			To Cutting Jacket	0 :1 :0
	April	29.	To a Frock & Pair drawers	0 :8 :0
	Nov.	17.	To making a Straight Bodyed Coat	0 :12 :0
	March	25.	To a Pair Striped Trowzers	0 :6 :6
	Oct.	16.	To making coat, Jacket & Breeches	1 :4 :0
	May	19.	To attiring Surtout Sleeves	0 :2 :6
1790.	Feby.	12.	To Cutting Coat & Jacket 1/4 & 8d	0 :2 :0
	April	8.	To Making a Coat for Stephn. Slosson	0 :12 :0
	May	27.	To Making a Surtout	0 :12 :0
			To Making a Jacket	0 :6 :0
			To Making a Pair Breeches	0 :6 :0
	Feb.r	10.	To Tow & Linen Cloth for 2 Shirts sent from ye Church by Eldr Davd.	0 :16 :0
	Nov.r	3.	To 1 yd Broad Cloth 31/6 & ¾ yd Baze 3/9	1 :15 :3
	June	24.	To sundr Cloathyers Work	3 :17 :6

A considerable business was also done in "dressing" (sizing or glossing) cloth and hats. A few sample charges are taken from the same manuscript (No. 8):

1789.	July	20.	To dressing 22⅓ yds. Cloth @ 3½	£ 0:6:8
	May	23.	To dressing a Hatt for the Apthycary	0:2:3
	Feb.	28.	To dressing 28¾ yds. Cloth @ 3d.	0:7:2
1790.	June	9.	To dressing 2 Skirts	0:6:3

The business of scouring flannel and of fulling and dressing cloth was carried on in the clothiers' shops and fulling mill during the first half of the next century, and provided constant employment for several brethren (Note 63). A close relationship was necessarily maintained between the sisters' weave rooms and these fulling shops. Cloth was dressed for other families in the community and often for the "world's people." Diaper and other cloth was sold in 1809 and regularly afterwards. Cotton and worsted cloth, shirting, drab cloth, worsted and flannel were being marketed in 1828, diaper and cotton shirting in 1837, and horse blankets in 1839. In 1835 the Church shops scoured quantities of flannel for the North family at the rate of 2¢ a yard, besides fulling and dressing large amounts of brown and mixed cloth.

The making of felt, colt's fur and wool hats constituted an important branch of the clothiers' trade, and it is evident that an experienced hatter was among the first Believers. Hundreds were sold in the first few years of the community's existence. After a time the bulk of the business was given over to the Hancock society, but occasional items as late as 1830 indicate that a few hats were still being made at New Lebanon. A felt or fur hat form used at Hancock is pictured in figure 43. Nine shillings was the usual price for a colt's fur hat in 1789. A colt's fur and wool hat cost ten shillings, a "caster" (beaver)

FIGURE 43 Straw hat for summer wear, and wooden form for brethren's fur or felt hat. Hat from Niskeyuna. New York State Museum.

FIGURE 44   Brethren's clothes, made and worn at Hancock.
Sometimes called "slip-on" clothes, such as were worn on Sundays,
or Saturday afternoons before meeting.   The plastered wall makes
indistinct the homemade white shirt of the right-hand costume.

hat, one pound and 12 shillings. Felt hats were listed at eleven graded prices depending on the size: 9s, 8s. 6d., 8s., 7s., 6s. 6d., 6s., 5s. 6d., 5s., 4s. 6d., and 4s. "Hatter's jacks" were sold in 1811 at the rate of $4.50 for 6½ pairs, and one item reads as high as $20.25 (MS. No. 9). By 1828 "fine wool hats" were sold for $1.75 apiece, and fur hats as high as $6. Later in the century, after the Civil War, the Mount Lebanon Shakers made hats, mittens and leggins from coon's fur, wool and silk. Straw hats like the one in figure 43 were also worn.

Eventually the Lebanon tailors and hatters confined their attention to making men's clothes and hats. The cutting and fitting of sisters' clothes became the function of the tailoresses; reference to this occupation will be made later in the section. A more comprehensive insight into the work of the clothiers may be gained from a description of the kind of garments first worn by the brethren, and of the changing styles of later periods (see figure 44). The following authentic account was written in 1858, evidently by one of the New Lebanon tailors themselves (The Manifesto, June '90, p. 121–23; July '90, p. 145–46):

GARMENTS

The early Believers accepted the simple, plain form of dress that prevailed among the common people of the world, and laid down no rules that should govern the Societies in this respect. The first American converts were extremely varied in the form, color and quality of their garments, but as they became more associated and united they inclined more to a uniformity, and were influenced largely by the manners of the first Elders.

After the organizing of the Church the uniformity of dress became a matter of much more consequence, and they adopted for the Sabbath, a dark blue coat, with a cape that came up to the neck, and lay upon the shoulders. Cuffs to the sleeves were six inches long. Pockets were cut at the waist and a large lid covered the horizontal pocket. The front edge of the coat was nearly straight, having some six or eight buttons of an inch in diameter, and button-holes three inches long. One half of these were for ornament and no place was cut through the cloth. On the back of the coat, at the lower extremity of each side seam, was a large double fold or plait, taking about three inches of cloth and folded twice. At the waist, on the back, was a large "square stitching" three or four inches long, and about one fourth as wide, and a button at the head of each fold, and another button at the bottom of the skirt, which came a few inches below the knee.

The vest was from the same cloth, the waist falling a little below the natural waist. The skirts were about seven or eight inches long. In front these were cut off to an angle of about forty-five degrees, from a point at the lower button. In the back, the skirt was divided into two sections, which overlapped each other one or more inches. The whole of the vest was made from the same piece of cloth. If the front was broadcloth the back would be of the same quality. A row of twelve buttons were arranged in front, and large pocket lids were set to the waist line.

The lower garment, especially for the Sabbath and for journeys, was black-lasting breeches which ended a little below the knee, these being supplemented by long black stockings. A row of four buttons ornamented the suit at the knee, while the breeches and stockings were secured in their proper places by a strap and a large brass buckle just below the knee in the front.

As the sleeves of the shirts were made large and very long, a blue silk ribbon, under the name of "sleeve tie" was fastened around the arm just above the elbow to secure them in place when the coat was laid aside.

The covering for the neck was called a "Stock." This was made of some very stiff material about two and one half or three inches wide and covered with white or blue silk, and fastened by a buckle on the back of the neck.

The white stocks were generally worn on the Sabbath, and were considered a part of the uniform, while the blue were for more common use.

In 1810 the white stocks gave place to white cotton, linen, or silk neckerchiefs which are used more or less at the present date (1858). The wearing of stocks was the general custom of the day and many of the portraits painted at that time will give a much clearer impression of the style.

The hats were made of fur or wool, with low crowns, about four inches high and brims five or more inches wide. These generally were colored black. The form of the hat has undergone some slight changes during the past forty years, and the crown now measures about five inches deep and the brim four or four and one half inches. The children generally wear caps.

The shoes were made of calf-skin and fastened with straps and shoe buckles.

The foregoing was generally termed the "Sunday Suit," and was preserved in the Society as quite necessary for several years.

For more common use, trowsers generally were worn, especially when engaged in manual labor, but the cloth was of a poorer quality and colored with a cheap dye. Surtouts and great coats were made for those who needed extra garments while on their journeys. The same provision was made for boots, overshoes, socks and mittens. Gloves were seldom seen.

This form of dress continued in use, without change till the year 1805. The Society was now resting on a more permanent foundation, and had been blessed with an experience of some eighteen years. From the first the Believers had been studying the advantages to be derived from the principle of Christian economy and utility, in all that pertained to a life in the Community.

At this date, the breeches and long stockings were laid aside on the Sabbath and the plain trowsers were substituted in their place. For several years, however, after this proposed change, individuals might occasionally be seen, who were on a journey, dressed as formerly, with long stockings, and with highly polished knee and shoe buckles.

In 1806 blue coats and vests began to give place to the steel-mixed, and this latter was adopted as the uniform color. Among the reasons for discontinuing the "blue" was partly on account of the expense of the Indigo, and the labor of making the garments. Trowsers for winter use were made of woolen cloth or of serge. For summer, Sabbath uniform, the trowsers were of linen or checked cotton, blue and white. Garments for manual labor were generally of tow cloth.

Another radical change was made in 1810 when the gray was laid aside and the coats and vests were made of drab-colored cloth. The form of the coat was also changed quite essentially. The double folds of the skirt were set aside, and a single fold adopted. The front edge was cut more circling, and fell back at the bottom of the skirt, some four inches. The pocket lids of the coats and vests instead of being cut with two scallops and leaving a point in the center, were cut with a curve on the lower, parallel with the upper edge.

A collar of about one and one-half inches wide, was added to the coat. This was made upright. Over this was a cape that extended to the edge of the shoulder. All the buttons and button-holes were now omitted, and for the fastenings of the coat in front, two or three pairs of "hooks and eyes" were substituted.

The vests were cut shorter in front, and the skirts reduced to correspond more closely with the height of the person, which made the medium length about seven inches.

By adopting the use of suspenders a slight change was made in the form of the trowsers, which had been, to this date, so formed at the waist as to hold themselves in place without any other aid.

Shoe buckles were laid aside, and strings of leather or cloth were used instead.

For several years the trowsers for uniform on the Sabbath in summer were colored with nutgall, but in 1820 these gave place to garments made of cotton, striped blue and white.

In 1832, the drab vest, which had been largely in use since 1810, was partially displaced by the introduction of a fine blue. While this color was generally used in the summer, the drab was retained for use in the winter. Blue seems to have been a favorite color for summer, and in 1854 they obtained a delicate, fine article of light blue, that was of foreign manufacture.

For winter use the blue was laid aside in 1840 and drab was established as the uniform color for vests, and continued to be used till 1854, when blue was again introduced.

From 1813 to 1840 the surtouts and great coats were made of drab-colored cloth, manufactured by the Society, then a finer quality of cloth was purchased and used till 1847, when a steel-mixed again was introduced.

The pressure of outside competition was more and more keenly felt as the century advanced. About 1866, in a Circular concerning the Dress of Believers, Elder Giles Avery of the central ministry wrote that the manufacture of cloth had seldom been a source of profit, and advised (p. 4) that the factory at Shakers' Society, New Lebanon, "be not rebuilt."

OCCUPATIONS OF THE SHAKER SISTERS

The emancipation of women from a position of social inferiority, and the investment of the Deity with feminine as well as masculine virtues, were fundamental principles in the Shaker theology. Ann Lee was convinced that by granting equal rights to women one of the chief evils of the existing social order would be corrected. Although she felt that such equality would be hastened by the liberation of women from the bondage of the marriage relation, a concept which was widely condemned by "worldly" critics, the ends she sought were nevertheless praise-worthy. The institution of Shakerism deserves acclaim on this account alone, that in it from the first women were coequal with men in all the privileges and responsibilities of leadership and labor (Note 64). The Shaker government was dual in every department, and women were as free as the men to speak in meeting or to write for publication. Under the management of various deaconesses, the sisters carried on occupations and industries of their own quite independently from the brethren, although they labored for a common cause.

Their accounts were also separately kept. The matter is thus explained in Seth Wells' "Importance of keeping correct Book Accounts" (MS. No. 37, 1836):

Tho' the Sisters have but little to do in the business of commerce; yet, being willing & desirous to do their part & bear their portion towards supporting the temporal interest of the Church or family in which they live & let their works be known, they are allowed to keep a Book account of the incomes of their own separate earnings & the expense of purchases made for their particular use. This is done by the Deaconesses at the Office. Of course, the money brought in by their own exclusive labors, is at their disposal, out of which they can make purchases of such articles as they need, exclusive of the general purchases made for the use of the family. Yet all these reciepts and purchases are entered on the Book of Incomes and expenditures kept by the Deacons; so that the whole amount of the reciepts & expenses of the family, both of the Brethren & Sisters, are regularly entered on book, & show at one view, what the real incomes & expenditures of the family are from year to year. This is the order & practice in the Church & Second Family at New Lebanon, & should be done in every family that feels an interest in keeping the order of the Gospel & supporting the united interest of the Family."

FIGURE 45. Wash-house or laundry at the New Lebanon Church Family. Weaving, spinning, hatcheling, dyeing, and other sisters' occupations were also carried on in this commodious structure.

Much of the time of the Shaker sisters was occupied by such domestic tasks as washing, ironing, cooking, cleaning, mending, "schooling" and taking care of the many girls who were placed in the care of the society. (See note 65. Figure 46 shows the early schoolhouse at the New Lebanon Church.) When one considers the size of the dwellings, the number of men, women and children living the communal life, and the almost religious emphasis placed on order and cleanliness, it can be seen that household occupations represented no small undertaking. The work was carefully organized, however, and through routine a high standard of efficiency was maintained. The system of rotation in such duties as those of the kitchen kept the necessary routine from being overarduous.

The Shaker sisters and younger girls also helped the brethren, especially in the herb and seed business. They printed the labels used on the herb packages and papers, and the gathering and "picking over" of the herbs and roots gave many sisters constant employment. The paper and cloth bags used in the seed business were also made in the sisters' shops. The final stages in the preparation of the renowned Shaker apple sauce and maple sugar were in their province, and their assistance in shelling the corn used in the dried sweet corn industry was invaluable.

Certain industries, spinning and weaving in particular, were taken over entirely by the sisterhood, the work being carried on at the wash-house or laundry (figure 45). The tailoresses made and mended the sisters' clothes. In the sisters' shops were made the palm-leaf bonnets, poplar baskets, table mats, knitware, Shaker cloaks, floor mops, and a long list of other fancy and useful articles.

Dairy products also yielded a steady income. The sis-

FIGURE 46 Schoolhouse, situated midway between the Church and Center families at New Lebanon. Erected, according to *The Manifesto*, in 1839.

ters did the milking and made the butter and cheese, and in the great kitchens barrels and barrels of apple sauce and pickles were put up each year. Tomato catsup and various preserves were also sold in large quantity, and wines found a ready market.

WEAVING AND THE MANUFACTURING OF CLOTH

New Lebanon was organized some time before the so-called "homespun" industries had given way to manufacturing establishments. Women who joined the society were often experienced in those many domestic arts practised in colonial homes, and it was natural that they should continue to spin yarn, weave and dye cloth, dip candles and engage in the countless occupations which made small industrial units of the homes of that period. In a very true sense the early Shaker community was but an enlarged colonial household.

Looms were constructed or used at the very outset (Note 66), and the attics of present-day Shaker dwellings hold many other devices and tools employed in the manufacture of cloth—"great" wheels, reels, swifts, skarns, flax foot-wheels, "pleasant spinners" and hatchels. Stored neatly away in boxes are the reeds, temples and shuttles of the once busy looms. Carding and spinning and the weaving of woolen, cotton and cotton-wool cloth were done exclusively by the sisters, who also for several years hatcheled all the flax used in making linen cloth (see figure 47). Until 1809, when a machine was invented for the purpose, the cloth was cut with shears made by the Shaker blacksmiths. A mill for carding wool was built, as we have noted, at an early date, and a clothiers' mill was constructed where fabrics were dyed. The looms were in constant use until about 1853, when the compara-

FIGURE 47 Flax hatchel on frame. Used for combing out the coarse parts from the fine fiber preparatory to spinning. From Niskeyuna community. New York State Museum.

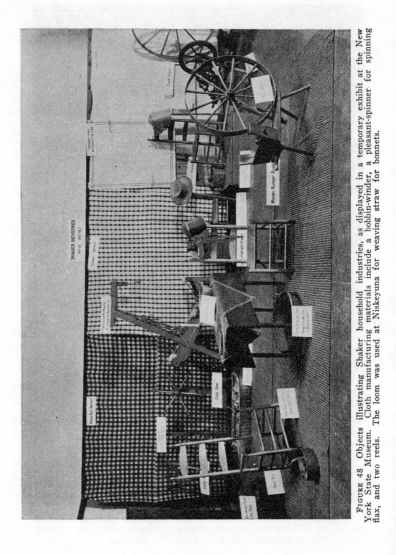

FIGURE 48 Objects illustrating Shaker household industries, as displayed in a temporary exhibit at the New York State Museum. Cloth manufacturing materials include a bobbin-winder, a pleasant-spinner for spinning flax, and two reels. The loom was used at Niskeyuna for weaving straw for bonnets.

tive cheapness of mill cloth made it seem uneconomical for the Believers to rely wholly upon their own product. For a long time after this, however, these looms were not wholly idle, and material for shag chair mats, toweling, serge trowsers, linen frocking, worsted gowns, cotton handkerchiefs, carpets, spreads etc. continued to be woven in the community. A glimpse of these household and sisters' shop industries is given in figure 48.

Before the writer are two weavers' records which date from the thirties of the last century. One is "A Weaver's Memorandum; or An Account of Weaving, etc. Kept by Hannah Treadway. D. 1833 & 34" (MS. No. 31). The other is a yearly account of weavings from 1835 to 1865; the recorder was Sister Joanna Kitchell (MS. No. 32). The memorandum serves as a guide to the technic of weaving. In the first part is reckoned the number of runs, yards, "overplus of quarters" and "remainder in half knots," depending upon the number of biers placed, these being computed from six to 60. The second part consists of a table of the number of biers, bouts and threads resulting from the number of spools used in warping, the table ranging from 10 to 44 spools.

Joanna Kitchell's record reveals what an all-inclusive program of work the early Shaker weavers set for themselves. In 1835 a total of 1205 yards of cloth was woven for frocks, surtouts, flannel shirts, habits, trousers, drawers, bags, garden sheets, serge, worsted serge for shoes, drugget gowns, drugget linings, drugget trousers, worsted trousers, worsted gowns, cotton and worsted jackets, jacket linings, worsted linings and wash aprons. In 1836, 1337 yards were woven for many of the above purposes, besides such additional uses as tow and linen frocks, barn frocks, boys' trousers, coarse flannel, linen ironing cloths, cotton and wool blankets, and narrow cotton and wool sheets. In 1837, 78 yards of horse blankets (wool with a cotton warp) were woven on the same loom, and 99 yards of checked linen "pocket hankerchiefs." In this year is the first mention of the characteristic red and blue cotton and worsted cloth which was used so commonly in Shaker dresses. Other items listed are cotton and linen "open frocks," "fine towels linen & tow," coarse strainers, drab habits, under coats, wide ironing cloths, scrub aprons, and cotton and wool, red and blue deacons' frocks. The total for this year was 2334 yards. Horse blankets of "doubled and twisted tow" were woven in 1838; also 51 yards of white linen handkerchief cloth, cotton check aprons, light striped gowns for the ministry, blankets for the ministry, "coppras" (copperas) aprons, butternut drawers and 120 yards of window curtain. Linen for stair carpets was woven in 1840, besides 43 yards of "crape," 30 yards of cheese straining cloth, 90 yards of rag carpeting, 19 yards of cloak head-linings, 54 yards of kitchen aprons, besides many materials already mentioned.

From 1841 to 1851 a total of 24,234 yards of material was woven. Serge, worsted, flannel, cotton, linen and drugget cloth constituted the main product. Hundreds of yards of blanketing, carpeting, toweling, bagging, shirting, lining and frocking were also woven. Horse blankets were sometimes woven with a linen warp. Serge blankets appear in 1841; blue and white trowsers, blue and white gown sleeves, "little boys frocks," hemlock gowns, butternut drawers, hand mittens, blue lasting for shoes and cotton bibs, in 1842; linen cheese strainers, cloaks, "butt" flannel drawers and serge and cotton blankets, in 1843;

FIGURE 49 Loom used for weaving narrow braids or tapes of cloth or straw. From Niskeyuna settlement. New York State Museum.

FIGURE 50 A two-treadle loom for weaving narrow braids of straw, palm leaf or cloth; from Niskeyuna. Andrews Collection.

linen and tow diaper cloth, wash gowns and cotton and wool sheets, in 1844; linen shifts, long frocks, meat strainers, oil cloth and linen wash house bags, in 1845; neckerchiefs, "stair cloths," bread cloths, meal bags and "grate coating," in 1846; "flag carpets," in 1848; "dish clothes" and "Sabbath blue & white trowsers," in 1849; linen table "clothes," cotton and wool "bread clothes" and "fine light collor'd gowns," in 1850; and "close" bags and cotton "caticue" aprons, in 1851. Whether these figures stand for the total cloth production of the family or for the output of Sister Joanna's loom alone is not clear in the original manuscript.

A noticeable decrease in production appears about this time. While the annual output varied from 1500 to 2000 yards before 1851, it was less than 1000 yards after this date, decreasing to 581 yards in 1861. The revival of the chair industry at the South and Second families is reflected in the weaving of the shag chair mats, which commenced in 1858 and continued until the journal's close in 1865, and in the few penciled items in another hand which carry the record to 1874. More carpeting was woven in these later years, as well as cotton cloth for handkerchiefs. In 1865 cotton-wool was still being woven in quantity; flannel cloth for gowns, drugget for trousers and jackets, fulled cloth for boys' frocking, and linen for trousers also kept the old looms from being idle (see figures 49 and 50).

Included here is a "Bill of prices" charged by the Shaker sisters for weaving cloth and making various articles of clothing (MS. No. 34). This old memorandum, undated but probably ascribable to the late 1820's or 1830's, is evidence of an organized occupation.

BILL OF PRICES

	$ cts.
Making worsted gowns	0 87½
" Drugget do	0 62½
Worsted cloth per yd.	1 00
Common Drugget per do	0 62½
Fine Cotton & Worsted per do	0 75
Coarse do per do	0 62½
Cotton & Wool Cloth pressed per do	0 37½
Woolen Frocking per do	1 00
Linnen do per do	0 44
Common Fulled Cloth per do	1 25
Fine do per do	1 50
Serge per do	1 25
Making Muslin caps, each	0 16½
Making do & finding thread & tape	0 25
" do & " cloth, thread & tape	0 31
Worsted Borders per yd	0 06
Cotton Cap tape wide per do	0 04
do do narrow per do	0 03
Mixed stocking yarn per knot	0 06
White do per do	0 05
Linnen cap tape wide per yd	0 05
do do narrow per do	0 05
Blue check neck Hkffs for Sisters each	0 87½
Light colored do for do ea	0 75
Fine check linnen pocket Hkffs. ea.	0 50
Fine do Cotton do do ea.	0 37½
Coarse do do do ea.	0 25
Cutting & making up Cloth for shoes	0 18½
Do Do & finding Cloth & thread for do	0 50
For Worsted Stocking yarn per knot	0 09

THE SISTERS' SEWING SHOPS

The cloth used for the brethren's and sisters' clothing
was woven on order from the tailors and tailoresses. Certain materials had certain definite uses and had to be
woven on given specification: for instance, frocking for
the smaller boys was woven with fewer biers than that
for the older boys. The width of the material was governed by its use. The actual making of the sisters' garments was done in the sewing or tailoring shops, just as
the brethren's clothes were made in the clothiers' shops.
The cloth was cut, pieced and sewed on the long counters

Figure 51 Sisters' dresses, for best wear, made and worn at Hancock. The dress at the right (lacking the collar) is cotton and worsted, dyed a dark butternut brown; the kerchief is silk and worsted. The other garment, a heavy worsted, is pictured without the kerchief. New York State Museum.

which were made for every sewing or tailoring room, while much of the finer work was done at the smaller sewing desks or cabinets. When a garment was completed, the initials of the one for whom it was made were worked into the fabric, and this person was henceforth responsible for its proper care. Other fabrics, such as towels, bags, cloth shoes etc. were similarly marked. To each brother was assigned a sister who washed, ironed and mended his clothes, and exercised "a general sisterly oversight" over his "temporal needs."

Paper labels printed on a Shaker press were also used on hats, bonnets, surplus boxes or drawers of clothing, and the like. In 1856 a "mall" of such labels was sent by a well-wisher signing her name "E" to the office sisters (MS. No. 36). The cover is thus inscribed:

> Dear Sisters at the Office, all,
> Will you receive this present mall,
> The best I have I give to you,
> And sure, I hope it well to do,
> In marking clothes and jars and pot;
> And other notions you have got.
> And should you wish for any more,
> Just write a list and hand it o'er!
>
> E.

The pages contain labels for such articles as drugget trousers, "summer footins," winter footings, winter shirts, fine shirts, summer shirts, drugget gowns, pocket handkerchiefs, "wollen stockings," "wollen shirts," winter coats, summer coats, socks, shoes, silk handkerchiefs (Note 67), "wollen mitings," "wollen gloves," leather gloves, "leather mittings," cotton worsted gowns, worsted gowns, light colored gowns, drab gowns, blue gowns and worsted trousers.

The dress adopted by the Shaker sisters varied in style with different periods (see figures 51, 52 and 53). The

Figure 52 Everyday linen dress, showing the manner in which the kerchief was folded up while the sister was at work. Bonnet and Shaker cloak.

FIGURE 53 North family group at Mount Lebanon. The picture, taken previous to 1893, shows late century costumes. The short, woolen or crocheted, outdoor wraps were common at this period.

same process of standardization that brought uniformity to the brethren's apparel applied to the garments of the other sex. The Manifesto (July '90, p. 146–47; August '90, p. 169) thus describes the various forms of dress worn by the sisters:

Many persons wore short gowns with short sleeves. These were made of light-colored, striped cotton. The stripes went around the sleeves, but lengthwise on the body of the dress. The waist extended to the hips, while the dress reached a few inches below the knees. For more common use the short gowns reached only some eight or ten inches below the waist.

Over the dress in front, was worn a checked apron, about one and one-half yards wide, cut circling at the top and gathered to about two feet in width. A white binding of an inch went across the upper edge which terminated in white tape-strings that were tied in front with a double bow. These aprons were an inch shorter than the dress or about two inches from the floor. Homespun linen was largely used till the year 1800, when the Sisters learned to card and spin fine cotton, and were able to manufacture their own dresses, aprons and kerchiefs.

The extended dress, or dress worn under the short gown, was generally black and fell to within one inch of the floor. After several years the black was partially laid aside and garments of blue were introduced. In 1811, the long outer dresses were adopted for summer and winter use, by all classes.

Black silk shoulder kerchiefs were worn for many years, when they gave place to fine, white lawn or linen, that were manufactured in the Society. In 1818 drab colored silk neck kerchiefs were used. Subsequently, some very beautiful silk kerchiefs were made by the Believers in the western and southern states.

For winter use the dress reached quite to the floor. These were made with two box plaits in the rear part of the skirt, and from these single plaits, of one-half inch in width, extended to a line from under the arm, where they met the plaits from the front part of the dress. The waist of these dresses extended several inches below the natural waist, and ended in a point on the back. Under the dress was a bodice, agreeably to the prevailing custom. These were abandoned in 1811. The sleeves ended just below the elbow, and were supplemented by plaited cuffs.

Blue and white checked aprons were largely used and blue cotton neck kerchiefs; these last were finished with two or three white borders, about three-eighths wide and one-half inch apart.

On the head the Sisters wore a fine lawn or linen cap. They were formed by plaiting and gathering, to adjust them to the head. These were trimmed in front with a border of open-work, one inch wide. Tape was passed through the back hem of the cap, and brought forward, then over the head, and return to terminate in a bow knot behind.

Muslin was used in the Society in 1806 and made into caps, and also into kerchiefs. Collars with a cape attached were worn in 1810, but previous to this date the neck kerchief only was used. Girls on accepting a head-dress have generally arranged the hair under a net woven for that purpose. The form of the caps changed quite essentially in 1819. A border in front of about three inches in width, made of leno, was attached to the cap and considered very beneficial.

As those who entered the Society wore high heeled shoes, the custom was continued for a great many years. The uppers were generally made of cloth, while the heels were formed from blocks of wood and neatly covered with leather. The shoes were secured to the feet by straps and shoe-buckles (Note 68).

In 1787 a hat braided of straw and styled a "Chip Hat" was generally worn by the women of the country and continued in use till 1805. It was covered, inside and out, with black silk. The crown was about one inch deep, covered with a band of silk of the same width, which was formed of fine plaits across the band. Silk ribbons were attached to the crown and brought down over the brim and tied in the rear of the neck. The brim of the hat was not less than six inches wide. From Chip Hats, the change was made to simple bonnets, similar to those worn by the Friends or Quakers. These were made of pasteboard and covered with light colored silk. The crown was made wholly of cloth and fitted to the head by plaiting, but were made without capes.

In 1827 the bonnets were made of palm leaf, and trimmed with a small silk cape and ribbons.

FIGURE 54 Cloth shoes with leather soles. Hancock Shakers.

The sisters were responsible for a definite allowance of wearing apparel. An order dated May 10, 1840, gave to "Females under 26" at the first order, New Lebanon: 2 outside gowns, 2 worsted gowns, 3 common winter gowns, 3 common summer gowns, 1 white gown, 2 cotton and worsted gowns, 2 light colored gowns, 2 cloaks, 2 winter petticoats, 3 summer petticoats, 1 white petticoat, 2 "good checkt aprons," 2 good winter aprons, 6 kitchen

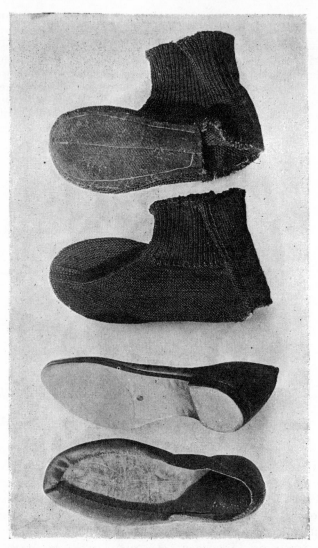

FIGURE 55 Knit gaiters with leather and felt shoes, for winter wear; New Lebanon. New York State Museum.

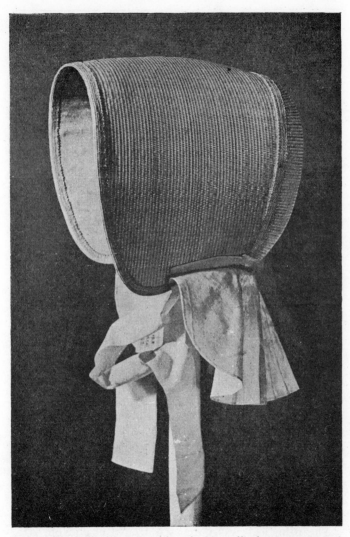

FIGURE 56 Straw bonnet, with pale blue silk bonnet-capes and ribbons; Hancock Shakers. New York State Museum.

aprons, 9 shifts, 3 palm bonnets, 1 pr. "nice" leather shoes, 1 pr. wash shoes, 6 pr. cloth shoes (figures 54 and 55), 2 pr. socks, 16 pr. stockings, 10 common neck handkerchiefs, 8 white neck handkerchiefs, 16 caps, 12 collars, 3 pr. undersleeves, 8 underjackets, 2 white handkerchiefs, 2 fine checked handkerchiefs, and common handkerchiefs "as many as needful." Females under 20 received a smaller quantity of clothing. The following articles were forbidden: checked collars, silk cushions, silk shoe or bagstrings, silk bonnet strings for every day, frills or ruffles on bonnets, pearl collar buttons, green aprons, bombazet aprons, clasp garters and "bought striped gowns with wider stripes than the good Church Order stripes" (Note 69).

PALM-LEAF AND STRAW BONNETS

The manufacture of palm-leaf and straw bonnets (figures 56 and 57) was an important Shaker industry, at New Lebanon and other societies, from the late 1820's until the Civil War period. The price varied slightly above and below $1. Children's bonnets sold for about $5 a dozen. In the journal kept by the deaconesses at the office of the Church family (MS. No. 30) an itemized account of bonnet sales is given covering a period from April 1836 to June 1837. In this time 1886 bonnets were sold to other societies and to the world, the account amounting to $1963.71. On October 27, 1838, a shipment of bonnets to New York and Philadelphia amounted to $528.95.

The following brief description of the early bonnet industry has been furnished by one of the Mount Lebanon sisters:

The palm leaf was purchased from Cuba (Note 70). It was first sized and dampened. The longest leaves were used for warp, and the shorter pieces for filling or woof. These were tied into hand looms to pieces of thread previously placed through a harness and reed. Then the weaver would tie the loose end of palm leaf to the apron rod of the loom and proceed to weave with short strands threaded through a wooden needle. When completed the woven pieces were known as "chips." In a much smaller loom were woven the braids. These were of two widths:

FIGURE 57 Palm-leaf bonnet covered with reddish-brown silk. The binding is a light tan tape. The bonnet-cape, extending as it does to the front, indicates an earlier style than that of the bonnet in figure 56. Andrews Collection.

FIGURE 58 Bonnet mold and stand. New York State Museum.

one, one-half inch wide, was called the crown braid and the other, an inch in width, the fore braid.

The chip was then treated to a flame of burning alcohol to singe off the fiber roughened by the sizing machine. Each "chip" was then varnished on one side, and a thin cloth pasted on the reverse side. Each "chip" made one front piece and crown piece; then pliable wire was sewed around the crown and front edge. The back edge of the front piece was securely sewed to the crown and the narrow ½ inch braid was sewed over the crown to cover the joining; the wider braid was doubled and bound over the front edge of the bonnet.

These bonnets were not commercialized after the Civil War [Note 71] but they have been and are now worn by the Shaker themselves. Most of the later ones were made of rye or oat straw.

Bonnets were made in graded sizes, 5's and 6's for the children, and 7's, 8's, 9's and 10's for the sisters. These sizes were regulated by cutting out the bonnet parts on paper, wooden or sheet iron patterns, and then piecing them together over wooden forms or molds (figure 58).

KITCHEN AND DAIRY INDUSTRIES

Shaker apple sauce was as well known in prebellum days in New England and New York as the Shaker bonnets, seeds, brooms or herb extracts. Apples were extensively raised by the Believers and large consignments were also received from the neighboring farms. "Paring bees" were held several times a week in the fall. The sisters trimmed and cored the fruit while the brethren ran the paring machines. The apples were then desiccated in the drying house; a large stove on the ground floor furnished heat, and the apples were stirred until dry in large bins located on the floor above. When cool they were packed away in barrels to be made later into apple sauce.

Inferior fruit was turned into vinegar or the cider was used in making the cider apple sauce. Sauce, presumably apple sauce, was being distributed at Hudson and other centers as early as 1814. Apple sauce and dried apples were sold by the barrel in the 1830's and perhaps earlier, and for 50 years this was an important industry. In 1848, 36 gallons of apple butter were prepared, and this product appears in the deaconesses' accounts for several years afterward. In 1855 apple sauce was sold for the equivalent of four shillings a gallon; in 1856 the price was $12 a barrel. Cider and vinegar were made in the 1820's and for many years afterward. In 1828 cider was sold for $1 and vinegar for $3 a barrel.

About the middle of the last century a lucrative maple syrup industry was developed which continued for many years. In 1853 the sales were so numerous that a separate section of the trustees' accounts (MS. No. 23) was devoted to this business. Entries appear amounting to $130, $136, $201, $250, etc. By 1860 at least, the product was being advertised the year round in certain newspapers. The making of maple sugar cakes, sometimes filled with butternuts, was begun at a slightly later date, but developed into an active household occupation about the time of the Civil War.

A large grove of maples was located at the north of the village. "The camp was on a side hill about two miles from the settlement," Sister Marcia recalled (Good Housekeeping, July '06, p. 36), "and here the great sheet iron kettles were arranged one above another and connected with pipes and faucets so that the boiling sap could easily be run from one to the other. In the early spring a detachment of sisters went out and washed all the buckets before they were hung upon the trees. The sap was first boiled down by the brethren at camp and then brought in on the ox sleds to the 'sugar shop,' where the sisters took charge of it. Shaker syrup is remarkably fine because it is clarified by the addition of milk, one quart to twelve gallons of syrup. . . . The syrup was stored in two-gallon jugs, sealed with resin, and one of these jugs was opened each Sunday morning for the family breakfast. In fact, the syrup was entirely for home consumption, though the sisters made quantities of little scalloped sugar cakes for sale, some plain, some with nuts. . . ."

The preparation of wines, sauces, jellies and preserves constituted another industrious household occupation during this same period. A package of labels, some dating before and some after 1861 (Note 72), shows that the following wines were made: blackberry, cherry, elderberry, grape, white currant, red currant and apple. Metheglin was also put up, as well as a tonic known as wild cherry bitters. The first mention of wine occurs in 1859, when ten gallons were concocted by the office sisters (Note 73). Two barrels were sold in 1860, and about the same annual quantity in the next few years.

Quince, peach, cranberry, raspberry, citron, pear, grape, pineapple, strawberry, "plumb" and tomato sauce were prepared by the sisters for home use and for sale. Currant, apple, raspberry and many other kinds of jellies were put up in quart containers which sold for the equivalent of eight shillings each; cherry, plum, crab-apple, cranberry and quince preserves were sold for four shillings a quart (Note 74).

A considerable business was also done in cucumber pickles and tomato catsup. Pickles were sold as early as 1811, and after 1818 such entries are not uncommon. The sisters of the Second order put up six and one-half barrels of pickles in 1840, and in the period 1840–55 more than 100 barrels had been sold. This business continued until 1870 or after. In 1848 the First order sisters prepared 43 dozen bottles of tomato catsup, and tomato sauce was sold in large quantities, by the bottle and by the gallon.

Dairy products were a household staple and also provided a steady although not large income. The sisters did the milking, except in stormy weather, and prepared the butter and cheese, the surplus of which was marketed after the family needs had been met. Cheeses were sold as early as 1810, the price at that time being four for $17.04. In 1841, 200 pounds of cheese were made by the First order sisters at the Church, and in the next 15 years these sisters had manufactured 5433 pounds. The current price in 1854 was the equivalent of one shilling a pound.

Other related industries added to the family's revenues. In 1841, the First order sisters sold 100 pounds of sausages. Ten years later strawberries were cultivated and marketed in some quantity. In 1853 currants were sold by the bushel, 24 bushels in 1853, 21 bushels in 1854 and so on. Gooseberries were also raised, and in 1865 five barrels of dried elderberries were put up. By 1860 a poultry business had been inaugurated: 160 fowls were "picked" by the First order sisters in this year, and 70 turkeys and chickens by the Second order. From 1863 on, the office sisters sold in their store quantities of preserved or sugared sweet flag root, sugared butternut meats, and sugared lemon and orange peel (MS. No. 30).

BOXES AND BASKETS, KNITTED WEAR AND MISCELLANEOUS PRODUCTS OF ·THE SISTERS' SHOPS

Besides the numerous occupations and industries already mentioned, the Shaker sisters engaged in the manufacture of many forms of wearing apparel and articles which appealed to the nineteenth century gift-seeker and housewife. The young women learned to sew and knit at an early age, and the aged busied themselves with such handicraft after they were unable to perform other occupations. For no one did the day's work end with the evening meal; the brethren had their outside chores, and the sisters and young people repaired to the dwelling workrooms to spin yarn, knit socks and gloves, braid rugs or make pincushions. A ready sale was assured of this varied fancywork. Visitors were frequent at the Shaker settlement. One of the chief diversions of sojourners at the fashionable Lebanon Springs nearby was to call at the Shaker shops and purchase mementoes of their visit, and the income derived from such patrons appreciably swelled the total resources of the society.

The writer does not know just when the two stores operated by the New Lebanon families were first established. The trustees' office and store was built in 1827, but fancy goods may have been sold before this date. Needlework, basketry, table mat, fan and duster making, and other similar occupations were carried on extensively in the second and third quarters of the last century. Certain occupations, such as whiplash braiding, "picking over" herbs, mop and mat making and basket weaving, engaged the time of the sisterhood at an even earlier period.

An important record of such sisters' shopwork from 1839 to 1871 is contained in the journal kept by the office deaconesses at the Church family in New Lebanon (MS. No. 30). In this journal was set down the annual output as well as the expenses incurred in running the shops.

In the first year covered by the journal the manufacture of palm-leaf bonnets constituted about 80 per cent of the shop's activity. Men's hats (39 in all) were also made, as well as baskets, gloves, socks and cushions. In the decade 1840-49, the following articles were manufactured: splint baskets, large braided baskets, "crown" baskets, palm-leaf "draw" [drawer] boxes and baskets, small baskets, work baskets or "portfolios," cup mops, cotton and tow floor mops, large and small "emera" [emery] balls, shag chair mats, feather and splint fans, palm salvers, "rheticles" [reticules], palm-leaf cup mats, pincushions, table mats, fancy brushes, bonnets and palm-leaf hats. Whiplashes were braided, beeswax whitened, wool hats trimmed, glove, mitten, footing and mop yarn spun, children's and adults' foot benches covered, thread and yarn gloves knitted, and thousands of paper and cloth seed bags made (Note 75). Hundreds of yards of linen and brown diaper, strainer cloth, and cotton and worsted cloth were also woven (Note 76).

In the next ten years the list includes pocketbooks (leather), knitting-sheaths, holders, penwipers, needlebooks, paper fans, wings, peacock-feather dusters, workstands, spool tables and spool stands, "popple" [poplar] fans, door mats, "little handled boxes of various kinds," small blankets and baby blankets, double-drawer boxes, gentlemen's cushions, box cushions, round cushions and toilet cushions. The sisters also engaged in the weaving of notched and fine braids, riddles and sieves, the knitting of silk head nets, and the "bottoming" of chairs.

The years from 1860 to 1871 reveal an even more complex shop activity. Articles made in the previous decades continued to be manufactured, and the following additional items are listed: napkin rings, thimble cases, satchels [leather?], toilet stands, pocket baskets, silk-top baskets, "bellows" baskets, quadrifoil baskets, peacock brushes, dove wings, "tomato" cushions, popple oval fancy baskets in many shapes and sizes, popple chests, small popple pails, popple hatboxes, hat plumes, large sacks, fur gloves and "Turkey Crop" court plaster. Baskets were "furnished," cushions ribboned, wax cakes "run," bath mitts and wristlets knitted, and thousands of letters marked on various fabrics and articles of clothing. In 1863 the Shaker sisters made 184 dozen candles and 12 barrels of soap.

The sale work done by the children and "caretakers" was separately listed. In 1860 they made 229 face braids, 1254 cushion linings, 109 cloth seed bags, 27,226 paper seed bags, and performed 48 days' work on yarn, hair etc. In 1861 they lined 449 round cushions and 1600 square cushions, made 110 tomato cushions, 48 wings and feather dusters, braided 167 yards of palm-leaf braid, and picked dandelion seed three weeks, "besides going to school." The children also hemmed and shagged, picked out walnut and butternut meats, footed stockings, made brushes and velvet cushions, cut labels, picked flowers, besides helping their elders in many other occupations.

A busy life! Small wonder for the inscription on one of the journal's pages: "Very little time, besides practicing Footology." These workers were indeed "Blessed Sisters of Industry."

DYEING

The bleaching and dyeing of cotton, linen and wool were complementary occupations which engaged the whole time of several Shaker sisters. In the very early days of the settlement dyeing was done not only for the family itself, but for outsiders and other societies. Such items occur as that for June 9, 1790, when yarn was dyed for Israel Talcott to the amount of two shillings. Indigo was then the common dyestuff. Later such dyes were used as logwood, copperas, camwood, madder, red tartar and fustic; the first three were bought by the barrel and redistributed to other families and societies. Sumac leaves were also employed. The most common native vegetable dyes were hemlock and butternut. These the Shakers prepared themselves.

From 1837 to 1855 a journal (MS. No. 33) was kept at the Church family in New Lebanon by Elizabeth Lovegrove and another sister whose name was not recorded (Note 77). In 1840 Sister Elizabeth was assigned, "as clay in the hands of the potter," to work at the washhouse, where she became so interested in the various operations involved in preparing raw flax and wool for weaving that she kept a memorandum of the activities in which she and her companions engaged. The journal reveals a very complex industry that was far from being standardized and that was replete with experimental procedures.

The work began each year in the month of April, when the flax and tow yarn were boiled and colored, the flax bucked and hatcheled, and the winter's wool sorted, picked over and washed (Note 78). Dyeing was one of the principal occupations. The diary continues:

May 1840

This month we commenced bleaching and whitning our cotton cloth, had about one thousand yards for the family and one hundred for the Office.

25. They began to shear the sheep.

This week we coloured about 60 yards of cotton cloth in hot butternut dye for frocks and trowsers, and 60 yards for linings.

28. Commence combing white worsted.

June

The first week in this month we put the butternut bark to soak.

6. finish combing the white worsted, had 36 lbs.

We put the wool into the butternut dye about the middle of the 2nd week in June and finished colouring butternut the 14th of July.

We finished combing the 29th of July.

The following disposition of the wool for 1840 was made:

Memorandum of worsted.

11	lbs. for stockings, grey and some white
36	for linings and fine crape white
9	for common crape Butternut
6	for Cloak head linings do fine
15½	fine worsted trowsers butternut
9	for linings for blue jackets, to fill on cotton
20	for Serge trowsers
12	for drugget trowsers
7½	for fine drugget gowns
7	for quality & sewing thread
6	for backings

Fifty-two pounds of wool were coloured blue, and ten pounds colored black for boys frocks.

Sent to the 2nd Families machiene this season.

41 lbs to be roped for coarse flannel
36 do do do   do   for surtouts
 9 do to be carded into rolls for boys footings.

By reason of a scarsity of water we had to send all the rest of our wool to be carded among the world this season.

```
 2 lbs. for  quality carded into rolls
30 do   do   footings  do        do
 3 do   for  fine stockings  do   do
22 do        common stockings do do
27 lbs.      fine flannel carded and spun
60 do   for boys frocks carded and spun and wove
15 do   drugget for trowsers carded and spun
11 do   fine drugget           do    do do
21 do   for boys trowsers warp do    do  do
26 do   to fill onto cotten    do    do  do
27 do   for carpet filling carded into rolls
22 do   to fill boys Trowsers carded & spun
16 do   for Searge filling     do  do do
 8 do   for mittens            do
 5 do   Stockings for sale     do
27 do   for chair mats do carded and spun
```

We finish spining the 29th of August.

We finish the wash house work colouring scouring boiling out yarn etc October 9th and the writer took a tour (turn?) in the kitchen.

In the succeeding years much the same routine was followed. A hot or cold butternut solution was the common dyeing medium. Carpeting and shagging were colored in a red and green dye. "Little girls gowns" were often colored in an old red dye. In 1844, 66 runs of cotton yarn were colored "hemlock" for little girls' gowns. Worsted linings were dyed drab. Horse blankets, carpets and shagging were sometimes colored blue with "pussly" [purslane]. Yarn was dyed blue for pocket handkerchiefs, footings, linings, window curtains, gowns, trousers, jackets and thread. In 1850 dye stuffs were used as follows:

Logwood	1 Brl.	Priessiate of Potash	1 Keg.
Fustic	1 Brl.	Sicely (Sicilian?) Sumac	100 cwt.
Catechu	1 Keg	Sugar of lead	20 lb.
Chromate of Potash	1 Keg	Cochineal	1 lb.

A few scattered items are selected to give a more intimate insight into the operations of the wash-house:

1844. July 29. The Wool is all greased.
Aug. 5. Boil the cloth for sheeting; put out 5 pieces of shirting to whiten.
Aug. 12. Scour the first piece of butternut worsted.
Sept. 20. We colour 3 runs of yellow yarn for the office.
Oct. 2. Fix and boil in lye a quantity of yarn.

1845. May 12. On account of a failure in the quality of the bleaching salts, all the coarse cloth except about 64 yards has been whitened in the sun & wind. . . .
May 25. We finish 75 runs of yarn in the blue dye that is partly coloured in hemlock dye.
27, 28. Two hired men shear the sheep. 210 in number.
June 5. Wash the wool to color butternut, and put the linen cloth in whey.
July 8. Commenced coloring copperas by the directions given at Harvard, but it looks very bad.

1846. April 17. We finish carding tow. We have had 17 carders besides the girls. . . . Our mop spiners this week have spun 100 mops.
April 20. Commence shrinking cloth and continue boiling yarn.
29. We have had a new reel made to rinse bleached cloth.
30. We sorted all the tag locks.
May 12. Dye seems quite too strong of Potash.
13. Only dip twice and conclude not to try to work the dye till it is in better order.
June 26. Several days previous to this we have put some lye in one tub of butternut dye but we cannot yet determine whether it does much good or not.

Aug. 21. Elizabeth Munson from the 2nd family came to assist us in coloring with camwood.

1847. April 19. go to washing and put down our first yarn to buck in the red rinsing tub.

June 1. We wash the wool to color blue. After scalding in the Liquor 20 min. we wash in warm suds, then rinse in cold waters.

June 17. We receive a pair of new Combing Tongs made by Arby.

Aug. 23. Prepare for coloring, logwood green.

Sept. 1. Coloured red for horse blankets with Nicwood and red wood, puting the yarn and chips in the kettle together, but long before we got cleaned up we promised ourselves never to do so again.

1848. June 1. Iron the rest of the cloth and color some copperas yarn to finish a piece of kitchen gowns.

8. Wash the Wool to color blue & drab. Commense at 5 oc. A. M. & Finish 7 oc. P. M.

17. Finish combing white & grey worsted.

19. Commence coloring conjurations.

Aug. 31. Finish coloring and clean the dye house.

Sept. 5. Make some composition of sumac & copperas for darkening colors.

1849. June 13. We commenced greasing worsted with lamp oil, very unpleasant, comb a little to try the grease. [Note 79]

Aug. 10. Color red and green, and filling for Ironing Blankets compound blue.

28. We madder our red yarn. [Note 80]

1850. April 19. We commence reeling and making our mops. We have a little machine made for tying on the mops by Charles Sizer.

May 29. An English man named John Robins, residing at Tyringham, comes to teach us about bleaching and colouring. He stays till friday noon and is very helpful, I write 33 receipts from his own mouth. He colors Blue yellow purple and orange on Silk wool & cotton. Bleaches a little linen and cotton cloth, makes several preparations such as Nitrate of Iron, Nitro Sulphate, Lac Spirit, Blue Spirit, etc.

June 8. We have this week bleached 600 yds. or 200 lbs. of cloth and 120 Runs of yarn.

19. The wool washer is set in operation.

27. The marino wool spoils the dye.

28. Scald the dye and stop coloring till next week, then cleanse the wool over in sal soda suds.

Sept. 24. Take some blue apron cloth thro sugar of lead and Bichromate of Potash.

27. Scour the last of our grey yarn.

Oct. 19. We have been spooling and geting out blue yarn to help the weavers.

1850. Sept. 30. This month has been spent in coloring. We colored 70 lb. of green on wool, Fancy Red for carpet binding, Yellow for carpet binding, but by using the same sizing which we used on our red it was spoiled entirely. Dyed a little purple, Catechue on wool, and Red on cotton. . . .

The diary records the sale at this time (1840 and after) of such products as checked pocket handkerchiefs, diaper, serge, drugget, horse blankets, strainers, crape and mop fabric.

Elsewhere it is remarked that the Shakers did not believe in bright colors or ornamentation of any kind. Their cloth was dyed in subdued colors. Rugs and carpetings were sometimes more positive in tone, but the feeling of restraint is evident even in these weavings. It is interesting to note that if there was a forced repression of that natural delight in exuberant color which is characteristic of the normal human emotions, this religious censorship did not always function. During the period when the Shakers inclined to spiritualism and its attendant visions and trances (1837–47), "gifts" or revelations from the spirit world were common. All such inhibitions on the longing for bright ornaments and colorful garments are removed in the vision of the "heavenly dresses" promised to the faithful in the City of Peace (Hancock) by the spirits of Mother Ann and Father William. The brethren were to receive "beautiful fine Trowsers, as white as snow; these resemble a garment of purity, with many shining stars thereon. The buttons of a sky blue color, and the appearance of them like glass. A Jacket of a sky blue color also, with gold Buttons thereon, and on these buttons are wrought in fine needlework, many elegant and pretty flowers, of different colors. A fine white silk handkerchief, bordered with gold, to tie about the neck. . . . A coat of heavenly brightness, of twelve different colors, which can not be compared to any natural beauties. . . . A pair of heavenly shoes, perfectly white, . . . A fine furr hat, of a silver color." The sisters' garments were to consist of a gown "of heavenly brightness" and of "12 very beautiful colors." . . . "A pair of silver colored shoes. . . . A fine muslin cap, with beautiful triming, also a pretty color and handkerchief for the neck. . . . A Bonnet of silver color, trimed with white ribbon, also a pair of blue silk gloves" (MS. No. 63).

SHAKER CULTURE AND CRAFTSMANSHIP

Thus far the Shakers have been viewed primarily as scientific agriculturists and industrialists. It has been pointed out that the sect was notable for its extreme industry and for the variety and high quality of its soil and shop productions. A portrait of Shakerism, considered from an occupational point of view, is not well-balanced or complete, however, if emphasis is not placed upon the spirit of fine workmanship which pervaded this industrial life and elevated it into a kind of guild enterprise where nothing but faultless craftsmanship was tolerated. As a prelude to an exposition of the chair industry, it will be well to review those factors in the social and religious culture of the society which actuated such ideals of craftsmanship and gave distinction to their utilitarian arts. Chairs were made for the market, and a study of this industry is pertinent to the present theme; what is said here is necessary also to an understanding of all Shaker furniture, architecture and decoration, and will likewise serve to give a more just appreciation of the entire occupational panorama.

A people who had withdrawn themselves from the world, as did the Believers in Christ's Second Appearing, relinquishing all personal claim to what they had accumulated and owned, renouncing all vanities and worldly ambitions, often breaking family and home ties before entering into this spiritual and communal fellowship, must before long have developed a more or less definite culture.

The early Shakers were a pioneering people. Their immediate task was to sustain their institution in the interests of survival. They were conscious of a particular destiny, an aloofness from the world, a kinship with a

divine plan, a fellowship of interests, but this consciousness was not at first refined into more than a general plan
of how to live. The situation was not unlike that of the
early New England religious towns; in order to advance
their religious welfare they had to spend long days, long
months and long years in clearing and cultivating land,
building dwellings and shops and barns, laying out roads,
raising cattle and horses, weaving cloth, grinding corn,
and inaugurating that complex agricultural and industrial
life which was necessary to insure ecomonic independence
and expansion. Under such conditions there was no
leisure for the intellectual or artistic expressions of a
secure civilization. Their first expositions of doctrine were
not elaborated until early in the last century, nor were
their laws and orders coded until nearly 50 years after the
first Believers settled in America.

The key to the early temporal activities of the Shakers
is given in Elder Giles Avery's dictum that "The most
important uses must necessarily engage [the] attention,
time and strength" (The Shaker, August '76, p. 58). The
comparison is drawn with "the pioneer settlers in a new
country." Protection against "hunger, cold and naked-
ness" came first, and time spent in such labors as "the culture of flowers" or the construction of "the merely ornamental in dress or architecture" was time misused. Elder
Frederick Evans, one of the chief spokesmen of the order
from 1830 until nearly the end of the century, voices the
same principle as it affected styles of architecture. The
Shaker buildings are well proportioned but plain structures, bare of design. "The beautiful," he once told the
historian Nordhoff, "is absurd and abnormal. It has no
business with us. The divine man has no right to waste
money upon what you would call beauty, in his house or

daily life, while there are people living in misery" (Nord-hoff, '75, p. 164–65). In building, the chief objects were light, an "equal distribution of heat," a "general care for protection and comfort," and other factors which pertain to "health and long life." Carpets and picture frames gathered dust, and pictures were useless (Nordhoff, '75, p. 165). Although flowers were beautiful, their true beauty lay in their usefulness (The Shaker, June '76, p. 46).

This philosophy of usefulness runs through all Shaker literature. Lamson reported: "This people are strict utilitarians. In all they do, the first inquiry is, 'will it be useful?' Everything therefore about their buildings, fences, etc., is plain" (Lamson, '48, p. 17). The same thought is found in Wells' remarks on education: "This life is short at the longest, and ought not to be spent in acquiring any kind of knowledge which can not be put to a good use" (MS. No. 65. Note 81). It was not the aim of the Shaker school system to make scholars, but to give the young people "as much letter learning as may be put to propper use, and fit them for business in the Society of Believers . . . to give proper exercise to their mental faculties, & turn those faculties into the propper channel of usefulness for their own benefit & the benefit of their Brethren & Sisters" (MS. No. 64. Note 82).

The correlate of this insistence upon literal usefulness was the rejection of what the Shakers liked to call "superfluities." Superfluities were as sinful as monopolies. Ornament was not only useless and "external," but impeded the spirit. Instrumental music was not employed in the early days of the sect. Like the Quakers, they repudiated also the idea of "steepled houses, with their costly cushioned pews, stained windows and elaborate ornaments, to attract the worldly minded, when the means for so doing were wrung out of the hard earnings of the poor laboring man and woman" (Note 83). Shaker meeting-houses (figures 3, 4 and 59) are plain but distinctive structures.

In the Millenial Laws, first formulated in 1821 (Note 84), a section was specially devoted to such superfluities. These orders show in what detail the daily life of the Believers was regulated (MS. No. 4):

1. Fancy articles of any kind, or articles which are superflously finished, trimmed or ornamented, are not suitable for Believers, and may not be used or purchased; among which are the following: also some other articles which are deemed improper, to be in the Church and may not be brought in, except by special liberty of the Ministry.

2. Silver pencils, silver tooth picks, gold pencils, or pens, silver spoons, silver thimbles, (but thimbles may be lined with silver.) gold or silver watches, brass knobs or handles of any size or kind. Three bladed knives, knife handles with writing or picturing on them, bone or horn spools, superfluous whips, marbled tin ware, superfluous paper boxes of any kind, gay silk handkerchiefs, green veils, bought dark colored cotton handkerchiefs for sisters use;—Checked handkerchiefs made by the world, may not be bought for sisters use, except head handkerchiefs. Lace for cap borders, superfluous suspenders of any kind. Writing desks may not be used by common members, unless they have much public writing to do. But writing desks may be used as far as it is thought proper by the Lead.

3. The following articles are also deemed improper, viz. Superfluously finished, or flowery painted clocks, Bureaus, and Looking glasses, also superfluously painted or fancy shaped sleighs, or carriages, superfluously trimmed Harness, and many other articles too numerous to mention.

FIGURE 59 The Church or meeting house at New Lebanon, raised July 3–4, 1822, and dedicated June 20, 1824.

4. The forementioned things are at present, utterly forbidden, but if the Ministry see fit to bring in any among the forementioned articles, which are not superfluously wrought, the order prohibiting the use of such article or articles is thereby repealed.

5. Believers may not in any case or circumstance, manufacture! for sale, any article or articles, which are superfluously wrought, and which would have a tendency to feed the pride and vanity of man, or such as would not be admissable to use among themselves, on account of their superfluity.

The religious strain so pronounced in all the Shakers thought and did is not absent in such pragmatism. Their goods were dedicated to God; the whole estate of the society was a consecrated possession, and the members had solemnly avowed in their covenant that they were "Debtors to God in relation to Each other and all men to improve our time and tallents in that Manner in which we might be most usefull." In the Shaker mind the right use of time implied not only the application of energy to useful enterprises, but such related factors as economy of time, materials and methods; constant industriousness; the maintenance of strict order, neatness and cleanliness; and devotion to the doctrine of that simplicity in speech, dress and craftsmanship which was not only consistent with, but which also advanced the cause of sanctified living (Note 85).

Few have ever visited a Shaker community without being impressed by such industry, such order and cleanliness. In his defense of the Shakers before the General Assembly of the State of Kentucky in January 1831, Robert Wickliffe proclaimed that "in architecture and neatness, (they) are exceeded by no people upon the earth." Their villages and towns, he added, "bear testimony everywhere of their skill in the mechanic and manufacturing arts. The whole society live in unexampled neatness, if not elegance—not a pauper among them—all alike independent. . . Who has visited one of the Shaker villages, that has not experienced emotions of delight at the peaceful, harmonious, but industrious movements of the villagers?" (Wickliffe, '32, p. 25). Hayward, surveying the towns and villages of New England in 1839, reported that the Shakers "have become a proverb for industry, justice and benevolence." In another place he notes: "They manufacture many articles for sale, which are remarkable for neatness and durability" (Hayward, '39). One of the keenest and most sympathetic observers of Shaker life and culture, Hepworth Dixon, gives us the following picture of New Lebanon (Dixon, '69, p. 304–5) :

No Dutch town has a neater aspect, no Moravian hamlet a softer hush. The streets are quiet; for here you have no grog-shop, no beer-house, no lock-up, no pound; of the dozen edifices rising about you—workrooms, barns, tabernacle, stables, kitchens, schools, and dormitories—not one is either foul or noisy; and every building, whatever may be its use, has something of the air of a chapel. The paint is all fresh; the planks are all bright; the windows are all clean. A white sheen is on everything; a happy quiet reigns around. Even in what is seen of the eye and heard of the ear, Mount Lebanon strikes you as a place where it is always Sunday. The walls appear as though they had been built only yesterday; a perfume, as from many unguents, floats down the lane; and the curtains and window blinds are of spotless white. Everything in the hamlet looks and smells like household things which have been long laid up in lavender and roseleaves.

On entering a Shaker dwelling (at Shirley), wrote William Dean Howells, "The first impression of all is cleanliness, with a suggestion of bareness which is not inconsist-

8

ent, however, with comfort, and which comes chiefly from the aspect of the unpapered walls, the scrubbed floors hidden only by rugs and strips of carpeting, and the plain flat finish of the wood-work" (Howells, '84, p. 110).

Shakerism, as well as other communistic systems, has often been indicted on the score that its severely regulated organization was not favorable to individual development and that its culture was so limited as to place restrictions upon individual growth and variation. While tending to "the development of some high qualities of character, such as obedience, resignation, loyalty, earnestness," and of "the talents which are exercised in mechanical invention," the system tended, in the opinion of Hinds, "to produce two distinctly marked classes; and that while one of them—the governing class, which holds the temporal and spiritual keys—has more than an average amount of shrewd good sense and thinking capacity, the other—the governed class, composed of the rank-and-file—does not compare favorably with the first in culture and general intelligence" (Hinds, '78, p. 101). Hinds noted, however, that important changes were taking place" in the internal character of Shakerism" and that "its leaders are more liberal and more tolerant than they were a quarter of a century ago. . . . It is also obvious that there is a growing party of progressives among the Shakers—men and women who, while firmly adhering to all that is deemed essential in the system, think it desirable that all non-essentials that stand in the way of genuine progress and culture should be modified or abolished" (Hinds, '78, p. 100-1). The matter is put thus by one of the Shakers themselves (Mace, '07, p. 74) :

The arts and sciences, in a future day, will flourish under the patronage of those living the highest life, the

Shaker life. Heretofore the work of drawing the lines between flesh and spirit has been so great that there has been no time to give to any other thought but that of watching all the avenues to keep out the evils that might enter and destroy the good that has been gained.

In the new heavens and new earth, all that is pure and elevating in art and the sciences will be understood and appreciated.

Although undoubtedly there is truth in Hinds' criticism and in the fact that there was opportunity for such an extension of liberalism, it should be recalled that the system always allowed for the conservation and development of native talent. The skills possessed by the newcomer into the society almost universally found a useful place in the varied economic life of the village. Minors were apprenticed to their elders in the home, shop or field. As no member was bound to remain in the order against his or her will, compulsion generally played a minor role in the cultural-economic scheme. It is true that education was narrowly utilitarian, and that literary opportunity was confined chiefly to books on religion—a situation reflecting the early overemphasis on doctrine. A keen theoretical as well as practical interest in the mechanical and agricultural sciences was apparent, however, at an early date, and books and periodicals of this nature were consulted by the brethren working in these fields. The Shaker system was founded primarily upon agriculture and horticulture; it was a progressive agrarianism, and it was Shaker policy and pride to keep abreast of the times. No obstruction to the betterment of his skill was placed in the way of the agriculturist, the herbalist or the shop mechanic. The cause of Shakerism was the great drive, and in this cause there was a place for individualism as well as collectivism. Throughout the history of the sect an interesting balance seems to have been maintained between the policy of rigid insistence upon obedience to leadership and the more enlightened principle of encouraging self-development and self-expression.

It is not surprising that certain elements in this culture of the Shakers—their high valuation of utility in all forms, their regard for order and cleanliness, their insistence on regulation, their prejudice against all ornament and superfluity, their glorification of labor and fine, durable workmanship of any kind, the union of an earnest, consecrated spirit with a considerable amount of shrewd but honest business acumen and an alertness in the application of the sciences—should be reflected in the various phases of their occupational life and in the quality of their manufactures. Whether their industrial products were made for their own consumption (most of their furniture, for instance), or for the world's markets, certain qualities are present. The product invariably functioned well. A high standard, one is almost tempted to say a religious, certainly an ethical standard of merit, was set, and nothing less praiseworthy was allowed to go forth as representative of Shaker workmanship (Note 86).

The finest craftsmanship of the Shakers was expended on their furniture, which is well represented by the following chapter on the chair industry. Here, in concrete form, are reflected typical elements in the culture of the sect: usefulness above all else, no excessiveness in either line or mass, restraint always, strength, porportion, a directness and straightforwardness in accomplishing the end sought, the most assiduous care that the essential function of the piece should be insured. When one views a Shaker chair or other piece of furniture, one feels that the elements of true artistic achievement were not lacking in such finely sustained craftsmanship. Inspired and guided by a passionate devotion to the life of the spirit, the society's chair and furniture makers wrought into their work a sincerity freed from all dross and marked by a great humility. In these labors the artistic coincided with the religious conscience, and in the end we find utilitarianism raised into the realm of undeniable charm and a quiet and pure beauty.

THE CHAIR INDUSTRY

When chairs were first manufactured in quantity at New Lebanon (about 1852) they were widely distributed, and many persons who are unaware that the Shakers made all their household furniture are familiar at least with the quaint slat-backs with their seats of varied colored webs. The world, however, is unacquainted with the fact that chair-making was one of the earliest industries of the sect, that the Shakers were pioneers in this occupation and "perhaps the first to engage in the business after the establishment of the independence of the country" (Note 87).

The prototype of the Shaker chair was the common slat-back which dated from early Colonial times. The strength and simplicity of this design appealed to the first cabinet-makers of the sect, under whose touch, however, the frequent crudities of those earlier chairs were refined and their utility greatly increased. A lightness was given to the frames without sacrificing strength, and their chrome yellow, red or natural finish gave them a charm which was heightened by the addition of woven seats in listing of many colors (Note 88). Because of this lightness and the simple turnings of all members, even the first chairs made are readily recognizable as a Shaker product. The arms of these early chairs

were crudely and poorly patterned, a defect which must
have soon been remedied, as few specimens of this type
are known. A turned collar on the base of the posts also
characterized this experimental stage. The arm-rests of
the typical Shaker armchair are delicate but strong strips
terminating in a modest scroll or fitting around and dow-
eled into front posts which are crested by the so-called
mushroom turning. Ordinarily the armchair (figure 60)
was a rocker having four slats; the side chair (with or
without rockers), only three slats (figure 61). The frame
was usually constructed entirely of native maple, grained
wood sometimes being employed; later other woods, such
as birch, cherry and butternut, were used, with cherry
sometimes employed in the slats. The back posts always
terminated in various shaped finials, sometimes of a
simple, always of a graceful pattern (Note 89).

At an undetermined date, probably in the first quarter
of the last century if not earlier, a large percentage of
the common Shaker three-slat sidechairs became equipped
by some ingenious mechanic with the famous "ball-and-
socket" device at the base of the rear posts, an example of
the many instances in which the active Shaker mind improved on the status quo. This device consisted of a
wooden ball fastened into the back posts by a leather thong
knotted at one end and fixed into the post by a wooden
dowel. By this arrangement one could tilt back or rock
in one of these sidechairs without danger of slipping; the
wear on carpets or the marring of floors was likewise pre-
vented. In what community these "tilting" chairs originated is not known. They were made in the New Hampshire and Massachusetts settlements as well as at New
Lebanon and Watervliet. Not only were these slat-backs
an esthetic improvement over the early country types,

FIGURE 60 Arm rocking-chair from the New Lebanon Church family. An early type: a label "01" on the back of one of the slats probably stands for 1801. The cut does not show the crude scrolling of the arms. Otherwise it possesses the peculiar lightness and charm of the typical Shaker armchair.

FIGURE 61 Three-slat or "common" chair made at New Lebanon and other Shaker communities; showing the method of hanging the chair on the peg-racks when the floors were being cleaned. From New Lebanon.

but they were made to fit every need of shop and home. The Shakers were among the first in this country to equip chairs with rockers. These were designed principally for the comfort of invalids and the aged. The rockers were short and gracefully cut in profile in the same manner as the arms, or as the legs of candle stands. Heavier rockers of the "sled" type were sometimes used for the brethren's chairs.

Chairs made for the market conformed more closely to a standard than those constructed for the varied uses of the shop and home. These latter were often characterized by interesting functional deviations from the norm. Several types prevailed, however, even in the comparatively small quantity consigned to early markets, and in all these forms the same note of delicacy combined with strength was maintained; whether intended for relaxation or some occupational need, each one may be identified as a product of Shaker craftsmanship.

It has been noted that the Shakers claimed to be pioneers in the chair business. A statement in The Manifesto (November '89, p. 252) places the first date of manufacture at New Lebanon in the year 1776, but the fact is not documented (Note 90). The earliest reliable evidence appears in the daybook of Joseph Bennet jr. On October 21, 1789, it is recorded in this book (MS. No. 8) that three chairs were sold to one Elizah Slosson for 11 shillings (Note 91). Subsequent entries on chair sales were as follows:

1790. To Daniel Goodrich. (Note 92) 4 chairs at 4/8   £ 0:18:8
     (May 6) To bottoming 6 chairs. (for Elizah
     Sacket)   0:7:0
1791. (Feb.ʸ) Delivered to Eliphelet Comstock, in
     Enfield, Conn...6 chairs (price not listed)
     (Febʸ. 2) To Eleazer Grant (Note 93) 6 chairs   1:0:0
     (Novʳ. 10) To Zebulon Goodrich (Note 94) 3
     chairs without Bottoms but Painted, at ¾   0:10:0

On a loose leaf inserted in this early ledger is an account between Bennet and John Spier. The account was "discharged" by the former on January 12, 1791, with the exception of a dozen chairs for which he was to supply the "bords."

Bennet's accounts end in 1791. In that year David Meacham was appointed to the office of senior trustee, and the succeeding daybooks were evidently kept by him or an assistant. Unfortunately the accounts covering the period between 1791 and 1805 have been lost, but there is every reason to believe that chairs were made intermittently during this time (Note 95). In the three-year period 1805–7, 286 chairs, "rockin," small, standard size and "wagain," were sold. Of this number only three were rocking chairs; 11 were small chairs, 54 were wagon chairs or seats (figure 62), and the rest were "common" chairs. In 1805 and 1806, 194 common chairs were sold, the number decreasing to 24 in 1807 (MS. No. 9).

The price varied slightly. Common chairs ordinarily sold for 6 shillings each; a few are listed at 6:3 and 6:4. A set of six chairs listed from £1:16:0 to £1:18:0; a set of three usually sold for 19 shillings. In 1807, the date in which the Shakers made the change from the old to the new currency, a set of half a dozen chairs sold for 75 cents apiece. "Rockin" chairs were priced at 16 shillings each; "wagain" chairs, from 12 to 15 shillings; and "small chairs" at four shillings, sixpence. A "great chair" is listed on April 22, 1807, for 12 shillings.

The largest single order was on February 12, 1806, from Hudson, N. Y., for 34 chairs. Many smaller orders were received from this town and from Albany. Frequent trips were made from the village at New Lebanon to these centers; less frequently to Poughkeepsie, Troy and Granville. Occasional visits were also paid, even at this early date, to Boston and New York. A wagon was loaded with merchandise, including such items as chairs, spinning wheels, tubs, pails, dippers, whips and whiplashes, wool-cards, brooms and brushes, seeds, nests of oval boxes, sieves, sole leather, refuse leather, calfskins etc. After the goods were sold or delivered the driver returned to the community bearing various necessities not produced by the Shakers, such articles as sugar, ginger, salt, pepper, molasses, tea, tobacco, ink, screws, tools, chalk, combs, almanacs and so on. Brother Nathan Slosson (Note 96) was assigned to such deliveries, although occasionally another member alternated with him. This regular route

FIGURE 62 Wagon chair, made to fit in the wagon box. The slats in this wagon seat are upholstered in leather. From the New Lebanon Church family.

system was adopted as early as June 26, 1790, on which date Nathan made a delivery of three wooden pails. This method of distribution was continued by all the societies until after the advent of the steam railroad. When the merchandise consisted of seeds, we have noted that these routes covered a large part of New York and New England.

The chair business at the Church family in New Lebanon dropped abruptly off at the close of the year 1807 (Note 97). Only two chairs are listed in the remainder of the book, which closes with items for 1823. It is quite possible that the expansion of the community and the influx of members necessitated the retention of the total output of the chair shop. On the basis of the sales recorded above, this output could not have been large, and it is probable that only one brother was then employed at this occupation. The next daybook consulted dates from 1817 to 1835 (MS. No. 10). Chair items appear again in 1820. The extracts below indicate that by this time chairs were sold to the trustees of other branches of the society as well as to outside markets.

1820.	(June	13)	To Elisher Gray. One Large Chair	$ 2 00
1821.	(Sept.	27)	To Luther Wells, 24 Chairs, @ 6/	18 00
1823.	(April	25)	To Ephraim Pierce, 6 Chairs @ 6/	4 50
1826.	(April	25)	To David Lear, one Smal Chair	75
1828.	(August	1)	To David Lear, one large Rocking Chair	2 50

In 1829 the Church family was buying chairs from Thomas Estes, who was the trustee at the East family in New Lebanon (Note 98). A bill for chairs on January 24th of that year amounted to $67.50. The items listed (from a fourth account, MS. No. 12) suggest that chairmaking was then more than a minor industry at Estes' family, known locally as "The Brickyard" or Hill family.

1830.	(Mar.	20)	By chairs and hides	$ 50 32
1831.	(Sep.	7)	By 2 Rocking Chears @ 20/	5 00
	(Dec.	31)	By 1 common rocking Chair @ 8/	1 00
1832.	(Jan.	13)	By 1 Rocking Chair without bottom	2 25
	(Mar.	17)	By 12 Chaire-fraims @ 5/	7 50
	(Mar.	19)	By 12 Chaire-fraims @ 5/	7 50
	(April	7)	By 6 Chaires @ 6/	4 50
1833.	(May	15)	By 6 Chaires @ 6/	4 50
			By 11 Chaire fraims @ 5/	6 88
			By 3 small do do @ 4/	1 50
			By putting bottom to a waggon chair	50
	(May	20)	By 6 chairs @ 6/	4 50
	(Aug.	3)	By 3 chairs @ 6/	2 25
	(Oct.	9)	By 8 chairs @ 5/	5 00
	(Dec.	4)	By 6 chair frames @ 5/	3 75
	(Dec.	13)	By 2 doz. Chairs @ 6/	15 00

On December 10, 1832, the Church supplied Estes with "turning Chizels for turning chairs" ($.88). In 1832 William Thrasher succeeded Estes at the East family, and for the next two years the credits are in Thrasher's name (Note 99):

1834.	(May 31)	By 1 Doz. small Chair fraims	$6 00
	(Aug. 13)	By 1 doz. Chairs @ 48/ pr. doz.	6 00
	(Sept. 6)	By 12 Chairs @ 6/	9 00
	(Oct. 8)	By 6 Chairs @ $10.00 pr. doz.	5 00
	(Nov. 3)	By ¾ doz. Chairs @ $10.00 pr. doz.	7 50
1835.	(Dec. 21)	By 2 Waggon chairs made & 1 repaired	5 75

In a fifth journal covering the years 1835 to 1839 (MS. No. 14) no chair items appear before the last named date. In that year the following items are listed in the Church records. It will be noted that for a period of 40 years there was practically no fluctuation in price.

Feb. 16.	1 Rocking Chair @ 20/	$ 2 50
Feb. 28.	½ doz. Chairs @ amt. 32/	4 00
Mar. 1.	1 Rocking Chair @ 20/	2 50
May 13.	8 Chairs @ 6/	6 00
	1 Chair @ 8/	1 00
Sept. 30.	10 Chair frames @ 6/ and 1 @ 20/	10 00
Oct. 3.	2 Chairs @ 6/ ea.	1 50

Our interest turns about this time to the chair-making industry carried on in the South and Second families at New Lebanon and at the Canaan families. On February 26, 1839, the Church purchased chairs amounting to $6.50 from the so-called Lower family at Canaan; and on November 4th, two rocking-chairs (at 30/) were bought from the same source for $7.50. That chairs were made in some quantity at Canaan is indicated by an account book kept by the office deacon at that place (MS. No. 23). In 1845, on July 7, appear these items:

Rec'd of Justice (Justus) Harwood for 2½ doz. chairs $28 50
Rec'd of Azariah for chairs   13 50

Chairs were also made at an early period in the South and Second families, but at just what time it is impossible to state. Fire has obliterated all but the records of oral tradition. According to this uncertain informant, chairs were first manufactured in a small mill on what is still known as Cherry lane. The mill was operated by water power. Here John Lockwood (Note 100) and other mechanics engaged in the making of chairs, other furniture and woodenware. On the road which leads from the South family to Canaan, sometimes called the Upper Queechy road, there formerly was another chair-mill in what present-day Shakers call "the very early days." The chief figure associated with this latter mill was James Farnham (Note 101). This shop was located about midway between the South family and the Canaan branches of the New Lebanon Shakers, and it is possible that the chairs produced and sold at Canaan were made here. It is also possible that some of the chairs sold by Estes and Thrasher from the East family were made either on the Canaan road or on Cherry lane. If these shops were turning out chairs as early as the first quarter of the last century, it would be difficult to account for the fact that some of them were not purchased by the large and growing Church order, and that a record of such transactions did not appear in the several daybooks of Bennet and his successors.

Although there is no record other than the Canaan items that chairs were manufactured between 1840 and 1850, it seems probable that the industry still continued in some part of the New Lebanon society during that decade. In the "Journal Kept by the Deaconesses at the (Church) Office" (M.S. No. 30) we find that from 1840 to 1871 there was a continuous although small industry in making chair mats or. cushions. The sisters made 51 in 1841, 50 in 1844, 50 in 1845, 26 in 1848, 10 in 1852, 17 in 1853, and so on. In one place the journalist speaks of "furnishing" chairs with these mats, and it is safe to assume that chair frames were provided.

The business of making chairs on a large, almost wholesale scale, goes back to about 1852. On March 2d of that year one of the brethren in the South family, George O. Donnell, secured a government patent on a type of chair equipped with a metallic ball-and-socket device, obviously based on the earlier invention in wood (Note 102). It seems evident that Donnell intended to manufacture these chairs on a wide scale (Note 103). Associated with him were D. C. (Clinton) Brainard and Robert M. Wagan (figure 63). Donnell left the society soon afterwards, and his name does not appear in any further records of the industry, which was taken over by Daniel Hawkins, Clinton Brainard and finally by Robert Wagan. Chairs were being retailed at the Second family office store as early as 1853. On January 6th of that year Hawkins sold six chairs to the Church family for $9. An April 12th, 14 chairs were billed to the same family for $14, and on November 12th, one chair for $1.38. This same year two small rocking chairs were sold to the Hancock ministry for $5, and six "setting" chairs for $15. On December 26th of the following year Hawkins sold the Church fam-

FIGURE 63   Elder Robert M. Wagan, chair maker at the South family, Mount Lebanon. Born in 1833; died November 29, 1883.

ily a dozen chairs for a dollar apiece. In 1857 the Second family sold to the Church "2 common sitting chairs" for $2, and "2 sewing Chairs the frames" for $2.50. Several additional items appear in 1858. The Church family bought $213.22 worth of chair frames and tape from some source, presumably the Second and South families, in 1860, and the occupation of "sacking" chairs and making chair cushions for the seats and backs revived at the Church about this time.

In a book of invoices covering this period the following transaction is recorded:

New Lebanon, Mar. 12 1860.

Edward Fowler (trustee at the Church) Dr. to Second Family.

6 Easy Chairs tape seat 24/	$ 18 00
2 Easy Chairs Splint 20/	5 00
2 Medium Size splint 16/	4 00
2 Sewing Chairs splint 16/	4 00
	31 00
less per Cash 10 p. c.	3 10
	27 90

Although Brainard soon transferred his activities to the flannel business and other Second family industries, he must still have exercised some supervision over the chair shop, for the Church family purchased a dozen splint-seat chairs of him on June 8th of this same year.

The South family, originally a branch of the Second family, became an independent organization in March 1863, with exclusive rights to the chair business. An inventoried stock of nearly $700 worth of chairs and stools was left at the Second family to be sold, but this latter Order required a large additional supply before the year was out. The South continued to sell to the Second in 1864–65, and smaller orders were received from the Church. During the period 1863–64 the South family sold to the Lower Canaan family in small quantities, and the next three years find a small business with the Church family. Prices in 1863 are listed in an order placed by the Second family on April 1st (MS. No. 54):

To 76 No. 3 Chair frames			8/	$ 76 00
13 No. 3	"	"	6/	9 75
36 No. 7	"	"	24/	108 00
12 No. 5	"	"	12/	18 00
38 No. 2	"	"	8/	38 00
25 No. 1	"	"	6/	18 75
24 No. 1	"	"	4/	12 00
22 No. 6	"	"	14/	38 50

On May 20, 1863, 24 revolving stools were sold to the Second family for $48, and on July 2d, 24 high revolving stools for $60. These were sometimes called "turning chairs" or "stool chairs." In 1864 chairs to the amount of $335.50 were sold by the Church family, and the next year, $200 worth. It is evident that the source of supply was the South Order or family, whose chair business had become well established by this time.

Records of the South family (MSS. Nos. 53–56) indicate that the wholesaling of chairs to city dealers began about 1868. After 1867 few orders were supplied to other families, and the South communal group became the sole manufacturers and distributors. An extensive mail-order business was built up with persons who had visited the Shaker colony and had become interested in the sect and its crafts. The charm of the light, graceful chairs became well advertised through such personal channels, and they were shipped singly or in small numbers to distant parts of the country. The chief consumers, however, were the city furniture dealers, and thousands of chairs were sold, from the late 1860's on, to such firms as Lewis & Conger (Note 104), Charles Jones, Jones and Hubbell, Scharles and Brothers, Newman and Capron,

Mathesius and Frey, and John E. Hubbell of New York City; Potter, Dennison and Co. of Providence, R. I.; Lawrence Wilde and Hull, Henry A. Turner and Co., and Blake & Alden of Boston; Green and Waterman of Troy, N. Y.; B. W. Wooster of Albany; Griffith and Page of Philadelphia; W. A. Porter of Racine, Wis.; and Thayer and Tobey Co. of Chicago. Smaller concerns took lesser consignments, and it was not long before Shaker chairs were widely known in eastern markets, and boldly advertised imitations were springing up in many places. The Shaker trademark served as a partial protection against such competition.

Credit for the development of the chair industry at the South and Second families belongs to Robert Wagan, a man of unusual mechanical skill and executive ability. The business so prospered under his administration that in the summer of 1872 it was found necessary to build a new factory on the Canaan road (Note 105); two years later catalogs were issued for the first time. A wider variety of chairs and stools was made, the designs being inspired by the models of the early Shaker craftsmen. Wagan applied for protection against the many imitations of chair styles which followed in the wake of the industry's success, and an ornamental trademark in gold transfer guaranteed to the purchaser the genuineness of his chair or foot bench.

According to the catalogs referred to above, the following chair prices prevailed in 1875:

With Arms & Rockers			With Rockers		
No. 7, per piece		$ 8 00	No. 7, per piece		$ 7 50
" 6, " "		7 50	" 6, " "		7 00
" 5, " "		6 50	" 4, " "		6 50
" 3, " "		4 50	" 3, " "		4 00
" 1, " "		3 50	" 2, " "		3 50
" 0, " "		3 25	" 1, " "		3 25
			" 0, " "		3 00

The compiler of this chair pamphlet stated that Shaker chairs combined "all of the advantages of durability, simplicity and lightness. Our largest chairs do not weigh over ten pounds, and the smallest weigh less than five pounds, and yet the largest person can feel safe in sitting down in them without fear of going through them." These chairs were generally finished in a dark stain. The material for the cushions was "woven in hand looms with much labor." Back cushions were priced from $1.75 to $4; seat cushions, from $1.75 to $4.50; back and seat cushions, from $3.75 to $8.50 a set. Foot benches, "twelve inches square on the top, with an incline to favor one's feet while sitting in the chairs, and . . . nicely adapted for the purpose of kneeling stools," sold for $1; cushioned, $2.75. Two-step benches were priced at $1.50, or $3.25 when equipped with a cushion. Floor rugs and mats woven on Shaker looms were made to order at 75 cents a square foot.

After Robert Wagan's death in 1883 (Note 106), the business was carried on for many years under the direction of Elder William Anderson. Eldress Sarah Collins, who succeeded him and who still maintains the industry, has her finishing, seating and sales shops in the buildings shown in figure 64. In figure 65 are illustrated various types of present-day chairs.

Before the subject of chairs is closed, reference should be made to this occupation in other Shaker communities. Most if not all the Shaker societies had among their membership skilled mechanics ably qualified to make furniture. This was particularly true in regard to chairs. Wherever one visits, the same general type of side and rocking-chair is found; a chance variation in finial turnings, perhaps, but no basic difference. Even tilting chairs

FIGURE 64 Chair shops at South family, New Lebanon; known to many lovers of Shaker chairs. The buildings are connected by a bridge, over which one passes from the display room to the shop where the chairs sent up from the Second family are finished and seated with colored braids.

FIGURE 65 Assemblage of various types of chairs and "foot benches," in the South family chair shop, New Lebanon. Some rugs are still woven at this family, as well as at the South family, Watervliet.

are found in many New England and New York settlements, at Harvard and Shirley, at Canterbury and the Enfields, and at Watervliet.

Gilbert Avery was employed at chair-making at the Canaan (N. Y.) family during the second quarter of the last century (Avery, '91, p. 13). Elder Philip Burlingame made chairs for the use of the different families at Enfield, Conn., before the Civil War. Richard Wilcox supplied the settlement at Hancock with chairs about the middle of the century. Father Job Bishop made chairs at Canterbury in the early part of the century. In "Gleanings from Old Shaker Journals" (at Harvard), Miss Sears extracted under date of January 28, 1843 the following item (p. 232):

An account of chairs made in this family in the years of 1841 and 1842, Elder Brother Thomas Hammond foreman in making chairs. Amount, including all sizes, 339. There was put at the office 38 common, 3 rocking chairs with arms, and 6 small ones—92 in all.

Chair-making as well as other forms of cabinetwork was carried on also in the Ohio and Kentucky settlements. Richard McNemar, one of the chief organizers of Shakerism in the West, was a mechanic as well as an able preacher and writer. "As a mechanic he could construct a lathe, make a chair, bind a book or weave cloth. From November 15th, 1813 to December 1817 he manufactured 757 chairs, 20 big wheels, 20 little wheels, 20 reels, besides spools and whirls. Up to April 15th, 1820, he had made 1366 chairs and from that time until May 1821, the number was 1463." (McLean: A sketch of the life and labors of Richard McNemar, '05, p. 50–51). A measured drawing of a sidechair in the Western Rerserve Historical Society at Cleveland indicates a close relationship to the eastern type (Note 107). The Ohio chair, however, has four slats instead of three, and the seat of leather is fastened to the frame with brass studs.

The early records of the Church family at New Lebanon indicate that chair-seating and the making of chair cushions were carried on in this family. On May 6, 1790, for instance, six chairs were "bottomed" for Elizah Sacket for seven shillings; and many years later, on February 29, 1832, one dozen chair cushions were billed to Frederick S. Wicker (trustee at Watervliet) for $5 (Note 108). Among the various businesses listed by the Manifesto was the making of chair and carriage cushions (The Manifesto, September '90, p. 194).

SHAKER INDUSTRIES SINCE 1890

As the United Society waned in numbers during the last quarter of the last century, the occupational life of the Shakers gradually assumed a different aspect. The forces of circumstance brought about the slow curtailment and eventual abandonment of almost every branch of manufacturing, and the sect became more and more exclusively a farming and fruit-growing community. It was inevitable that agriculture should thus have survived the shop industries. Fewer and fewer brethren were available to carry on the many skilled and semiskilled trades which entered into the complex economic fabric of an earlier day, and more reliance was naturally placed upon the soil to provide the family's essential needs. The land was there, well cared for for a century, and there was no dearth of farm buildings, farm machinery or available hired labor. Fruit trees and berry plants and bushes had also been planted and carefully cultivated for years. New Lebanon had always been basically an agricultural settlement, and the virtues of farming eulogized by Evans and other leaders had strengthened a tradition which remained virile long after the settlement had passed the zenith of its material development.

The decline in numbers was also accompanied by an ever-increasing ratio of women to men, and the sisters' industries gradually assumed a new economic importance. Boys were still welcomed into the novitiate, but they seldom remained long, whereas greater success attended the reception of girls. The community stores inaugurated earlier in the century proved in this later period, as today, to be one of the chief avenues of income, and these dispensaries have been stocked chiefly with the handicraft of the sisterhood.

A fairly clear industrial profile of the Mount Lebanon society during the 1890's may be obtained by a brief survey of what the Church, Center, South, Second and North families were doing during this period.

The tendency in farming was "more fruit and fewer animals." Although some stock was kept, and poultry raising had become established at the North and other families, attention was turned more and more to fruit and berry culture and to the kitchen and market gardens. Vegetarianism appealed strongly to the Shaker mind, and there is ample evidence that toward the end of the century this cult had been widely adopted. The placing of emphasis on fruit growing rather than on stock raising was believed to be "in the line of physical and moral evolution."

In favorable seasons thousands of bushels of apples were raised in the Church and other families. In 1891 the South stored away 200 bushels, dried three and one-half barrels for sale and made 700 bushels into cider. In 1894 the Church family sold hundreds of bushels "on the ground" for ten cents a bushel. There was an abundance of this fruit in 1896; in this year the Church family shipped 200 barrels of fall apples to England. The next year "prime apples" were delivered at $1 a barrel. Cherries were also grown on a large scale in the various families, and the short cherry-picking season was a busy one. Plums, pears and peaches were likewise cultivated. In 1894 the North family planted some 137 pear trees and 24 plum trees, and the Church family set out 120 peach trees.

Berries, strawberries in particular, were raised extensively during the last half of the century. Raspberries and blackberries ("dewberries") were also cultivated, and wild huckleberries were picked and preserved or canned. In 1891 the North family picked 37 bushels and 19 quarts of strawberries, preserved 55 gallons, sold seven bushels and 22 quarts, and gave away two bushels and 26 quarts. The Church family grew 23 bushels in 1891, 15 bushels in 1894, 33 bushels in 1897 and a similar amount in 1899. In 1898 Calvin G. Reed of the Church family set out a new strawberry bed "of between 2000 and 3000 plants," chiefly Bubach No. 5, "with an admixture of Lovett as fertilizers." In 1891 the South family preserved and canned 150 gallons of "black and blue huckleberries," and in 1896, 21 bushels were picked by the Church family. The North family planted 750 raspberry sets in 1894; in 1897, nine bushels of raspberries were picked at the Church family. Currants were also grown in the several families, and cranberries were raised near the top of the mountain. In 1892 the Center family picked 100 bushels of cranberries, and in 1896 the Church family produced nearly 300 bushels. Accounts of hoeing "cranberrys" go back to 1846 or earlier.

The vegetable and root gardens received the proverbial Shaker care. Probably the most important vegetables were tomatoes, asparagus and potatoes. In 1891 the South family "put into stone jugs" 150 gallons of tomatoes, pickled three gallons and preserved three gallons. In 1896 the Church family stewed 213 gallons for family use, and put up 600 gallons in tin cans to supply a single order. Most of the families had asparagus beds, the Church alone growing 74 bushels in 1899. Potatoes constituted a staple crop. The South family stored 300 bushels for winter use in 1891, and sold 700 bushels. Squash, turnip, carrots, onions, peas and other vegetables were also grown, largely for family use. Oats and rye were grown at the Church family and elsewhere in the village.

The dried sweet corn industry was still carried on at the South and Church societies during the last decade of the century. In 1891 the South family dried between 35 and 40 barrels. In October 1897 a correspondent of this group reports that "sweet corn drying is the chorus of our morning, noonday and evening song." The sweet corn industry was carried on at the Church family under the direction of Robert Valentine until about 1910. This brother, in association with George Turner, engaged in the manufacture of brooms until about the same date.

The Shakers at this time purchased most of the machinery they used on the farm, but they kept abreast of the times, and their agricultural methods were modern. Daniel Offord of the North family observed in 1891 that "It costs a good deal to keep up with all the various improved machinery; but I rather think it would cost more to keep on in the old way." This was a characteristic attitude.

Bee-keeping was experimented with late in the century at the Church and North families. Amelia Calver had eight swarms of bees at the Church family in 1897, and five swarms were kept at the North family. A small business in butter and eggs was also carried on in certain family groups.

Many articles issuing from the sisters' shops in the middle of the century continued to be manufactured in the 1890's and after. In an undated catalog published by the Church family early in the present century are such items as shopping and work bags, Shaker dolls (with bonnet or cloak), bureau cushions, basket cushions, oblong, octagon and square poplar work boxes, poplar silk-lined work boxes, poplar handkerchief and jewel boxes, oblong and oval "carriers," wool dusters, spool stands, doll's straw sunbonnets, melon cushions, daisy and strawberry emerys, chamois penwipers and eyeglass cleaners, bookmarks, iron-holders, needlebooks, pintrays, knitted table mats and knitted washcloths. Yarn mops for hardwood floors were still made, selling for $1.

A considerable business was also developed at the Church and Center families in making cloaks and coonskin fur gloves. The brethren and sisters together performed the arduous task of picking and pulling the skins until the hair was soft and fine enough to be mixed with silk or wool to be made into glove yarn. In 1898 it took three weeks for all available help to divest 200 coonskins of fur and hair. After the yarn was prepared the gloves were knitted by the sisters. In 1891 one sister at the center family knit 47 pairs.

The North family sisters were engaged at this time in shirt-making, rug-weaving and the making of rug and carpet whips. In 1891 the family had "on hand 200 doz. shirts to make." The next year their correspondent to The Manifesto (July, '92, p. 159) reported that 200 pounds of wool was being sorted (after which it was cleansed and dyed "in the old fashioned indigo blueing tub") and that 400 yards of cotton cloth was being bleached in chloride. Carpet beaters or whips were made in quantity in 1898 and after; 500 were made in one day during this year. Shaker products were distributed through the family store on special orders and were often displayed at such country fairs as those at Chatham.

The oldest surviving industries at Mount Lebanon today are the medicinal herb business at the Church-Center family and the chair business at the South-Second families. In the 1890's the former pursuit still provided a considerable annual income to the producers, and as late as 1899 Alonzo G. Hollister, who had charge at this time, reported that a new boiler was being installed at the "extract laboratory." Although several kinds of extracts were being manufactured, as before noted, Norwood's Tincture was the main product, thousands of the four-ounce bottles being sold annually. The small paper wrappers for these were made on wooden forms by the sisters; the thousands of paper boxes for "sending out" the various medicines were also made by the sisters, with some help from the brethren. "Mother Seigel's Curative Syrup" (Note 109) and a preparation known as "Seven Barks" were also manufactured.

The public demand for the "far-famed" Shaker chairs and foot rests continued to be a brisk one during this final decade of the century. Orders were received "from all points of the compass." In The Manifesto's "Home

Notes" for July 1898 (p. 108), the South family correspondent advertises their "beauty, perfection and comfort," ending her letter with the verse:

> Should any one care
> For a good Shaker chair,
> At Mount Lebanon, N. Y. let them call,
> We have them just right,
> Cherry color and white,
> And can suit both the great and the small.

Farm and shop activities have continued along similar lines until the present time. As the Shakers at Mount Lebanon have decreased in numbers, farm labor has been taken over more and more by hired men, and smaller quantities of fruit and vegetables have been available for market. Some work in cloak making, in poplar-weaving for fancy baskets, in the lining of oval boxes and baskets, etc. is still done at the Church family, and fancy work of various kinds is also carried on by the North family. The Center family has been absorbed by the Church family. At the Second family, chairs, foot rests and oval boxes are still made in the tradition of 75 years ago. The chairs are finished, seated and sold at the chair shop in the South family. The braids, listing or webbing used by Eldress Sarah Collins in the seating of the frames are no longer woven by the Shakers themselves, but the occupation retains much of its old time leisurely charm, and is the oldest continuous industry of any importance in the settlement.

INDUSTRIAL AND STATISTICAL SURVEY OF THE NEW YORK AND NEW ENGLAND SOCIETIES

In the foreword to this study it was observed that an exposition of the industrial life of the New Lebanon community would illuminate the economic activities of the other communes established by the Shakers in the East. Lamson, ('48, p. 18) was correct when he wrote "that whatever is described of one family or society of Shakers, in which they differ from the world at large, is equally applicable to every other family or society. It is a description of the denomination. There is an almost perfect uniformity among them, of dress, language, manners, forms of worship, government, etc."

The data given below, while not exhaustive, will serve to support this contention. All these communities depended to a considerable extent upon farming and the growing of fruits and vegetables for their own needs, and agricultural products were also marketed. Shop industries also tended to assume similar patterns; as one family or community took up a certain line of manufacturing and prospered, other places soon fell in line. The various branches of the sect were in close rapport with one another, and the tendency of every society to conform to the same religious and social principles carried over into temporal affairs.

As early as 1815, according to the New Hampshire Gazetteer of that date, the Canterbury society was manufacturing linen and woolen spinning wheels, measures, sieves, candlesticks, brooms, woodenware, boxes of wood, whips, cooper's "set-work," cards for wool and cotton, rakes and snaths, and leather "of different kinds." Garden seeds were also being raised at this date, and soon afterwards Thomas Corbett was laying the foundations for the medicinal herb industry. A rack of herb labels in the author's possession shows that this business was an extensive one; a comprehensive line of extracts and powders was also prepared at this community. Hand cards were made in Canterbury as early as 1796, and at a later date such articles as pipes, sand shakers and turned boxes. Reference has elsewhere been made to the cheese vats and to the Improved Shaker Washing Machine manufactured by this society. This machine, as well as a screw-operated mangle, was designed particularly for laundries, hotels, hospitals and other large institutions. On the occasion of the Philadelphia Centennial, the washing machine received a special award "for size, strength, simplicity and capability, for extensive uses."

The New Lebanon industries are again reflected in the report sent by the Enfield, N. H., trustees to John Hayward for his "Book of Religions" published in 1843. In this communication they state (p. 78): "In our occupation we are agriculturists and mechanics. The products of the garden may be said to be as important as any; which are principally seeds, herbs, etc., from which this section of the country is chiefly supplied. Our manufactures are woodenware, such as tubs, pails, half-bushel and other measures, boxes, etc.; also whips, corn-brooms, leather, and various other articles. We keep from 1200 to 1500 sheep, mostly Saxon and Merino, which afford wool for our own wear, and is likewise a source of small trade with us." Nordhoff ('75, p. 188) mentions the early manufacture at this place of spinning wheels, rakes, pitchforks and scythe snaths, and credits the Enfield Shakers with being among the first to put up garden seeds. At a later period they made maple sugar and apple sauce; the sisters also sewed shirts; and drawers, socks and flannel shirts were made on knitting machines. The same historian refers to their woolen and gristmills and to their carpenter, blacksmith, tailor and shoemaker shops.

The Maine societies engaged in similar occupations. Like other communities, they manufactured chairs and other articles of furniture for their own use. The New Gloucester or Sabbathday Lake society is said to have made chairs for sale. Both the Alfred and New Gloucester societies raised garden seeds and made brooms and brushes at an early date. The Alfred Shakers kept a tanyard, a sawmill and a gristmill, and manufactured sieves and such woodenware as dry measures, nests of boxes, dippers, tubs, pails, churns and mortars. Rakes, combs, hats, and linen and wool wheels were also sold. The sisters made fancy baskets and boxes of poplar wood. Sieves and measures were also made at New Gloucester, and spinning wheels were manufactured until after the Civil War. At the time that Nordhoff was writing (1875) the "most profitable" industry at this latter society was the manufacture of "oak staves for molasses hogsheads, which are exported to the West Indies" (p. 182). The poplar basket industry was also followed at this community, and a Shaker brother here invented a planing machine for shaving the poplar into strands for weaving. A preparation known as "Tamar Laxative" was made exclusively at Sabbathday Lake. In 1864 the herb industry was sufficiently important to warrant the preparation of a "Catalogue of Herbs, Roots, Barks, Powdered Articles, Etc."

One of the most important of the Shaker garden seed businesses was located at Enfield, Conn., where it was

9

developed on a wide scale under the able supervision of Jefferson White. The Civil War cost the society a serious setback in this industry, as a large trade had been developed in the Southern States.

Harvard may be taken as an example of the close industrial correspondence between the various Shaker communities. Here, by the 1830's at least, the pressing and preparation of herbs was developing into an important business which reached its greatest expansion at about the same time as at New Lebanon, that is, the decade before the Civil War. Elisha Myrick, whose interesting journals (MSS. Nos. 66, 67 and 68) are fine records of this vigorously prosecuted industry, was at the head of the Harvard herb department for a long period. The broom and garden seed industries were also carried on at this society, and at one time Shaker chairs were made in some quantity. In the brethren's shops were made such familiar products as wooden boxes and sieves, and in the sisters' shops such handicraft as palm-leaf hats and palm-leaf and turkey feather fans. Here the famous Shaker apple sauce was also made, and apples were dried. Rose water, powdered pumpkin for pies, and elderberry and currant wines, were all prepared. The fruit tree nurseries of the Harvard Shakers likewise provided a considerable income. Miss Sears ('16, p. 223) also records the manufacture of spools and knives. An apiary was being maintained in 1843.

The broom industry was carried on in the other Massachusetts settlements at Shirley, Hancock and Tyringham. At Shirley we encounter the familiar occupation of sweet corn drying. Nordhoff ('75, p. 194) reports that "the main business" at this colony was the making of apple sauce, "of which they sell from five to six tons every year." The sisters also made maple sugar, jellies and pickles; preserved fruit; and engaged in the manufacture of fancy articles for sale.

Reference to the society at Hancock has frequently been made. This settlement lies just over the mountain from Mount Lebanon, and it is not strange that the two communities should have followed similar pursuits. Here again, broom-making and the raising of garden seeds were numbered among the chief occupations. Blacksmithing and the dressing and fulling of cloth were early industries. The fur and wool hat business was concentrated at Hancock during the first quarter of the last century, and an extensive industry in swifts was carried on for a long period. Sweet corn drying was engaged in until early in the present century, as was the making of Shaker cloaks. A map of the East family drawn in 1880 shows a cooper shop. The dominance of the interest in agriculture is indicated by the number of buildings (shown in this map) devoted to farming and stock-raising: a horse barn, a sheep barn, a cattle barn, a calf barn, a hoghouse, a henhouse, a grain barn, a corn barn, a cornhouse, a wagon barn and a repair shop.

Watervliet, and later Groveland, were in the same New York bishopric as the New Lebanon community. The Lebanon ministry had direct supervision over the affairs of the two other societies, and there was frequent intervisitation between these three places. References already made to the Niskeyuna or Watervliet commune make it evident that the industrial life of this settlement was in most respects a duplication of that in the mother colony. The major occupations of broom-making, the growing and distribution of garden seeds, and the preparation of medicinal herbs, roots and barks were followed from an early period. The Watervliet colony also maintained a tanyard and dried sweet corn; the products of the brethren's and sisters' shops were similar to those manufactured at New Lebanon. An important activity during the latter half of the last century was the preserving of fruits and vegetables in tin cans. As at New Lebanon, the settlement at Watervliet was founded on an agricultural basis, and farming and stock-raising have always been its chief industries.

The situation was the same at Groveland. This society was originally founded at Sodus Point in 1826, moving to Groveland ten years later. The Shakers' farm at this place consisted of 2000 acres, and farming, gardening and cattle-raising were their chief employments. They also raised broom corn, made brooms, and dried sweet corn and apples. The sisters engaged in the manufacture and sale of fancy work.

The growth of the United Society of Believers was somewhat spasmodic for the first 25 years or so after the arrival of Ann Lee and her followers in America. The Baptist revival of 1780 brought in the first accessions, just how many is not known. The decade of 1780–90 was one of patient preparation, the results of which were not apparent until the various New England and New York societies were organized. From the time the last of the New England group was thoroughly established (1794) until the first western society was organized (1805), progress was again slow. The greatest numerical gain was achieved during the next two decades, that is, from 1805 to 1825. From 1825 to 1850 development was moderate, but a gradual increase in numbers is apparent from the various reports of observers during this period. The peak was probably reached about the middle of the century and maintained until the Civil War. After the war, applications for membership in the society fell off to a considerable extent, and by the end of the third quarter of the century, the numerical deterioration of the order became definitely apparent. This decline gained such momemtum that by 1900 the population of the various communities of Shakers was less than half of that reported in 1878. At present there are not more than 200 Believers in the six surviving settlements at Mount Lebanon, Watervliet, Hancock, Canterbury, Sabbathday Lake and Alfred (Note 110).

The author's intention is not to inquire exhaustively into the causes of this decline of Shakerism, except to point out that they were economic and social as well as purely religious. White and Taylor ('05, p. 205–6) wrote that after the Civil War, "Man, in America, felt himself a young giant just come to a knowledge of his might. Of the earth, earthy, he paid less attention to religious thought. The spiritual struggles of a former day were unknown to him. He turned to external interests and when the religious instincts moved it was in the direction of physical activities . . . The question of his soul's salvation or the gaining of Heaven became absurdly irrelevant." Such interests as "the development of material comforts" and "opportunities for commercial enterprise" undoubtedly had much to do with vitiating the spiritual temper of the age. The country as a whole was being transformed by the application of science and invention to industry, and it is not to be wondered at that a communistic and religious institution such as that of the Shakers, depending as it did upon converts, the results of occasional revivals and placements of orphans and the poor, should become more and more isolated and reduced by such factors as the institutional care of children by the state and especially by the growth of capitalistic and competitive methods in business and industry and the accompanying emphasis upon an extreme economic individualism. Moreover, the Shakers composed a relatively small group who were always opposed to such dominant social ideas as those regarding marriage, participation in politics and the bearing of arms. As a minority order, they were often on the defensive in these issues, which sometimes were fought out in the courts. The same misunderstanding and opposition that accompany all radical social experiments fell to the lot of the United Society. The extreme position taken on various social and religious issues kept the society from ever attaining a large membership, and became an increasingly serious handicap in an age apathetic in religion and negligent of the golden rule in industry.

The following data on the growth and decline of the United Society is based upon the reports of Green and Wells, White and Taylor, Benedict, Hayward, Nordhoff and Hinds. It is impossible to compute the number of members at any given period with exactitude. According to Lamson ('48, p. 13), it was "manifestly the policy of the "Lead" to keep the matter a secret, not only from the world, but also from the lay members in the denomination." Secessions as well as additions were constantly occurring, and it can be understood that it was not policy to advertise the former. The heads of the order today are also naturally averse to making known their poverty in numbers. Lamson himself, writing in 1848, estimated (p. 13) that the total population of the society was then between 4000 and 6000, but "supposed" that it had "considerably diminished within the last 15 or 20 years." This is putting the beginning of decline at too early a stage, but the fact is mentioned as showing in what obscurity the matter of population lay.

**Number of Believers In the United States
At Different Periods**

1774	9	
1780	10 or 12	(Note 111)
1800	1000	(Note 112)
1823	4000 to 4300	(Note 113)
1828	5400	(Johnston, '51, p. 267. Johnston obtained his data from Rapp's Religious Denominations in the United States.)
1843	6000	(Hayward, '43, p. 84)
1874	2415	(Nordhoff, '75, p. 179–214)
1878	2400	(Note 114)
1902	1000	(Note 115)
1931	200?	(Note 116)

The largest communities in the United Society were those at New Lebanon, N. Y., and Union Village, Ohio. The population of each of these villages in 1823 was estimated at about 600 members. It is not probable that the New Lebanon commune ever exceeded this figure. The report of the trustees of this society to the New York State Senate in 1850 is based on a population of 550, and Nordhoff, whose book was published in 1875, reported that in the seven families there were then only 383 members. The turning point in this community, as it was in most others, thus lay in the 25-year period between 1850 and 1875.

It may be of interest to list the names of the earliest recorded membership at New Lebanon. A verbal covenant was entered into by the members of the New Lebanon Church in 1788, but it was not until after seven years "experience" that the covenant was "committed to writing." This important document (MS. No. 1) is still preserved at the church, signed by the following forty-two persons: David Darrow, Joseph Green, John Farrington, Eliab Harlow, Jethro Turner, Samuel Spier, Benjamin Bruce, Hezekiah Phelps, David Slosson, Joseph Bennet, Abiathar Babbit, William Safford, Isaac Crouch, Peter Pease, James Louge, Stephen Markham, Ebenezer Bishop, Moses Mixer, Artemas Markham, Richard Spier, Ruth Farrington, Anna Spencer, Rachel Spencer, Hannah Turner, Azubah Tiffany, Desire Sanford, Rebekah Moseley, Eunice Goodrich, Desire Turner, Mary Andrus, Jane Spier, Ruth Hammond, Mary Tiffany, Chloe Tiffany, Salome Spencer, Lucy Bruce, Lucy Spencer, Martha Sanford, Betty Mixer, Eunice Belling, Hannah Cogswell and Lucy Bennet. David Darrow was appointed first elder of the western societies in 1805. In 1806 Ruth Farrington assumed her position as first eldress in the western ministry. John Farrington was one of the earliest converts to Shakerism, receiving the faith from Mother Ann Lee in 1780; in 1805 he succeeded David Darrow as elder at New Lebanon. Eliab Harlow's name has already been mentioned as an early, and probably the first physician of the society. David Slosson was the first tailor at the Church family. Joseph Bennet was the first trustee of this family, serving unofficially until the appointment of David Meacham. Isaac Crouch was also a physician at the Church order. Peter Pease was one of the early organizers of the Hancock community. Elder Ebenezer Bishop (with Eldress Ruth Landon) succeeded Mother Lucy Wright in the New Lebanon ministry. Rachel Spencer in 1805 was appointed to succeeded Ruth Farrington as first eldress at New Lebanon.

CONCLUSION

Two factors which are almost entirely absent in present-day American industrialism contributed most to the continuous success of every branch of agriculture and manufacturing adopted by the Shakers—the reliance upon cooperative methods and the religious actuation which dominated the occupational life.

The various societies paid practically no attenion to "worldly" individuals or concerns whose products competed with theirs in the general market. In a few cases, as has been noted, the leaders took steps to protect their economic rights. The rule, however, was to produce the very best article that could be made, and to let this article speak for itself. The Shakers seldom resorted to advertising or spurious methods of introducing their manufactures, but a discriminating public soon began to associate their name with an invariably high quality of merchandise. The sect did not desire or expect quick returns, but as each society was setting the same standards of honestly made goods, it was not long before all of New England and New York had begun to respect their products, and Shaker businesses which had begun as small ventures developed into large scale enterprises. The sound organization of these societies enabled them to maintain their ideals of a finished product even during the period when sales were limited, and the flexibility of their occupational economy was such that workers could be shifted at will into those trades which demanded at any given time the · most attention. By this system of "rotation" of work and such capacity for adjustment to market conditions, a successful balance between the forces of production and consumption was permanently maintained.

The spirit of cooperation, ably organized by the leaders of the sect's temporal affairs, arose out of the consciousness of a divine and consecrated fellowship of interests. No motivation could exceed this one of religious devotion to task. The Shaker brethren and sisters were ever aware that theirs was a high calling, and that they labored for the greatest Employer of all. With such meaning attached to their work, wages and hours were insignificant, the honor of the vocation everything. Those whose sincerity was found wanting in such a test of true service soon tired of the rigorous regime and left to pursue their own aims in their own ways. The faithful carried on with zeal, practical idealists who realized for a surprisingly long time a Utopian commonwealth of peace, equality and prosperity (Note 117).

NOTES, SUPPLEMENTARY TO THE TEXT

1 White and Taylor, '05, p. 19. This vision was undoubtedly conditioned by Ann's personal experiences. She was married against her own wishes and had four children, all of whom died in infancy.

2 The Testimony of Christ's Second Appearing. Albany, 1810, p. 498. In this important work, often referred to as the Shaker's Bible, the birthplace of American Shakerism is spelled "Niskeuna." Other spellings are found in early Shaker literature, but the one adopted is supported by established usage.

3 The Manifesto, August 1889, p. 169. "Unmarried persons and adults free from debt, or independent of all

obligations to others were generally admitted, and also some of the children by the free consent of their parents."

4 A bishopric was a grouping of two or more societies for the purpose of facilitating their administration. Societies were founded in the early nineteenth century in the following places: in Ohio, at Union Village in Warren county, in 1805; at Watervliet, in 1810; at North Union, eight miles northeast of Cleveland (now called Shaker Heights), in 1822; and at Whitewater in 1824 (Nordhoff (p. 206) gives this date as 1827); in Kentucky, at South Union, between 1807 and 1809, and at Pleasant Hill, in Mercer county, between 1805 and 1809. A settlement was made at Burso, called West Union, in Indiana, the covenant bearing the date of February 25, 1815; also at Eagle Creek and Straight Creek in Ohio (first gatherings in 1805). The Believers at these two places moved to established communities in 1809; those at West Union, in 1827. A society was founded at Sodus Point, in Livingston county, New York, in 1826, removing to Groveland in 1836.

5 David Meacham was born in 1744; died in 1826.

6 From the original manuscript (Andrews MS. No. 1). See section on Industrial and Statistical Survey (p. 264) for list of names affixed to the document.

7 The distinction is sometimes made between the novitiate or first order and the junior or second order. The novitiate or probationary members lived in a separate order, and were "prepared for advancement in Shakerism" under the special instruction of Novitiate Elders (Robinson, '93, p. 33). The second order were "untrammeled by the embarrassments of those of the matrimonial class"; members of this order could donate part or all of their property to the family in which they resided

or could "consecrate it forever to the support of the institution" (Robinson, '93, p. 34. See also Green and Wells, '46, p. 9–12).

8 "This dedication does not end with the lives of those who thus dedicate it, but descends in perpetuity to a regular heirship, who can never apply it to any other purposes than those stipulated in our constitution or covenant" (Green and Wells, '46, p. 35).

9 State of New York. [Document] No. 198. In Assembly, April 2, 1849, p. 7. The report states (p. 7) that "During a period of more than seventy years, not a legal claim has been entered, by any person, for the recovery of property brought into the Society; but all claims, where they have been found to exist, have been amicably settled, to the satisfaction of the parties concerned.

10 The indentures varied slightly with the family, society or period. Often a particular occupation was specified. Thus, a nine-year-old girl was to be taught "the art and mystery of Dress-making," a twelve-year-old boy, "the art and mystery of Farming," and so on. The society promised to provide these minors with "comfortable Food and Clothing, and an education including reading, writing and the principles of common arithmetic, a new Bible and "two suits of good and decent wearing apparel."

11 Shaker and Shakeress, July 1873, p. 49. "Hence Families, or Communities, and even Societies, which are aggregations of Communities, may be, comparatively, rich or poor. But, in a poor Family, the poverty is entirely nominal, inasmuch as, so long as the organization lasts, the physical wants of such are quite as amply provided for as are those of a rich Family or Society . . . The

worst than can happen is, that the waning Family becomes broken up, and its members absorbed in other Families of the Society" (p. 49–50).

12 White and Taylor, '05, p. 310. "Nearly all of their many valuable inventions have been unpatented. To the Shaker, patent money savors of monopoly, the opposite of the Golden Rule."

13 The invention of this machine is open to question. In a document dated June 2, 1831 (Andrews MS. No. 48), it is recorded that William Cobb of Norwich and Jacob Coller of Northfield, "in consideration of" $150 granted to Stephen Munson and Jonathan Wood of New Lebanon "the full and exclusive right and liberty "to use one of Smith's revolving timber-planes. Letters patent on this machine, whose purpose was the straightening, squaring and smoothing of "Timber, Plank, Boards, Etc.," had been granted to one David N. Smith on December 28, 1826. This particular machine was therefore not a Shaker invention, and the document gives hesitancy to a too hurried attribution of other devices.

14 Another case in which credit is probably not due. Jeremiah Wilkinson, of Cumberland, R. I., as early as 1776 made cold or cut tacks for use on hand cards. They were first sheared from a chest lock and later from sheets of iron. He subsequently made larger nails for shingling and lathing. (See letter of Samuel Greene to the secretary of the R. I. Historical Society, July 19, 1827. Printed in Report of the Commissioner of Patents for the year 1852. Washington, 1853, p. 443.) The Shakers were nevertheless pioneers in the cut-nail industry, as their early account books clearly show.

15 Patented January 26, 1858 by David Parker of Canterbury. Credited to Canterbury by White and

Taylor ('05, p. 313), and originally by Buckingham. The latter writer corrects himself thus in the October 1877 issue of The Shaker (p. 77): "It (the Shaker Washing Machine) originated in the Society at Mount Lebanon, N. Y., and was used by them many years previous to its being patented. The Society at Shaker Village, after having made considerable improvements in the original, in agreement with the originators thereof, got it patented with their improvements." As early as 1811, one Sylvester Noble of Hoosick, N. Y., sold to Nathan Kendall of the New Lebanon Shakers for $1 the right to use or make "a new and useful improvement in the Washing Machine" which he [Noble] had patented in 1810. This machine may have been the original model of the ones later made at Canterbury (MS. No. 43).

16 Credited by D. A. Buckingham to the Watervliet colony (The Shaker, August '77, p. 59).

17 At least one framed house, that owned by the Bishops at the south of the settlement, was there when the gathering of the Shakers took place.

18 The results of the inquiry were found not to warrant legislative interference or the repeal of the Shakers Trust Act of 1839 whereby the society through its trustees was given the legal right to execute all deeds of trust in relation to real and personal estate. This right was subject to the provision that the society should not become "beneficially interested in any real or personal property, or acquire any equitable right or interest in any such property, either directly or indirectly, the annual value or income of which, after deducting necessary expenses, shall exceed five thousand dollars . . . " (Assembly No. 198, p. 10). For an account of the various appearances of the New Lebanon Shakers before the State Legislature, see The Manifesto for November 1890, p. 241–42).

19 The reference here is to articles produced at New Lebanon.

20 An illustrated catalog and price list of the Shakers' chairs, foot benches, floor mats, etc., '75, p. 9. "This we consider good policy," Wagan adds, "and a safe way of doing business, checking speculative or dishonest propensities, and averting financial panics and disasters."

21 Unfortunate investments and legal fleecings in particular (See MacLean, '07, p. 17–18).

22 "The joint and several answers of Daniel J. Hawkins and John Mantle, Defendants to the Bill of Complaint of Henry Baker, Complainant" (Andrews MS. No. 62).

23 For a comparative view of the communistic societies of the United States, see Nordhoff, '75, p. 385–418.

24 Greeley, Horace. In "Hints Towards Reform." Quoted by F. W. Evans in Shaker Communism, '71, p. 118.

25 In 1837 the following routes were taken by the Hancock salesmen: the western or canal route, the New York route, the Westfield route, the mountain towns route, the Ramapo route, the Coxsackie and Columbiaville route, the Fishkill route, the Norwalk route, the Northampton route, and Pittsfield (Andrews MS. No. 57).

26 From an old manuscript printed in The Manifesto, February 1881, p. 45. The New Lebanon signers were Stephen Munson, Jonathan Wood and John Wright.

27 On October 3d, 3000 copies of this manual were sold to Jefferson White of the Enfield (Conn.) colony, who conducted one of the most enterprising seed businesses in New England. The issuing of this catalog marked the first attempt of the Shakers at New Lebanon

to advertise their seed business. As with other products, they were usually content to let the merit of the commodity speak for itself, and the prices asked for seeds, medicines etc., while often higher than prevalent market prices and by some observers termed "exorbitant," were usually justified by the consistently superior quality of the goods.

28 For several years prior to the Civil War, the seed accounts, which then varied from $3500 to $5500 yearly, were kept by William Calver. Henry Calver had charge in 1863. For five years or so after the war, the seed gardens at the Church family were managed by Thomas D. Drake; after 1872 the "first gardener" was William Anderson.

29 One of the reasons given by the Shakers for the failure of the seed business lay in the practice of outside firms putting out seeds in fancy colored papers and boxes (See MacLean, '07, p. 257). Dixon's statement that the Shakers of Mount Lebanon were the only seedsmen in the State just after the Civil War, can hardly be termed accurate (Dixon, '69, p. 302).

30 William Anderson issued as late as 1882 an 84-page "descriptive and illustrated annual catalogue and amateur's guide to the flower and vegetable garden"; and catalogs are known to have been distributed by the Shaker Seed Company of one family as late as 1888. The garden seed business was probably the most lucrative of all Shaker industries during the first three quarters of the last century. Medicinal herb preparations and tannery products were also important sources of revenue, but neither they nor the products of the broom and brush shops can be ranked as having a comparable economic value. The garden seed industry was older than either the herb or broom business. While not yielding an income

as evenly sustained as the tanyards, the seed business was prosecuted much more widely than either the tanning or broom businesses, which were more local in character; on the other hand, its profits, while perhaps not reaching the heights achieved by the herb department during its mid-century heydays, were yet more reliably fixed over the protracted period of 75 years. The comparative importance of these industries during the period 1840–47 may be calculated in the inventories, or "bills or stock," taken by the trustees of the Church family at New Lebanon (MS. No. 50). For these seven years the stock of "garden seeds put up in bags or remaining on hand," "garden seeds out on commission," and "seed bags, paper and boxes on hand" amounted to $79,879.07. Compared with this, the stock of medical roots, herbs and extracts on hand, and the stock "in hands of agents" (principally in New York, Philadelphia and Baltimore) amounted for the same period to only $26,050. The total stock "in tannery, bark, etc." was listed at $19,491. The yearly stock entries of brooms, brushes, broom twine, brush and handles on hand are incomplete, the total in this case amounting to only $1844.75. It should be recalled that these figures do not represent incomes from sales, but merely the value of stock on hand or out for sale.

31 From an article in the Chatham (N. Y.) Courier printed in The Manifesto, April 1879, p. 88. The description applies to the industry conducted by the Second family. A similar enterprise was carried on at the Church family.

32 The last "agent" for the Shakers' dried green sweet corn at the Church family was Robert Valentine. On the labels he prepared for the packages are the following directions for its use: "Soak in water for six or eight

hours; after which it should be slowly boiled in the same water for two hours. Make dressing of cream, butter, salt and pepper. A teacupful of the Evaporated Corn will make about three teacupsful when ready for the table."

33 The comparison has been made by such historians as Dixon ('69, p. 302) and Robinson ('93, p. 3–9) between the Shakers and the ancient communistic sect known as the Essenes. These ascetics were also celibates and held purity of life and thought among the highest virtues. In their occupational life they were also seedsmen and florists. Although the parallelism is striking, there is nothing in the teachings of Mother Ann and the first leaders of Shakerism to suggest that they were directly influenced by the Essenian doctrine or manner of living.

34 Nathan Slosson was delivering rose water to Albany and other centers as early as 1809. The price then was 50 cents a bottle. Similar items occur at several later dates (Andrews MS. No. 9).

35 Several orders for bilious and digestive pills and "eyewater" attest to the profession of the early managers of the herb industry at New Lebanon (Andrews MS. No. 22).

36 The author has recently come upon the following eight-page pamphlet: "Catalogue of Medicinal Plants and Vegetable Medicines, prepared in the United Society, Watervliet, N. Y. Hudson: printed by Ashbel Stoddard, 1833." This is the earliest medicinal catalog to be recorded. On the title page is the couplet:

> Why send to Europe's distant shores
> For plants which grow at our own doors?

A note reads: "Orders for simples should be forwarded as early in the season as July; this will give an

opportunity for collection in their proper season . . . "
The catalog contains the names and prices of 137 different
plants (seeds, roots, leaves, barks, flowers), 12 extracts
(boneset, butternut, cicuta, cow parsnip, dandelion, henbane, hop, garden lettuce, wild lettuce, deadly nightshade,
garden nightshade and thorn apple), and four ointments,
(elder, marsh mallow, savin and thorn apple). Functions
of the following preparations are described: vegetable
bilious pills, cephalic pills, digestive pills, compound vegetable cough balsam, concentrated syrup of liverwort, vegetable cough drops, compound concentrated syrup of sarsaparilla, compound syrup of black cohosh, rose water,
superfine flower of slippery elm, and peach water.)

37 Professor Benjamin Silliman of Yale College, writing about the New Lebanon Shakers in 1832, remarked,
"They take great pains in drying and packing their medical herbs, and so highly are they valued that they have
frequent orders for them from Europe to a very large
amount" (Silliman, '32, p. 7). White and Taylor ('05,
p. 316) note that shipments were made to London as late
as 1905.

38 In the Fowler interview in the American Journal of
Pharmacy the annual product was stated at "about six or
eight thousand pounds, but since (the) improvement in
apparatus and manipulation, this amount has been greatly
increased, and the quality improved" (American Journal
of Pharmacy, N. S., 18:90).

39 The Shakers did not cultivate conium, but collected
"that of spontaneous growth, believing it to be more
active" (American Journal of Pharmacy, N. S., 18:90).

40 In a recent exhibit at the New York State Museum,
an herb store room from the Watervliet colony was re-
stored in part. In it, among other objects, was an herb

press, a label printing press and an herb cutting machine—
all Shaker products. This Museum has the most comprehensive collection yet assembled of objects illustrating the
industrial history of the Shakers.

41 The journals "kept for the use and convenience of
the herb department" by Elisha Myrick of the Harvard
Church from 1849 to 1853 (Andrews MSS. Nos. 66–68)
are among the most interesting personal documents of
Shakeriana.

42 Superfine flour of slippery elm. This important
product was first ground in the 1820's; in 1839, 600 elm
flour labels were bought.

43 "Though a few prominent New England physicians
had used veratrum in their practice in the early part of
the past century, and considerable local attention was
directed toward it in 1835 by an essay written by Dr
Osgood, who had used it to advantage in pneumonia, yet
it was not very generally prescribed until the emphatic
proclamation of its virtues was made to the public by Dr
W. C. Norwood, of Cokesbury, S. C., in 1850" (Materia
Medica and Therapeutics of Norwood's Tincture of Veratrum Viride. Mount Lebanon, N. Y., 1904). The tincture was made from hellebore and used extensively in pul-
monary diseases. Before Doctor Norwood died he gave
the business entirely into the hands of the Shakers.

44 The example owned by the author is set into a
charming piece of Shaker craftsmanship, a graceful dove-
tailed pine box with an arched cover, the whole box set
on a slight splayed frame strengthened at the base by
gracefully turned stretchers.

45 An electric battery, presumably for therapeutic use,
is credited to Thomas Corbett of the Canterbury society
as early as 1810. Except that this was a decided improve-

ment on one built in 1800, no further data on this device can be found.

46 One of the finest mechanics at the Church and North families was George M. Wickersham, the record of whose life is perpetuated in a small pamphlet, "How I Came to be a Shaker" (East Canterbury, N. H., 1891).

47 The author of this and other historical sketches appearing in the Manifesto in the year 1890 was probably Henry C. Blinn of Canterbury, the editor at that time. Apparently the material was based upon an earlier account compiled in 1858 by an anonymous writer. For an instructive account of the early tanning industry in New York state, see Van Wagenen's chapter on "The Old-Time Tanner" ('27, p. 69–73).

48 Some of the tanning terms used in this journal are almost obsolete and are not even mentioned in such descriptions of the treatment of leather as that given in the Encyclopaedia Brittannica (New Werner Edition, Vol. XIV, Akron, Ohio, 1905, p. 380–92). Conversation with an old-time tanner has elicited the following explanations: Patnas ("patnays") were imported skins, generally sheep or goat, which were made into a light leather. The "leach" was the pit where the tan-liquor was mixed by soaking the bark in hot water, thereby extracting from it the tannic acid. A cord of bark constituted 128 feet; bark used to be purchased by the cord rather than by weight. A lime solution was the customary ingredient for soaking the hair preliminary to shaving. The "handlers" were reels fixed on top of the liquor vats for drawing out the hides after they had been steeped in the tanning liquor. The grain ("grane") side of the hide or skin was the hair side; the other side was known as the flesh side. Oak bark gave a lighter finish to the leather than the more

commonly used hemlock bark. "Glass off" meant to "smooth off," the term being derived from the glass blade of the hand tool employed in this dressing process; the term is apparently synonymous with the word "slick" used on January 14th. To unhair ("unhear") was to shave the hair off the hide. A slaughter side was a side of leather fresh from the slaughterhouse, not salted or dried. To beam ("beem") a hide was to shave, curry or finish it on a heavy board called a tanner's beam; the first processes connected with finishing leather took place in what was known as the beam house, in contrast to the tan house, where the actual tanning was done, and the currying shop where the leather was given its finish. To board a skin was to soften it by rubbing with a tool known as a "raising-board." The knife used in removing hair was called a "grainer"; the term also applied to a solution used in softening the leather. After the hair was taken off the leather by the use of lime, the hide was "bated," that is, the lime was removed, generally with hen or pigeon manure. African sides were half-hides imported from Africa. To wheel a hide was to soak it in a "pin wheel," which consisted of a revolving box fitted on the inside with wooden pins; the box was filled with water to which melted tallow was sometimes added. Lamp black was used in blackening leather. Putting on grease (often made up of tallow and cod oil) to soften the leather was termed rough stuffing ("ruff stuf") the hide. To size a skin was to treat it with a sizing fluid in the polishing process.

49 Broom corn was raised at Watervliet as early as 1781, but it was grown in the garden like other corn. The first brooms sold for 50 cents each (Buckingham: Epitomic History of the Watervliet Shakers. In the Shaker, July 1877, p. 50).

50 Earle, Home Life in Colonial Days, '98 p. 256. According to this author, Levi Dickinson, a Yankee farmer living in Hadley, Mass., was the first person in the States to grow broom corn. An entry in a small account under date of October 27, 1817, reveals that broom brush was purchased by the Shakers from this town. On this day "Hezekiah Hammond and Jonathan Wood went to Old Hadley after Broom Corn and returned the 2d of November with about one tun of Corn" (Andrews MS. No. 21).

51 A broom sizing machine was used at an early period, indicating that at least ten sizes were manufactured.

52 The splinter brooms referred to were probably the same as the "besoms" to which Elkins referred (Elkins, '53, p. 49). The manufacture was a "dusty occupation," but with a characteristically loyal spirit this brother kept at his task, making 2500 brooms from one late fall until spring.

53 On January 4, 1833, the Church family paid Thomas Estes $2.63 for turning 263 "close pins" at 1 cent a piece. On April 8, 1835, the Church shop turned 56 "Banisters" for a Thomas Bowman jr for 2 cents apiece. The lathe for turning broom handles was the invention of Jesse Wells, a New Lebanon Shaker (White and Taylor, '05, p. 314).

54 Buckingham, D. A. In the Shaker, July 1877 p. 50. Later in the century Shaker broom-winders were sold under that name by commercial houses. One such machine was sold to Justice [Justus?] Harwood of the Canaan family by F. F. and A. Van Patten of Schenectady in 1859. The price was $24.

55 The Church family did not seem to be so well supplied with lumber (or labor for cutting timber) as some of the other sections of the village. They were con-

stantly buying lumber for building purposes, and maple logs for boxes. On April 11, 1807, a maple log was purchased for eight shillings; on March 10, 1818, $1.25 was paid for a maple tree; on April, 1834, $4 was paid to Joseph Allen for "2 Maple Logs, for Boxes," etc. etc. (Andrews MSS. Nos. 9 and 12).

56 This order of five tubs and 12 keelers was consigned to Frederick S. Wicker, trustee at Watervliet. A 17 per cent discount indicates that special prices were sometimes given in intercommunity trade.

57 Cheese hoops or rings were used in pressing the curds after they had drained in the open-weave cheese baskets. The hoop was lined with cheesecloth, and after being filled with the curds, was placed in the press, which was screwed down at intervals until the cheese was hard. The Shakers made their own presses and cheese baskets.

Dry measures as well as cheese hoops were made of tough, hard wood, generally ash. At Hancock measures were made either with or without covers, a difference which probably accounts for the terms "sealed" and "unsealed." Occasionally they were fitted with handles.

58 Van Wagenen ('27, p. 59) states that one Arthur Scholfield, an Englishman, who established a carding mill at Jamaica, L. I., about 1801, began shortly after to manufacture these machines at Pittsfield, Mass. It was undoubtedly one of Scholfield's first machines that the Shakers purchased in 1809 (Smith, '76, p. 162–80). Smith refers (p. 171) to "the superfine Berkshire broadcloth which was spun and wove in a superior style by the Shakers . . . " Van Wagenen's description of the woolen industry, which includes sections on shearing the sheep, treatment of the wool, carding, the wool spinning wheel, the fulling mill, dressing the cloth and dyeing, affords an

interesting technical analysis of the various operations involved. See also Alice Morse Earle's chapter on "Wool Culture and Spinning" (Earle, '98, p. 187–211).

59 On June 4, 1830, 22 horses' manes were sold to Joseph Allen for 22 cents. On December 11, 77 cows' tails were sold to Hawkins for one cent each. In 1835 the price for horse hair was 20 cents a pound.

Daniel Jackson Hawkins was for a long time a leading figure in the industrial life of the Second family, and his contribution to the economic as well as the spiritual welfare of this family and the whole society ranks with that of such Church family deacons as Joseph Bennet jr, David Meacham, Amos Hammond, David Osborn, Jonathan Wood, Stephen Munson, Edward Fowler and Benjamin Gates. He was born October 27, 1781, in New Lebanon, soon after his father and mother, who were on a visit to the town, "set out in the Gospel." At the age of 11 years, he went to live at the East family, where, in 1808, he succeeded Israel Tallcott jr as foreman of the farm. Two years later he removed to the Second family office, where he remained nearly 50 years, serving for the greater part of this period as the leading trustee. In January 1859, he was appointed first elder at the South family, where he lived till his death on January 15, 1873.

60 Boxes with wooden handles were made with and without covers. They were often used to carry lunches when the sisters were berrying or gathering herbs. They served also as invalids' trays. Oval boxes were put to a great many other uses by the Shakers themselves, especially in the herb and extract business.

61 The Shaker Manifesto, January 1879, p. 20. In its reply, The Scientific American reported that it was unable to find any record of the manufacture of metal pens in

America as early as 1820. A correspondent of the Scientific American, however, contributed the following information in the issue of February 8, 1879 (Vol. 40, No. 6, p. 84):

The letter of Mr G. A. Loomis, in the Scientific American of November 23, 1878, with regard to the early manufacture of metal pens, reminds me of the following note which appeared in the Boston Mechanic for August 1835:

" 'The inventor of steel pens,' says the Journal of Commerce, 'is an American, and a well-known resident of our city (N. Y.), Mr Peregrine Williamson. In the year 1800, Mr W., then a working jeweler at Baltimore, while attending an evening school, finding some difficulty in making a quill pen to suit him, made one of steel. It did not work well, however, for want of flexibility. After awhile he made an additional slit on each side of the main one, and the pens were so much improved that Mr Williamson was called to make them in such numbers as to eventually occupy his whole time and that of a journeyman. At first the business was very profitable, and enabled Mr W. to clear a profit of $600 per month. The English soon borrowed this invention and some who first engaged in the business realized immense fortunes.' "

HENRY G. CHANDLER

Concord, N. H.

62 In 1789, a few scythe snaths were sold for one shilling each (Andrews MS. No. 8). The industry was later well established at Canterbury.

63 The fulling of cloth was a process distinct from and antecedent to the dressing or glossing of the material. When woolen cloth came from the loom it was apt to be saturated with the grease or oil applied to the yarn before it was woven. Sometimes the warp had been strengthened by treating it with a starch sizing. The fullers often used "fullers earth" as an absorbing agent to clean off this oil or sizing. Such cleansing was the first step in the finishing of cloth. Following this, the cloth was shrunk and thickened in the fulling mills by immersing it in hot soapy

water and beating it with "paddles" or heavy stocks, rubbing it together, or pressing it between rollers. It is said that most of the cloth manufactured at New Lebanon was fulled at the Hancock society. Cloth was dressed by inserting it between hot iron rollers.

64 Not only was the founder of the society a woman, but a woman (Mother Lucy Wright) presided over its ministry for 25 years during a period of great prosperity (1796–1821). Mother Lucy's ministry dated from 1788.

65 It was the custom among the Shakers to charge certain sisters with the responsibility of caring for and educating the girls taken into the society, and certain brethren with a like oversight over the boys. The "common branches" were taught at New Lebanon, even though somewhat irregularly, from the outset of organization. In 1808 or soon after, evening schools were established, attendance at which, however, was voluntary and the sessions rather intermittent in character. It was not until 1815 that the Shaker school was settled on a firmer basis, and in 1817 a public school on the Lancastrian plan was formed for the benefit of all the children. The girls were taught for a period of four months in the summer, and the boys for a similar period (November to March) in the winter. Reading, spelling, writing, geography, arithmetic and grammar were the common subjects. At a later date such subjects as music, algebra, astronomy and agricultural chemistry were added to the curriculum. A schoolhouse was built at the Church family in 1839. From the first the Shaker schools were inspected by district officials and conformed to the general school laws of the district and state. Each family at New Lebanon sent its own children to the school at the Church family, and tuition was charged to respective family deacons at the end

of the year. Such charges in 1833–35 were as follows (Andrews MS. No. 12):

Dec. 31, 1833. Daniel J. Hawkins, Dr.

To tuition of 18 boys during the last winter		$ 23 47
To do 9 girls during the summer		10 12½

Joseph Allen, Dr.

To tuition of 8 boys last winter		10 43
To do 4 girls last summer		4 50

Dec. 31, 1835. Daniel J. Hawkins, Dr.

To schooling 16 boys and 9 girls in 1834		29 03
To do 22 boys and 8 girls in 1835		37 60

Joseph Allen, Dr.

To schooling 16 boys in 1834		11 70
To do 7 boys in 1835		8 91

Charles Bushnell, Dr.

To schooling 1 Boy and 5 girls in 1834		6 95
To schooling 2 Boys and 1 girl in 1835		3 75

William Thrasher, Dr.

To schooling 1 girl in 1834		1 16
To do do 1835		1 20

In 1833, Thomas Estes, deacon at the East or "Hill family," paid for the tuition of two girls by making three chairs for the Church family.

66 Occasionally a loom was made for sale. On July 17, 1790, the Church family sold to Absolem Jenings "sundr Bricks & Loom" for £4:13:4. Several small looms for weaving tape etc. were made by Henry DeWitt.

67 A few silk handkerchiefs were made for sale at New Lebanon in the 1820's and 1830's of the last century. In 1830 the price for making a handkerchief was 12 cents. The silk was obtained from the South. The manufacture of silk handkerchiefs was an important industry in the Kentucky societies, where silk worms were raised as early as 1832.

68 At an early period "oversocks" were made to be worn over the shoes in cold or stormy weather. The tops were of knitted worsted applied to the sole by a leather rim.

69 Hervey Elkins ('53, p. 77–78) describes in some detail the allotment of clothes to the boys at Enfield, N. H. Elkins' exposition (p. 77–80) of the management and occupations of indentured boys under the Shaker system is probably the most complete account yet published.

70 In 1839, palm leaf came in bales priced by the leaf. On April 15th, six bales containing 1800 leaves were bought for four cents a leaf.

71 The effect of the war on the bonnet industry was instantaneous. At the Church family, New Lebanon, 533 were sold in 1859, 470 in 1860, and 238 in 1861. The next year only a dozen were made. That some bonnets were made for sale after the war is evident, however, from a schedule of prices on bonnets set by the office deaconess at Mount Lebanon, 1869. According to this schedule, straw bonnets were worth "from three to five dollars when trimming is furnished by ourselves." Palm bonnets were priced from $2 to $2.50.

72 The date when New Lebanon became known as Mount Lebanon. The Shaker village at New Lebanon was originally part of the town of Canaan, and some of the early settlements or "discharges" of accounts were signed "Canaan." The town of New Lebanon was formed from Canaan in 1818. The Shaker section of the town was customarily known as New Lebanon, however, from the time the society was first organized.

73 The earliest record of distilling spirits is in the form of a license granted to Jonathan Wood of the Church family on April 18, 1814. The license allowed this family to distil spirits "from Domestic Materials" for a term of two weeks.

74 The fact that the price of such products as apple sauce, jellies, preserves, catsup, stewed tomato and cheese are computed in the early shilling currency inclines one to the belief that these commodities may have been prepared for market at an early date.

75 In 1846 a total of 24,700 paper seed bags were made; in 1848 production amounted to 206,000 bags.

76 Dolls were made for sale in 1834 and 1835, but there is no mention of them after this date. They were sold for $1 apiece. Dolls dressed in Shaker costume are an important item in the present-day community stores.

77 Elizabeth Lovegrove died in 1844.

78 The word "buck" is a bleaching term. The flax was cleaned by being beaten with a stick or bat while it was in the water. Then it was steeped and boiled in lye.

79 A new dyehouse was erected this year.

80 Several old receipts for coloring madder red testify to a more common use of this dyeing medium than one would suppose after reading Elizabeth Lovegrove's diary. Red was a favorite color with the Shakers, who used it often on their furniture. One of the receipts in the author's collection is dated November 14, 1826, and is signed by one James C. Hutton. (Andrews MS. No. 35). It reads thus:

The proportion for 20 lbs. of wool or flannel take for the preparation 5 lbs of Allum and $2\frac{1}{2}$ of Read tartar or arga (argol) put them in clear watter Boiling when dissolved run your cloth or yar(n) boiling for one hour air and run again if the strength is not out of the liquor. then rince and shift your liquor from the copper fill with fair (?) watter nearly full leaving room for six gallons of bran watter which a peck of wheat bran has previously been boiled in. heat moderately scalding hot then introduce the madder ten pounds which has been wet with some of the bran watter 6 or 8 hours before and after a fiew minutes

put in your goods as evenly as possible and keep constantly stirring them for one hour then are (air) and
simmer your dye a little after which run again untill the
strength is well out of the dye and the . . . pretty strong
on the redd then drye it and schour it in tolerable strong
soap suds so as to raise the colour and take all the loose
dye off leaving a small quantity of suds in it. which should
be dryed as soon as possible after raiseing if it is flannel
etc this will be a cleare and dureable Red. It will do with
out the tartar and with 2 lbs less of Madder but better
with it.

81 Wells, Seth, Remarks on Learning and the Use of
Books. (Andrews MS. No. 65. March 10, 1836. Watervliet.) In his instructions to teachers he adds: "Letter
learning is useful in its place, provided a good use be
made of it by those who possess it. But there is much
useless learning in the world, which only tends to clog the
mind and sense, and shut the gifts of God out of the soul."

82 Wells, Seth Y., Letter to the elders, deacons, brethren and sisters of the society in Watervliet. Jan'y. 26th,
1832. (Andrews MS. No. 64). Before joining the
society, Wells had taught in the Albany public schools
and at Hudson Academy. In 1821 he was appointed
"General Superintendent of Believers' Literature, Schools,
etc. in the First Bishopric, which included Watervliet,
Hancock and Mount Lebanon" (White and Taylor, '05,
p. 132–33).

83 White, Anna, Instrumental Music. (In The Manifesto, August 1890, p. 177–78). The earliest worship of
the Shakers, however, was attended by chant and song
as well as by rythmic, but often unrestrained dancing.
The songs were said to have been inspired. The first song
book, "Millenial Praises," was printed by Josiah Talcott
in Hancock in 1813.

84 Millennial Laws, or Gospel Statutes and Ordinances ....Recorded at New Lebanon, August 7th, 1821, p. 72–74. (Andrews MS. No. 4.)

85 The Shakers often refer to their religion as a practical faith, combining "science, religion and inspiration." (The Manifesto, March 1886, p. 63). When Charles F. Wingate, editor of the Sanitary Engineer, visited New Lebanon in 1880, he was informed by the elders "that their careful attention to hygiene has a theological basis," and that they believed "that science and religion, 'truly so called,' are one and the same." (Wingate, '80).

86 "The Trustees were very particular in regard to [all] articles when sent to the market. Everything must be free from blemish while that which was defective must be retained at home or given to the poor" (Perkins, '93, p. 22).

87 The compiler of the chair catalog here quoted was Elder Robert Wagan.

88 This listing or webbing was woven on small braid looms. Sometimes the selvage of the broadcloth was used. Webbed chair seats were made at a comparatively early date (before 1840). The earliest chairs were seated in narrow, closely woven splint. Rush was rarely used; cane, but seldom.

89 Exceptions are the low one-slat and two-slat dining chairs used at Hancock and New Lebanon, and those later chairs equipped with a cushion rail at the top. Dining room chairs were suspended on the pegs along the wall when not in use.

90 The authority is the Canterbury and Enfield (N. H.) ministry. In as much as the Shakers at New Lebanon were not organized until 1786–87, and Shakerism itself in 1776 was isolated in the little group at

Niskeyuna, the latter date can hardly be accepted. The craft of course may have been plied in the vicinity, and by one or more persons who later joined the society.

91 On the occasion of one Mary Dayley's separation from the society on December 8, 1788, the trustees, according to custom, delivered to her a "bill of articles", which contained, among other items, six chairs valued at £1:10:0 (Andrews MS. No. 38).

92 The Goodrich family were early members at Hancock.

93 Grant was a local magistrate at New Lebanon (See White and Taylor, '05, p. 56–58).

94 See note 92.

95 In November 1792 Elizah Slosson sold a table, bedstead and eight chairs to Timothy Edwards. In 1798 a bill of articles delivered to John Shapley included one "house chair" (at five shillings) and one sadler's chair (also at five shillings). (Andrews MS. No. 39). The author owns an early rocking chair bearing on the back of one of its slats an old printed label "01." According to the Shaker custom, only the last two numerals of a date were used in marking pieces.

96 Nathan may have been a brother to Elizah and David Slosson.

97 In a quaint record of "Artikels Rec^d of the Church & families for the Poor office for the year 1807" (Andrews MS. No. 3), we find among other "artikels" lent on March 5th to Moller Wiley; 4 Chairs as well as 1 Chest with Draws, 1 Bedsted, 1 Tabel, 1 Great Wheele, 1 Linnen Do, 1 Real, 1 wooddenbole, 1 Earthen pot, 4 Tinpans, 4 plates puter, 3 plates Earthen, etc. etc.

98 Thomas Estes was born in 1782. His name is given as a member at Savoy, Berkshire county, Mass., in Sep-

tember 1819. (For an account of the small, short-lived community at Savoy, see White and Taylor, '05, p. 137–38.)

99 William Thrasher died in 1896 at the age of 100. In an article, "How the Shakers Live," in the New York Times, August 6, 1899, the writer states that Thrasher moved to the Canaan family in 1821, at which place he stayed for 19 years.

100 Born in 1791; died at Groveland, N. Y. in 1878.

101 James Farnham was born in 1780 and died in 1857. He was buried in the Shaker cemetery at Canaan, and seems to have been associated for a while at least with the families there. (See reference in A compendious narrative, elucidating the character, disposition and conduct of Mary Dyer . . . Pittsfield, 1826, p. 75–79.)

102 The patent number was 8771. The United States Patent Office record includes the following statement of the patentee:............"I...................have invented a new and improved mode of preventing the wear and tear of carpets and the marring of floors, caused by the corners of the back posts of chairs as they take their natural motion of rocking backward and forward . . . . The Nature of my invention consists in a metallic ferrule, ball, and foot piece, combined; and applied to the back posts of a chair in such a manner, as to let the chair take its natural motion of rocking backward and forward, while the metallic foot piece rests unmoved; flat and square on the floor or carpet." The report of Examiner of Patents J. H. Lane includes the following observation on this device: "We have had chairs made with the hind legs retreating so as to interdict the occupant from the luxury of leaning back in his chair; but the patentee, with a more accomodating spirit, has provided

the legs with ball and socket joints and flat steps at their lower ends" (Report of the Commissioner of Patents for the year 1852. Part 1. Washington, 1853, p. 423).

103 Apparently not many chairs with the patent feet were made. One is owned by the author and a few others are known. They were a simple, three-slat type with cane seats. Examples are in the New York State Museum collection.

104 Lewis and Conger were the chief urban distributors of Shaker chairs. They placed their first order in 1868. In 1870, this firm purchased chairs to the amount of $893.61; in 1872, the account was $1051.81; in 1873, $1013.09; in 1874, $540.67; and in 1875, $1383.28.

105 This was equipped with "A thousand dollar engine from Haskell's Albany works . . . to drive the machinery" (The Shaker, September 1872, p. 71).

106 For an appreciation of the life and work of Robert Wagan, see The Manifesto, January 1884, p. 22.

107 See also illustration of interior of guest house at Pleasant Hill, facing page 78 in the book, Ye Olde Shaker Bells. Several western chairs are here depicted.

108 The initials "F. W." stamped in a square on the top of one of the front posts of several sidechairs found at Hancock and New Lebanon may have indicated· that these chairs were consigned to the trustee of the Watervliet family. In the constant removals of members from one settlement to another these chairs could have found their way into other societies.

109 The story of Mother Seigel's Syrup is contained in an eight-page undated advertisement, "Life Among the Shakers," published by Horace Bush, Lowville, N. Y.

110 Since this was written, the two Maine societies have consolidated at Sabbathday Lake.

111 Green and Wells, '48, p. 75. The statement is added that all of these first Shakers came from England.

112 Estimated. Calvin Green and Seth Y. Wells, the authors of A Summary View, state (p. 75) that between 1780 and 1787 there was "a gradual and extensive increase in numbers."

113 Green and Wells, '48, p. 76–84. The authors write that "The number of believers contained in all the Societies, both in the eastern and western states, exceeds 4000. Two-thirds, at least, of this number, have been added since the commencement of the present century; and the number is gradually increasing" (p. 84). Eldresses White and Taylor, on the other hand, state that in the 20-year period 1805–25, 1800 persons joined the western societies, and during the same period 1600 were "gathered" into the eastern communities ('05, p. 152). If the 1823 figures are substantially correct, and not allowing for deaths and withdrawals during this period, the number of Believers at the opening of the century would be roughly calculated as being between 600 and 900. Benedict, whose figures seem to have been based in part on "A Summary View," estimates the number in 1824 to be 5000, but this total includes 750 (comprising in part members of the Harmony Society) "not gathered into their societies" (Benedict, '24, p. 300–1). Nordhoff's figures are also apparently based on "A Summary View."

114 Hinds, '78, p. 81. This estimate includes the family of 20 colored persons living in Philadelphia.

115 Hinds, '02, p. 26. This estimate does not include the late Shaker settlements at Narcoossee, Fla., and at White Oak, Ga.

116 An estimate of 500, by Stewart M. Emery in The New York Times, November 28, 1926 (v. 76, section 9, p..9), is probably greatly in excess of the actual number of Believers five years ago.

117 A comparatively early résumé of the worth of the cooperative principle as illustrated by the Shaker system of religious communism is contained in a little known account of these people written by the Englishman, J. S. Buckingham, in 1841. He writes as follows ('41, p. 75) :

As far as the history of the Shakers can establish the fact, it has certainly shown that, where property is held in community, and not individually, the disposition to bestow it in works of charity and benevolence to others is greatly increased. And that the property itself is better managed for accumulation and preservation, no one can doubt who has watched the progressive advancement which this society has made in the augmentation, as well as improvement, of its possessions, and in the neatness, order, and perfection by which everything they do or make is characterized; this is so much the case, that over all the United States, the seeds, plants, fruits, grain, cattle, and manufactures furnished by any settlement of Shakers bears a premium in the market above the ordinary price of similar articles from other establishments. There being no idleness among them, all are productive. There being no intemperance among them, none are destructive. There being no misers among them, nothing is hoarded, or made to perish for want of use; so that while production and improvement are at their maximum, and waste and destruction at their minimum, the society must go on increasing the extent and value of its temporal possessions, and thus increase its means of doing good, first within, and then beyond its own circle.

10

SELECTED BIBLIOGRAPHY
BOOKS AND PAMPHLETS

The J. P. MacLean bibliography of Shaker literature ('05) includes 523 titles. This list is made up of books, pamphlets and broadsides. Added to this compilation is a number of journals which contain accounts of the Shakers. Recent investigation has shown that there are a hundred or more titles not included in the above bibliography, as well as many additional magazine articles. Several books and pamphlets have also been published since 1905. From this abundant material the following items of printed matter have been selected. The list covers the references in the text and furnishes as a whole an adequate historical background. See also below: "List of Works in the New York Public Library Relating to Shakers," 1904.

The items are arranged in alphabetical and chronological sequence. All unsigned printed matter is listed alphabetically under the caption "Anonymous."

Andrews, Edward D.
1930 The New York Shakers and Their Industries. Circular 2. New York State Museum. 8p.

Anonymous
1904 List of Works in the New York Public Library Relating to Shakers. 10p. Reprinted from Bulletin, November 1904.

1904 Materia Medica and Therapeutics of Norwood's Tincture of Veratrum Viride; 11th ed. Mount Lebanon, N. Y. 32p.

1852 New Lebanon: Its Physic Gardens, and Their Products. Amer. Jour. Pharmacy, v. 24, n. s., v. 18, no. 1, p. 88–91, January 1852. Philadelphia.

1853 Report of the Commissioner of Patents for the Year 1852. Part 1. Arts and Manufactures. 484p.

1849 State of New York. (Document) No. 198. In Assembly, April 2, 1849. 13p.

1850 State of New York. (Document) No. 89. In Senate, March 19, 1850. 14p.

1843 The Gardener's Manual; containing plain instructions for the selection, preparation, and management of a kitchen garden; with practical directions for the cultivation and management of some of the most useful culinary vegetables. Published by the United Society, New Lebanon, N. Y. 24p.

1857 The Shakers. *In* Harper's New Monthly Magazine, v. 15, no. 86, p. 164–77 (On herb industry)

1907 The Story of Shakerism. By One Who Knows. 16p. (Pamphlet). Shakers, East Canterbury, N. H.

—— Catalogue of Medicinal Plants, Barks, Roots, Seeds, Flowers and Select Powders. With their therapeutic qualities and botanical names; also pure vegetable extracts, prepared in vacuo; ointments, inspissated juices, essential oils, double distilled and fragrant waters, etc. etc. Raised, prepared and put up in the most careful manner, by the United Society of Shakers at New Lebanon, N. Y. (No date is on this copy. MacLean refers to a catalog with similar title dated 1860, published at Albany; Nordhoff records another dated 1873)

—— Products of Intelligence and Diligence. Published by Shakers, Church Family, Mount Lebanon, N. Y. 16p.

Avery, Giles B.

1866? Circular Concerning the Dress of Believers. Mount Lebanon. 12p.

1891 Autobiography of Elder Giles B. Avery. East Canterbury, N. H. 33p.

Baker, Arthur

1896 Shakers and Shakerism. New Moral World Series. London. 30p.

Barber, John W.

1839 Historical Collections, being a general collection of interesting facts, traditions, biographical sketches, anecdotes, etc., relating to the history and antiquities of every town in Massachusetts, with geographical descriptions. Worcester. 624p.

Benedict, David

1824 A History of All Religions. Providence. 360p.

[Bishop, Rufus, & Wells, Seth Y.]

1816 Testimonies of the Life, Character, Revelations and Doctrines of Our Ever Blessed Mother Ann Lee, and the Elders with Her; through whom the word of eternal life was opened in this day of Christ's second appearing: collected from living witnesses. Hancock. 405p.

Blinn, Henry C., *ed.*

1882–83   Shaker Manifesto. v. 12–13. January 1882 to December 1883. Shaker Village, N. H.

1884–99   The Manifesto. v. 14–29. January 1884 to December, 1899. Shaker Village, N. H. (Also called Canterbury or East Canterbury.)

Buckingham, J. S.

1841   America, Historical, Statistic, and Descriptive. v. 2. New York. 516p.

[Bullard] Sister Marcia

1906   Shaker Industries. In Good Housekeeping, July 1906; v. 43, no. 1, whole no. 333, p. 33–37.

Campbell, *Mrs* **Sylvia**

1855   Practical Cook-Book: containing recipes, directions, etc. for plain cookery, being the result of twenty years experience in that art. Cincinnati. 113p.

Crossman, Charles F.

1836   The Gardener's Manual; containing plain and practical directions for the cultivation and management of some of the most useful culinary vegetables; to which is prefixed a catalogue of the various kinds of garden seeds raised in the United Society at New Lebanon; with a few general remarks on the management of a kitchen garden. Albany. 24p.

Darrow, David, Meacham, John, & Youngs, Benjamin S.

1810   The Testimony of Christ's Second Appearing; containing a general statement of all things pertaining to the faith and practice of the Church of God in this latter day; 2d ed. Albany. 620p. (The actual writing of this book is credited to Benjamin S. Youngs, although the names of David Darrow and John Meacham are also signed to the preface. The second edition was revised by Youngs with the help of Seth Y. Wells.)

Dixon, William Hepworth

1869   New America. Philadelphia. 495p.

Eads, Harvey L.

1849   The Tailor's Division System, Founded Upon, and Combined with Actual Measurement: containing thirty diagrams and designs, reduced to mathematical principles. Union Village, Ohio.

Earle, Alice Morse

1898 Home Life in Colonial Days. New York. 470p.

Elkins, Hervey

1853 Sixteen Years in the Senior Order of Shakers: a narration of facts concerning that singular people. Hanover, N. H. 136p.

Emery, Stewart M.

1926 Shaker Sect Reduced by Its Own Doctrines. New York Times, v. 76, section 9, p. 9. November 28, 1926

Evans, F. W.

1871 Shaker Communism; or, Tests of Divine Inspiration. London. 120p.

[Evans, F. W.]

—— Shakers as Farmers. Broadside. Reprint from Chatham (N. Y.) Courier

Evans, F. W. & Doolittle, Antoinette, *eds.*

1873–75 Shaker and Shakeress. v. 3–4, January 1873 to December 1875. Mount Lebanon, N. Y.

[Green, Calvin, & Wells, Seth Y.]

1846 A Brief Exposition of the Established Principles and Regulations of the United Society of Believers Called Shakers. Improved edition. New York. 36p.

Green, Calvin, & Wells, Seth Y.

1848 A Summary View of the Millennial Church, or United Society of Believers, Commonly Called Shakers; 2d ed. Albany. 384p. (First edition published in 1823)

Greene, Nancy Lewis

1930 Ye Olde Shaker Bells. Lexington, Ky. 83p.

Greylock, Godfrey [J. E. A. Smith]

1852 Taghconic; or Letters and Legends about Our Summer Home. Boston. 228p.

Hayward, John

1839 The New England Gazetteer; containing descriptions of all the states, counties and towns in New England; also descriptions of the principal mountains, rivers, lakes, capes, bays, harbors, islands, and fashionable resorts within that territory. Boston

1843 The Book of Religions. Concord, N. H. 443p.

Hinds, William Alfred
1878 American Communities. Oneida, N. Y. 176p.
1902 American Communities. Chicago. 433p.

Holmes, James
1850 A Collection of Useful Hints for Farmers. And many
       valuable recipes. West Gloucester. 120p. (First edi-
       tion, without title, published in 1849)

Howells, William Dean
1884 Three Villages. Boston. 198p. (Contains a sketch of the
       Shirley Shakers, p. 69–113)

Johnston, James F. W.
1851 Notes on North America. Agricultural, Economical and
       Social. In two volumes. v. 2. Boston

Lamson, David R.
1848 Two Years' Experience among the Shakers: being a
       description of the manners and customs of that people;
       the nature and policy of their government, their marvel-
       ous intercourse with the spiritual world, the object and
       uses of confession, their inquisition, in short, a con-
       densed view of Shakerism as it is. West Boylston.
       212p.

Lomas, George A., *ed.*
1871–72 The Shaker. v. 1–2. January 1871 to December 1872.
          Shakers (Watervliet), N. Y.
1876 The Shaker. v. 6. January 1876 to December 1876. Pub-
       lished jointly at Shakers, N. Y. and Shaker Village,
       N. H.
1877 The Shaker. v. 7. January 1877 to December 1877.
       Shaker Village, N. H.
1878–81 The Shaker Manifesto. v. 8–11. January 1878 to De-
          cember 1881. Shakers, N. Y.

Mace, Aurelia C.
1907 The Aletheia: Spirit of Truth. 146p. Farmington, Maine

MacLean, J. P.
1905 A Sketch of the Life and Labors of Richard McNemar.
       67p. Franklin, Ohio
1905 A Bibliography of Shaker Literature, with an introductory
       study of the writings and publications pertaining to Ohio
       Believers. Columbus, Ohio. 71p. (Items Nos. 159–85
       refer to pamphlets and circulars advertising Shaker
       medicinal preparations, seeds, chairs etc.)
1907 Shakers of Ohio. Columbus. 415p.

[McNemar, Richard]

1846 Investigator, or a Defence of the Order, Government and Economy of the United Society Called Shakers, against Sundry Charges and Legislative Proceedings. Addressed to the Political World, by the Society of Believers, at Pleasant Hill, Ky. New York. 84p. (Includes: Some account of the proceedings of the legislature of New Hampshire in relation to the people called Shakers, in 1828. 19p.)

Nordhoff, Charles

1875 The Communistic Societies of the United States. New York. 432p.

Noyes, John Humphrey

1870 History of American Socialisms. Philadelphia. 678p.

Perkins, Abraham

1893 One Hundredth Anniversary of the Organization of the Shaker Church, Enfield, N. H., October 18, 1893. Enfield. 37p.

Reist, Henry G.

1932 Products of Shaker Industry. New York History, v. 13, no. 3:264–70. July 1932

Robinson, Charles Edson

1893 A Concise History of the United Society of Believers, called Shakers. Shaker Village, East Canterbury, N. H. 134p.

Sears, Clara Endicott

1916 Gleanings from Old Shaker Journals. Cambridge. 298p.

[Silliman, Benjamin]

1832 Peculiarities of the Shakers, described in a series of letters from Lebanon Springs in the year 1832, containing an account of the origin, worship and doctrines of the Shaker's society. By a visitor. New York. 116p.

Smith, J. E. A.

1876 The History of Pittsfield (Berkshire County), Massachusetts, from the Year 1800 to the Year 1876. Springfield. 725p.

Van Wagenen, Jared, jr

1927 The Golden Age of Homespun. Agricultural Bulletin 203. N. Y. Department of Agriculture and Markets. June 1927. 45p.

[Wagan, Robert M.]

1875   An Illustrated Catalogue and Price List of the Shakers' Chairs, Foot Benches, Floor Mats, etc. Lebanon Springs, N. Y. 12p.

[Ward, Durbin]

1869   Shaker Income Tax. Application to Commissioner Delano. Brief of Durbin Ward, counsel for applicants. Albany. 21p.

White, Anna, & Taylor, Leila S.

1905   Shakerism: Its Meaning and Message. Embracing an historical account, statement of belief and spiritual experience of the church from its rise to the present day. Columbus, Ohio. 417p.

Wickliffe, Robert

1832   The Shakers. Speech of Robert Wickliffe. In the Senate of Kentucky January 1831. Frankfort, Ky. 32p.

Wingate, Charles F.

1880   Shaker Sanitation. Broadside. (Reprint from The Sanitary Engineer, v. 3. September 1880. New York)

MANUSCRIPTS IN THE ANDREWS COLLECTION

In the present investigation considerable use was made of manuscripts. The author has assembled an extensive collection of trustees' and deaconesses' accounts, various communications and pronunciamentos from and to the ministry, private journals of many kinds, copy books, memorandums of varied religious and secular experiences, letters, notes, indentures, wills, discharges etc. From this collection the following list is selected as bearing directly on the substance of the present study. A serial number has been given to each of these manuscripts, which are grouped as nearly as possible by subject matter and in chronological order. Items treating of the industrial life in other families than the Church at New (Mount) Lebanon, or of industries in other societies, are placed at the end of the list.

Andrews MS. No. 1

1795   Order and Covenant of a Church in Gospel Order. First written covenant of the United Society. New Lebanon

Andrews MS. No. 2

1780–1854   A Record of Deaths at New Lebanon, Watervliet and Hancock (First-bishopric death-book)

Andrews MS. No. 3

1806–17   Account Book of Articles Received of the Church and Families for the "Poor Office" for the Years 1806–17

Andrews MS. No. 4

1845   Millennial Laws, or Gospel Statutes and Ordinances; Adapted to the Day of Christ's Second Appearing. Given and established in the Church for the protection thereof by Father Joseph Meacham and Mother Lucy Wright, The presiding Ministry, and by their successors the Ministry & Elders. Recorded at New Lebanon Aug. 7, 1821. Revised and Re-established by the Ministry and Elders, Oct. 1845. (Undoubtedly this code of regulations is the most important unpublished record in the history of the sect)

Andrews MS. No. 5

———— A Memorandum of Things Carried to the North-House by Samuel and Elisabeth Johnson in the Year 1793 for the Use of the Famaly. New Lebanon

Andrews MS. No. 6

1776–89 Joseph Bennet, Jun[rs] Day Book, Begun July 29th A. D. 1776

Andrews MS. No. 7

1789–92 Church Book of Accompts Kept by Benj[n] Bruce & Nich[s] Lougy. Lebanon 25th March A. D. 1789 (Smith's Day Book No. 1)

Andrews MS. No. 8

1789–92 Trustee's Account or Day Book, 1789–92. New Lebanon Church family

Andrews MS. No. 9

1805–23 Trustee's Account or Day Book, 1805–23. New Lebanon Church family

Andrews MS. No. 10

1817–35 Trustee's Account or Day Book, 1817–35. New Lebanon Church family

Andrews MS. No. 11

1823–28 Trustee's Account or Day Book, 1823–28. New Lebanon Church family

Andrews MS. No. 12

1830–36 Trustee's Account or Day Book, 1830–36. New Lebanon Church family

Andrews MS. No. 13

1834–41 Trustee's Account or Day Book, 1834–41. New Lebanon Church family

Andrews MS. No. 14

1835–39 Trustee's Account or Day Book, 1835–39. New Lebanon Church family

Andrews MS. No. 15

1853–57 Trustee's Account or Day Book, 1853–57. New Lebanon Church family

Andrews MS. No. 16

1863–76 Trustee's Account or Day Book, 1863–76. New Lebanon Church family

Andrews MS. No. 17

1795–1884 Book: Seeds Raised at the Shaker Gardens. 1795–1884. New Lebanon Church family

Andrews MS. No. 18

1807 Price List of Seeds

Andrews MS. No. 19

1840 A Journal of Garden Accounts Commencing July 27, 1840. New Lebanon Church family

Andrews MS. No. 20

1857–67 Farmer's Journal (Includes an annual "recapitulation" of sales, stock, events)

Andrews MS. No. 21

1817 Johnathan Wood's Book for the Year 1817

Andrews MS. No. 22

1827–38 Ledger No. 1, 1827 Herb department, New Lebanon Church family

Andrews MS. No. 23

1834–38 Ledger, 1834–38. (Herb department, New Lebanon Church family. (Includes also trustee accounts at Canaan Lower Family, 1838–68, and miscellaneous Church records)

Andrews MS. No. 24

1844–48 Ledger, 1844–48. Herb department, New Lebanon Church family

Andrews MS. No. 25

1846–73 Ledger, 1846–73. Herb department. New Lebanon Church family

Andrews MS. No. 26

1849–53 Church Scratch Book Kept by J. Wood & Co. 1849–53

Andrews MS. No. 27

1835–78 Tannery Journal and Account Book, 1835–78. New Lebanon Church family

Andrews MS. No. 28

1838–47 A Journal of Domestic Events Kept by Benjamin Lyon, 18, Began, Dec.ʳ 21st, 1838

Andrews MS. No. 29

1873–88 Journal, 1873–88. Writer unknown

Andrews MS. No. 30

1830–71 Journal Kept by the Deaconesses at the (Church) Office. 1830–71 New Lebanon

Andrews MS. No. 31

1833-34 A Weaver's Memorandum; or An Account of Weaving, etc. Kept by Hannah Treadway, A. D. 1833 & 34

Andrews MS. No. 32

1835-65 Weaver's Journal. Beginning in the year 1835

Andrews MS. No. 33

1837 Journal Kept by Elizabeth Lovegrove. Begun in March 1837

Andrews MS. No. 34

——— "Bill of Prices" for Making Cloth and Clothes. New Lebanon Church family

Andrews MS. No. 35

1826 A Receipt for Colouring Madder Red. Signed by James E. Hutton

Andrews MS. No. 36

1856 Labels Presented to the Office Sisters (Church family) by "E"

Andrews MS. No. 37

1836 Importance of Keeping Correct Book Accounts. By Seth Y. Wells (Copy of original MS.)

Andrews MS. No. 38

1788 Mary Dayley's Discharge. Together with A Bill of Articles Delivered to Mary Daly

Andrews MS. No. 39

1798 John Shapley's Discharge. Together with A Bill of John Shapley, Sadler Tools

Andrews MS. No. 40

1797 Note on Clothing Shears from Ebenezer Kellogg

Andrews MS. No. 41

1808 Receipt for Bark Mill

Andrews MS. No. 42

1810 Authorization To Build, Use or Sell a Patent Bark-grinding Wheel. Signed by Benjamin Tyler jr and John Tyler

Andrews MS. No. 43

1811 Authorization To Make a Machine for Washing Clothes. Signed by Sylvester Noble

Andrews MS. No. 44

1814 Authorization To Make, Use or "Cause To Be Used" an Improvement in Looms. Signed by Ebenezer Jones

Andrews MS. No. 45

1816 Authorization To Use a Roller for Compressing and Extending Leather. Signed by William Edwards

Andrews MS. No. 46

1824 Wilkes Hyde's Conveyance of the Spinner

Andrews MS. No. 47

1830 Deed of Patent Door and Window Springs. Signed by Marquis G. Selkirk

Andrews MS. No. 48

1831 Authorization To Use Smith's Revolving Timber-Plane. Signed by William Cobb and Jacob Coller

Andrews MS. No. 49

1843 Letter Concerning Planing Machines. From W. Willard to Jonathan Wood

Andrews MS. No. 50

1840–47 Bills of Stock Belonging to the Church. New Lebanon

Andrews MS. No. 51

1846–59 Trustee's Account or Day Book, 1846–59. New Lebanon Second family

Andrews MS. No. 52

1864–71 Trustee's Account or Day Book, 1864–71. New Lebanon Second family

Andrews' MS. No. 53

1863–78 Trustee's Account or Day Book, 1863–78. New Lebanon South family

Andrews MS. No. 54

1863–85 Trustee's Account or Day Book, 1863–85. New Lebanon South family

Andrews MS. No. 55

1863–1907 Trustee's Account or Day Book, 1863–1907. New Lebanon South family

Andrews MS. No. 56

1878–85 Trustee's Account or Day Book, 1878–85. New Lebanon South family

Andrews MS. No. 57

1831–46 Trustee's Account or Day Book, 1831–46. Hancock

Andrews MS. No. 58

1857–67 Trustee's Account or Day Book, 1857–67. Canaan West family

Andrews MS. No. 59

1776 Jehiel Markham's Minute Book. Early Enfield (Conn.) business accounts

Andrews MS. No. 60

1787–88 Jehiel Markham's Minnit Book No. 7. Hancock

Andrews MS. No. 61

1822 Letter to Brother Daniel (Goodrich) from Brother Morrell. Dated Watervliet, December 26, 1822

Andrews MS. No. 62

—— The Joint and Several Answer of Daniel J. Hawkins and John Mantle Defendants to the Bill of Complaint of Henry Baker Complainant. New Lebanon Second family. No date

Andrews MS. No. 63

1842 A Little Book Containing a Short Word from Holy Mother Wisdom, Concerning the Robes & Dresses That Are Prepared for All Such As Go Up to the Feast of the Lord, or Attend to Her Holy Passover. Copied July 20, 1842. For the Ministry of the City of Peace

Andrews MS. No. 64

1832 Letter to the Elders, Deacons, Brethren, & Sisters of the Society in Watervliet, Watervliet Jany 26th 1832. Signed by Seth Y. Wells

Andrews MS. No. 65

1836 Remarks on Learning and the Use of Books. Watervliet, March 10, 1836. Signed by Seth Y. Wells

Andrews MS. No. 66

1847–54 Account Book of Elisha Myrick. Harvard Shakers

Andrews MS. No. 67

1850 Day Book Kept for the Use & Convenience of the Herb Department. By Elisha Myrick. Harvard Church. 1850

Andrews MS. No. 68

1853 A Diary Kept for the Use & Convenience of the Herb Department by Elisha Myrick. Harvard, Mass. January 1, 1853

Andrews MS. No. 69

1815 Copy of Second Family, New Lebanon, Covenant, 1815

Andrews MS. No. 70

  1827 A Concise Statement of the Faith and Principles upon which the joint Union and Covenant Relation of Believers are formed, the Nature of that Relation, and the order and manner of attaining and entering into it. [Also] The Covenant of the Second Family. [Schedule E] of the New Lebanon United Society, 1827. With names of members of that family. 16p. Copy

Andrews MS. No. 71

  ——— A Second Book copied from Br. Alonzo G. Hollister's Manuscripts

Andrews MS. No. 72

  1855 Memorandum of Baskets, etc. Kept by the Basket Makers. Recorded from 1855. (New Lebanon)

INDEX

Adams, Dr Charles C., acknowledgment to, 15

Agriculture, basis of social system, 27; beneficial influence, 38; cultivation of soil considered ritual, 61; expansion of gardening activities, 22; farming and gardening basic functions of, 60; gradual abandonment of industry for, 248; measure of development, 45; medicinal herb industry outgrowth of interest in, 87; scope of activities before Civil War, 65

Albany, market for Shaker goods, 49, 234

Alden, Ebenezer, 67

Alfred, Maine, society at, organization, 20; original properties, 22; survey of industries at, 257

Allen, George, 75

Allen, John, 75

Allen, Joseph, 118, 124, 280, 281

Allen, Phineas, 91

Anderson, William, 244, 272

Andrews, Edward D., cited, 294

Andrews collection, manuscripts in, list, 301–7

Apiary, 258

Apple butter, 206

Apple-drying kiln, described, 84

Apple growing, 249

Apple-paring machines, 86

Apple sauce, 182, 205

Armchairs, 230

Avery, Gilbert, 247

Avery, Giles, circular concerning dress of believers, 179; quoted on relation between beauty and use, 220; variety of occupations, 118; cited, 295

Babbitt, Sarah, invention, 42

Baird, Daniel W., invention, 40

Baker, Arthur, quoted, 39; cited, 295

Baptists, 17, 22

Barber, Franklin, 75

Barber, John W., cited, 295

Barks, used as herbs, 94

Barrels, 141, 145

Barter of goods, 48; examples of, 52

Basket-making, 164; in sisters' shops, 210; prices, 166; variety of baskets, 164

Bates, Theodore, invention, 44, 130

Bedell, Abner, inventions, 42

Bee-keeping, 252

Believers, see United Society of Believers

Benches, 244

Benedict, David, cited, 295

Beneficial influence, 38

Bennet, Joseph, jr, chair sale recorded in daybook of, 233; first trustee, 48, 264; ledger of accounts of clothier shop, 171

Bennett, Henry, invention, 40

Berry culture, 208, 249, 250; see also Strawberries

Besoms, 279

Bibliography, 294–300

Bill, Aaron, 124

Bishop, Amos, invention, 40

Bishop, Ebenezer, 264

Bishop, Father Job, 247

Bishop, John, 18

Bishop, Rufus & Wells, Seth Y., cited, 295

Bishop, Talmage, 17

Bishoprics, 22, 57, 267